English metaphysical poetry, from Donne to Marvell, is conspicuously witty. A. J. Smith seeks the reason for the central importance of wit in the thinking of the metaphysical poets, and argues that metaphysical wit is essentially different from other modes of wit current in Renaissance Europe. Formal theories and rhetorics of wit are considered for both their theoretical import and their appraisals of wit in practice. Prevailing fashions of witty invention are scrutinised in Italian, French and Spanish writings, so as to bring out the nature and effect of various forms of wit: conceited, hieroglyphic, transformational, and others from which the metaphysical mode is distinguished. He locates the basis of Renaissance wit in the received conception of the created order and a theory of literary innovation inherent in Humanist belief, which led to novel couplings of time and eternity, body and soul, man and God. Yet he finds that metaphysical wit distinctively works to discover a spiritual presence in sensible events; and he traces its demise in the 1660s to changes in the understanding of the natural world associated with the rise of empirical science.

METAPHYSICAL WIT

METAPHYSICAL WIT

A. J. SMITH

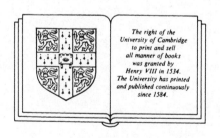

CAMBRIDGE UNIVERSITY PRESS

CAMBRIDGE

NEW YORK   PORT CHESTER

MELBOURNE   SYDNEY

Published by the Press Syndicate of the University of Cambridge
The Pitt Building, Trumpington Street, Cambridge CB2 1RP
40 West 20th Street, New York, NY 10011-4211, USA
10 Stamford Road, Oakleigh, Melbourne 3166, Australia

First published 1991

Printed in Great Britain at the University Press, Cambridge

British Library cataloguing in publication data
Smith, A. J. (Albert James) *1924*–
Metaphysical wit.
1. Europe. Poetry
1. Title
821.309

Library of Congress cataloguing in publication data
Smith, A. J. (Albert James), 1924–
Metaphysical wit / A. J. Smith.
p.   cm.
Includes index.
ISBN 0 521 34027 6
1. English poetry – Early modern, 1500–1700 – History and criticism.
2. English wit and humour – History and criticism. 3. Literature,
Comparative – English and European. 4. Literature, Comparative –
European and English. 5. Metaphysics in literature. 1. Title.
PR545.M4S6 1991
821'.409384 – dc20   90–28119   CIP

ISBN 0 521 34027 6 hardback

To Gwyneth, and the memory of Sergio Baldi
Conosco i segni dell'antica fiamma

CONTENTS

PREFACE

This essay concludes the study of a metaphysical sentience in Renaissance poetry which I carried forward in two earlier books, *Literary Love*, 1983, and *The Metaphysics of Love*, 1985. Wit focuses an interest in the rendering of our ambiguous state when sensation and idea interfuse in the language itself, opening an absolute consequence in the momentary encounter and registering the shock of metaphysical predicaments posed in the play of the senses.

Versions of poetic wit evolved in Europe from the fifteenth century on. To ask how these versions bear upon the wit of the English metaphysical poets is to seek the qualities which distinguish that mode of wit. The enquiry is of more than literary concern. Wit followed out divergent expectations of the created order, as of poetry. When metaphysical wit simply ceased to have point in the later seventeenth century, an entire way of thinking had changed.

A few expositors of English metaphysical poetry have allowed that the poems owe their general character to a distinctive metaphysical apprehension. The argument that follows engages with the discussions which serve to further it, notably those by James Smith, S. L. Bethell, W. J. Ong and Robert Ellrodt. In contesting an issue with these savants I implicitly acknowledge a debt and a shared – if unfashionable – concern.

I have modernised the spelling of poems in English but otherwise followed the form of my source-texts. Translations of poems in French, Italian and Spanish aim to bring out the wit rather than render the elegance of the original.

ACKNOWLEDGMENTS

I gratefully acknowledge the support of the following institutions: the Leverhulme Trust; the British Academy; the British Council; the English Speaking Union; the Folger Shakespeare Library; the Gladys Krieble Delmas Foundation of New York; the University of Wales; the University of Florence; the University of Keele; the University of Southampton.

Permission to reproduce the hieroglyphs and imprese in chapter 4 has been granted as follows: 'How they denote a Watchful Person' and 'How an Amulet' from *The Hieroglyphics of Horapollo Nilous*, translated by A. T. Cory, 1839 (Cambridge University Library); *Impresa* of the Porcupine from Paolo Giovio, *Dialogo dell'imprese militari*, Lyons 1574 (British Library).

1

DRASTIC DEVICES

On Tuesday 5 November 1616 Bishop Launcelot Andrewes preached his annual Gunpowder Treason sermon before the King at Whitehall, as he had done since the first anniversary of the discovery of the plot. Both the Bishop and King James himself, as well as many present, were among the intended victims of the plot and would not have been there at all in 1616 had it succeeded. On this occasion Andrewes took what seems on the face of it a capriciously remote text from Isaiah 37: 'the children are come to the birth, and there is not strength to bring it forth'. His sermon is entirely built upon the conceit that the Gunpowder Plot was a failed birth, which he bears out wittily by the elaboration of correspondences between the two predicaments in the teeth of the apparent unlikenesses, and unlikeliness. This process is carried through quite openly and even (so to say) on the hoof, with a sense of real revelation as more and more points of likeness disclose themselves to his mind:

The more I think of it, the more points of correspondence do offer themselves to me, of a birth and coming to birth, and that in every degree: 1. The vessels first give forth themselves, as so many embryos; 2. the vault as the womb, wherein they lay so long; 3. they that conceived this device were the mothers, clear; 4. the fathers were the fathers, as they delight to be called, though oft little more than boys – but here right fathers, in that they persuaded it might be, why not? – might be lawful, nay meritorious then: so it was they that did animate, give a soul, as it were, to the treason; 5. the conception was, when the powder as the seed was conveyed in; 6. the articulation, the couching of them in order just as they should stand; 7. the covering of them with wood and faggots, as the drawing a skin over them; 8. the *Venerunt ad partum*, when all was now ready, train and all; 9. the midwife, he that was found with the match about him for the purpose; 10. and *partus*, the birth should have been upon the giving fire. If the fire had come to the powder, the children had come to the birth, *inclusivè*, had been born. But *Non erant vires*, which I turn, there was no fire given; and so, *partus* they wanted, as God would.[1]

A clinching justification of his witty use of the text is an intricate play
on the terms of the Vulgate version, which he sustains throughout the
sermon, making the most of any incidental correspondences of letters,
sounds, ideas:

This *pariendi* was indeed *pereundi*, the bringing forth a quantity of powder, the
perishing of a whole parliament. They were not, but put case they had come
forth, (it is well we are in case to put this case) certainly they had been
Benonis, 'Sons of sorrow', to this whole land, Ichabods right; our glory had
been gone clean. For what a face of a commonwealth had here been left?
Exclusivè they came *ad partum*; if *inclusivè* they had, their *inclusivè* had been our
exclusivè. We had been shot off, and that out of this life and this world every
one, *Venerunt*, if they had come *ad partum*; if they *ad partum*, we *ad perniciem*.
Non erant vires; if there had, these *vires* had been *virus* to us, and their *pariendi*
our *pereundi*. If those children had not been lost, many fathers had been lost;
many children had lost their fathers, and many wives their husbands. There
had been a great birth of orphans and widows brought forth at once. What
manner of birth should this have been, first in itself, then to us?

On the face of it all this ingenuity may seem to do little more than
bear out the dismissive presumption of eighteenth-century commentators that the essential shallowness of Court life in the decades before
the Civil War is shown in the way Court preachers played with words
and conceits. Yet Andrewes was not a shallow man, and the occasion
decidedly did not call for flippancy. We must ask ourselves why he is
so concerned to make an abortive birth of the Gunpowder Plot, or at
least, why he needs to labour the identity so.

Notorious parallels offer themselves in seventeenth-century poetry.
Donne derives the decay of the entire cosmos from the recent death
of a young girl; or he finds a present enactment of Christ's crucifixion
in his journey to visit a friend on Good Friday; or he portrays his
fevered body as a flat map over which the physician-cosmographers
must pore as they struggle to chart a particularly hazardous progress.
Herbert takes Christ's stretched sinews on the cross for the strings of
a lute which must be tuned up to the right pitch to set the key for the
entire consort. Vaughan finds the promise of a bodily resurrection in
the physical make-up of a printed book. Marvell depicts the soul in
the body as a prisoner hung up in chains of nerves and sinews, which
hold it helpless to resist the torturing head and heart. No one who
knows the writings of the time will take these conceits for passing
whimsies. They witness an engrained habit of mind, and epitomise a
mode of conceited wit which prevailed in seventeenth-century
English poetry.

Conceited wit itself was no innovation. It had flourished in Italy, Spain and France from the late fifteenth century, and Renaissance rhetoricians took it for a requisite of some styles of writing well before the seventeenth-century theorists codified it as the pattern of creative thought. If we do not speak of metaphysical wit in reference to Italian or Spanish poetry it might be because our customary use of the term is conventional, without precise meaning. Certainly the use was arbitrarily established. When Dryden spoke of Donne as affecting the metaphysics he plainly took Donne's metaphysical manner for no more than a casual way of sporting with oversubtle ideas.[2] For Johnson metaphysical wit is an artificial trick of style, an arbitrary coupling of unlike images in the manner of Marino which shows off ingenuity.[3] Coleridge shrewdly characterises the diverse energy of Donne's wit, and often takes issue with Donne on metaphysical questions; yet he nowhere proposes that the wit itself may work a metaphysical end.[4]

Nineteenth-century historians of taste in Italy and Spain presumed the ascendancy of a European cult of *secentismo* or *concettismo* which comprehended all the forms of poetic wit.[5] They take the style of the metaphysical poets, where they know of it, for nothing more than a local nuance of the mode of conceited wit which prevailed in Europe from the late fifteenth century on. Nearer our own day Mario Praz lumped Donne with Marino, Gongora and Lyly, taking their writings for aspects of a single cultural phenomenon, so many phases 'of the taste which is commonly designated as *secentismo, marinismo, gongorismo, eufismo, Poesia "metafisica"*'. He finds that seventeenth-century literary theory simply bears out the thinking of the times, which brings the entire universe 'under a mode of wit'. Praz holds that Donne pillaged the witty Italians and Spaniards for his conceits, and the mediaeval schoolmen for his ideas. He allows that Donne's ingenuity is more than the arbitrary cleverness of a Marino, being the habit of a complex mind which generates its own intellectual excitements. Yet the metaphysical ideas simply sustain the ardour.[6] More crudely, D. L. Guss has argued that Donne was an out-and-out Petrarchan whose wit simply develops the conceited ingenuities of such Italian court poets as Serafino d'Aquila.[7]

Given the arbitrary emergence of the designation 'metaphysical' itself it is not surprising that commentators who disrelish metaphysics have been slow to allow it any real substance. J. C. Ransom, in 1941, characterised the metaphysical conceit as a 'functional or structural metaphor'. The metaphysical poets are distinguished not by some special way of thinking and feeling but by the mode of metaphor they favour.[8] Rosamund Tuve shows no specific concern with wit in her laborious study of Elizabethan and metaphysical imagery; but she defines metaphysical images purely in terms of their logical basis and development, and their rhetorical function. She claims that Elizabethan and metaphysical conceits alike draw upon the categories of the Aristotelean logic, and vary only in the number and complexity of the logical parallels they discover. Metaphysical wit would thus be distinguished from earlier modes of wit just by its greater logical complexity.[9]

T. S. Eliot quietly adjusted his view of wit as he grew more interested in spiritual presence than in the workings of his own mind. In his celebrated 1921 *TLS* review Eliot points out two distinguishing features of metaphysical poetry, which he appears to connect with each other. One is the agile management of figures of speech, especially those figures which call for the rapid association of unlike objects. The other is the peculiarly close association, if not actual fusion, of feeling and thought, sensuous experience and intelligence, sensation and idea. Eliot posits that the seventeenth-century poets, in common with their predecessors back to Dante and the *dolce stil nuovo* poets, possessed an all-devouring mechanism of sensibility which subsequent poets have forgone.[10]

Some five years later, and rather less publicly, Eliot sought to differentiate Donne's poetry from Dante's. Donne is a metaphysical poet, Dante a philosophical poet. Donne, Poe and Mallarmé share a passion for metaphysical speculation but they do not necessarily subscribe to the ideas they entertain as Dante and Lucretius believe in their ideas; indeed Donne's ideas serve just to refine and develop his sensibility.[11]

By 1927 Eliot was pointing out a fundamental shift of attitudes to love which occurred between the time of Dante and the *dolce stil nuovo* poets and the time of Donne. The Italian *trecentisti* aspire to the pure contemplation of a transcendent beauty whereas Donne argues for union and possession, following out a formal dualism between the body and the soul which is wholly alien to the thirteenth century. Eliot thus reserved for a Clarke lecture which was published only obscurely in French his tacit recantation of the cultural theory of the dissociation of sensibility. Nonetheless he has tellingly come to surmise that the distinctive sensibility of the metaphysical poets, the peculiar fusion of thought and feeling in their wit, may have something to do with a particular understanding of the relationship of body and soul.[12] Eliot's developed pondering of the intersection of the timeless with time must be sought in his own poetry and playwriting from *Ash Wednesday* on.

James Smith's essay in *Scrutiny* in 1933 attempts the first explicit justification of the term 'metaphysical' in the entire course of its use, and reflects Smith's preoccupation with some metaphysical issues in Aquinas. Smith argues that Donne is properly called a metaphysical poet because his verse is overwhelmingly concerned with metaphysical problems, such as derive from or resemble the problem of the Many and the One. Yet Donne is not a Dante or a Lucretius. Metaphysical propositions occur in Donne's verse in a peculiar way. What makes him a metaphysical poet is not just that he entertains such propositions but that he finds metaphysical problems lurking behind any action, and is continually excited or disturbed by this apprehension. He holds opposite possibilities in play, maintaining a balance between rival claims to reality.[13]

Father W. J. Ong suggestively links the English metaphysical poets with such mediaeval Latin hymnologists as Aquinas and Adam of St Victor, who found witty paradoxes and puns at the heart of Christian truth, not least the truth of Christ's double nature.[14] J. A. Mazzeo and S. L. Bethell also discover a true metaphysical disposition in metaphysical wit. They more or less concurrently followed out Croce's induction to a body of seventeenth-century discussions of wit. Mazzeo rehearses the ideas of some theorists who claim that wit is the means of discovering, or recovering, the hidden correspondences which link the entire creation in a providential interchange of love. This view makes a witty poem an embodiment of occult truth, which differs from a talisman or a magical hieroglyph only in that it does not seek to activate the power of love.[15]

Bethell believes that seventeenth-century wit is a revival of patristic wit, whose end is to reveal the exquisite order of the universe. He finds support in the contemporary theorists for the view that witty conceits are in essence logical sophistries – 'urbane cavillations' – which deliberately flout the decorum of the established categories of matter in the service of a higher truth. Bethell takes wit for a sacramental agent in that it works to offer us a double view of events in the world, as at once historical and timeless. The understanding implicit in his argument is that metaphysical wit is quite precisely so called because it discovers the presence of the spiritual order in the sensible experience.[16]

The most rigorous demonstration of a metaphysical intent in the verse is that attempted in Robert Ellrodt's magisterial study, *Les Poètes métaphysiques anglais*. Like James Smith before him Ellrodt distinguishes metaphysical poetry from philosophical poetry and poetry which merely entertains metaphysical propositions. He thinks that true metaphysical poetry registers a particular kind of experience or perception. It follows out a sense of double natures simultaneously apprehended whose warrant is Christ's own nature, the union of man and God. We are body and soul together. Metaphysical wit seeks to hold in a tense equilibrium two orders of being which are irremediably distinct yet indissolubly bound together.

Donne and Herbert incarnate in the instant a concrete and living intuition of spiritual truth. They discover a spiritual presence which underlies all human experience and makes the eucharist itself a continual sacrifice. They are true metaphysical poets because their poetry uncompromisingly follows out the sense of a double nature. Ellrodt judges that Crashaw, Vaughan and Marvell fall short of that sense in various ways. He finds that other poets who have been taken to exhibit metaphysical traits of style, such as Herbert of Cherbury, Traherne, and Cowley, do not sustain such a doubleness at all.[17]

A range of expectation which takes us from a wanton figurative ingenuity to the apprehension of the timeless in time leaves scope for enquiry. Some large questions propose themselves. What accounts for the emergence of witty poetry in Renaissance Europe, and why did the conception of wit which shaped that poetry not outlast the seventeenth century? What distinguishes metaphysical wit from the other modes of wit which burgeoned in the sixteenth and seventeenth centuries? Any answer which can be given to these queries must come partly from the poetry itself. But it might also be sought in the thinking about literature which attended the poetry.

2

MIRROR OF CREATION

The re-emergence of classical discussions of discourse loosed a flood
of critical theory in the sixteenth century, some of which directly
fostered poetic wit. Two considerations dominate these sixteenth-
century exchanges and need to be put in focus at the start. One of
them is the conception of perceived truth which shaped contemporary notions of metaphor. The other is the drive towards literary
emulation which followed out the conceit of a rebirth of ancient
wisdom. These concerns were formulated in cognate modes of
imitation.

Imitation of nature curiously advanced the imitation of classic
authors. The idea of imitating nature had metaphysical consequence
when art was taken to mirror the order of the creation, or further our
attempts to apprehend it. To imitate an ancient masterpiece might be
to come nearer that ideal order when we seek to make the earlier
writer's truth our own in some novel application, as it were revitalising the pristine vision. Both modes of imitation put in question our
present capacity to comprehend the creation and our own nature.
Both raise the issue of the relation of form to matter.

Renaissance thinking about discourse is ordered by Aristotle's
schematic account in the *Organon* of the nature of the material universe. The sections of that work known as the *Categories* and *Topica*
offer an analytic categorising of matter by qualities. This analysis is
grounded in an absolute discrimination between essential qualities and
accidental or contingent qualities. The essential qualities of a thing
define it, giving it its distinct nature and making it what it is and not
something else. The accidental qualities of a thing are not essential to
it but may or may not be present in any particular specimen of that
class of thing. The essential qualities of a thing are its defining characteristics, those attributes which it shares with all other members of its
kind. The accidental qualities of a thing are contingent upon circumstance. In Aristotelean terms they might fall within some subclass of

the general categories of quantity, relation, place, time, position, state, activity, passive condition and the like.

From Aristotle's categorical analysis of matter follows his scheme of logic, based in the syllogism, the form of reasoning which shows what relationships are deducible within the scheme. Dialectics becomes the master-discipline of thinking, investigation and argument. In separating substantial or essential qualities from accidental or contingent qualities this analysis cleanly distinguishes form from matter, opening the way to the differentiation of soul and body, style and content. The characteristic effect of the Aristotelean physics is the distinction between shaping form and formless mass: 'out of this, which is bronze, we make this other, which is a sphere . . . we bring form into this particular matter, and the result is a bronze sphere'.[1]

Cicero directly exploited the Aristotelean scheme when he ordered the categories of matter in some forty topics or places and made them the necessary instruments of legal pleading and oratory. In manuals by Cicero or attributed to him, such as the *De Inventione*, *Topica*, *De Oratore*, *Ad Herennium*, orators were shown how to resort to particular categories or places for appropriate means of legal suasion. They might draw upon personal disposition, motive, intention, opportunity, probability, manner, antecedents, causes, effects, consequents and so on, measuring one person's actions against another's in degrees of likeness, or difference, or contrariety.

The sixteenth-century logician Thomas Wilson exemplifies the relentless systematising which followed out Cicero's scheme. Wilson orders the material of reasoning under five broad heads called predicables. These predicables are genus, species, differentia, proprium and accidents. Then he works steadily through each predicable, proliferating such subclasses as definition, whole, parts, power, will, passions, cause, effect, action, antecedents, consequents, similitudes, synonyms, contraries.[2] Ultimately he has an instrument for analysing and classifying every property and relationship of matter, at least to the extent that objects may be treated as the sum of their properties:

> Therefore ye must needs have these predicaments ready, that when so ever ye will define any word or give a natural name unto it, ye may come to this store house, and take stuff at will . . . As for an example, if ye will know what a man is, ye must have recourse to the place of *Substantia*.[3]

This is no arbitrary aid to legal pleading. Wilson takes the entire network of properties thus projected for a blueprint of the providential order of creation, to which the processes of logic provide the key. 'We

know hereby, that God hath ordained nothing in vain, and that everything is ordained for some one end'.[4]

Wilson demonstrates his scheme with the term 'magistrate', systematically dredging the places to throw up every conceivable quality
which might be attributed to a magistrate under such heads as
definition, general rule, kind, words yoked, adjacents (necessary and
causal), deeds, thing containing (by which he means the names of
magistrates as David, Moses, Edward VI), efficient cause (God),
second efficient cause (rebels, criminals and the like), ends, effect,
authority, things incident, similitude (the shepherd to his sheep,
master to his ship, head to the body), things compared (as servants are
to masters so men are to magistrates), and many more:[5]

Ye may see by this one example that the searching of places, ministereth
arguments plentifully.[6]

He goes on to debate a specific question concerning magistracy,
culling syllogisms from the places both to advance his own cause and
destroy an adversary's, and making confirming arguments from
comparisons, similitudes, and other such places of relation.

The key to an apt literary use of the system of places was the
classifying of kinds of oratory according to circumstance and occasion,
which followed out the assumption that certain places better serve
some purposes than other: 'Those kinds of speeches, then, which have
different ends and purposes cannot have the same rules'.[7] Appropriate
places were assigned to specific ends and manners of oratory,
epideictic, deliberative, forensic or whatever. Minturno used the
places to categorise styles and characters in a set system of decorum by
which he gauged the rhetorical skill of poets, ancient and modern.[8]
Major sixteenth-century poets measured other poets by their
judgment in accommodating styles and places to the subject matter in
hand, as Bembo did in Book 2 of the *Prose della Volgar Lingua*, and
Tasso did in Books 4 to 6 of the *Discorsi del Poema Eroico*.

The supplying of the places and use of apt matter from them became
a Humanist preoccupation which prompted Erasmus's *De Duplici
Copia Verborum ac Rerum*, published at Paris in 1512. The places were
treated as storehouses of oratorical provender and used as the basis of
analytical thesauruses in which material was systematically ordered by
its conventionally ascribed properties and qualities. Much of this
categorising became prescriptive, and the prescribed characters of
things acquired moral force in oratorical use. Natural lore, gathered
from Pliny or Diodorus Siculus or whoever, became fossilised in stock

figures and emblems which were rhetorically more effective when they could command general acceptance. Theological and literary matter went into the databank with the rest. F. Panigarola, Bishop of Asti, showed how to make the places into a vast storehouse of over a thousand compartments – 'quasi una selva' – from which preachers might fetch apt conceits for their sermons.[9] F. Alunno made a much-reprinted thesaurus of 'voices' from Dante, Petrarch, Boccaccio 'and other good authors' whose ten books covered the estates of the entire universe, God, heaven, the world, the elements, the soul, the body, man, quality, quantity, hell.[10] Giulio Camillo discovered in the scheme of places nothing less than a universal network of correspondences which discloses 'the secrets of God under obscure veils' and mirrors the eternal mind.[11] An exposition of the use of the places became standard in Renaissance manuals of discourse.

The scheme of categories could authoritatively be taken for a map of the creation. By the middle of the sixteenth century it had been scholasticised in a providential order of love,[12] Neoplatonised in transcendental hierarchies of being,[13] hermeticised in a system of occult correspondences.[14] The system had come to present a universe of settled qualities in which understanding alone is free, a hierarchy of values which rational beings are uniquely at liberty to range: 'If the intellect can trace the very totality of being, and as it were divide it into all its members by their degrees, diligently comparing them now to each other and now to the sum . . . how much more will it be able to run through the broad range of the whole!';[15] 'Admirable felicity of man! to whom it is given to have what he wishes, be what he will'.[16] The vast consonance of natural and supernatural being was taken for a picture of a universal order to which the degeneration of our reason denies us a ready key:

It is as difficult for man to pursue his bliss when he is set outside his place in nature as it is easy for him to follow it when he is restored to his natural place.[17]

The discovery of truth entails the restoration of our understanding of nature to what it was, if not the rectifying of Nature herself to what she was. Our search for truth requires the renewal of our wits to the point where they may seize upon the links in that infinitely subtle web of correspondences which constitutes the harmony of creation, discerning 'the likeness and conformities between things which seem diverse in themselves'.[18] Bringing together attributes which unexpectedly couple we reassemble the disjointed fragments, recover the order which God created. True knowledge comes by the disclosing of hidden relationships between categories which seem distinct, and the disjoining of things which are only arbitrarily brought together. Such hidden patterns of relationship may disclose themselves in the work of men of uncorrupted wit, especially those men of antiquity who retained so much more of the pristine vision than we do. Ancient myths embody divine mysteries which they yield to us now only in allegory, as Boccaccio demonstrates when he finds all four levels of allegorical meaning in the episode of Perseus's slaying of the Gorgon.[19]

The projection of the categories into a universal order gave prominence to our human means of apprehending and controlling our state. Poetic invention itself amounts to a rediscovery of the hidden articulation of the creation, the recovery by human wit of the infinitely subtle interconnection of all the forms of being. Yet this exalted office of wit is inseparable from the humdrum task of exploiting the system of places for legal and oratorical ends. Discovery and persuasion share their procedures.

The three major arts of thinking and discourse, logic, rhetoric and poetry, were each allowed their distinctive ways of managing the Aristotelean scheme. In effect they disposed and exploited the relationships between created things themselves. They were commonly grouped together, yet formally differentiated by their means and ends. Commentators generally agreed that all three arts depend upon an apt resort to the categories or places; and invention in rhetoric and poetry was judged to be a matter of handling the places wittily so as to produce new and ingenious conjunctions and recombinations of things by their discovered possession of like attributes. This manner of invention is 'a skill which one cannot take from others, on the contrary it is an index of an acute wit in whoever does it well; for the apt transporting of things from distant places calls for nothing other than a shrewd perception of the likenesses of things'.[20] The end of logic is truth, so that its task will be proof and its means the syllogism. The end of rhetoric is persuasion, its particular work being argument and its means the enthymeme, which is simply an abbreviated and less rigorous form of syllogistic reasoning. The end assigned to poetry is the amendment of civil life by moral instruction, which poets seek to bring about by conveying truth delightfully in memorable fables and fictions: 'Poetry is nothing else than antique philosophy, which with its arguments and precepts covered by the veils of fables, verses, and harmony moved the minds of those early beings and drew them into institutional life by pleasing them';[21] 'Truly the poet will wish to do no other than to teach the true way to live and behave, now openly and now by speaking in fables';[22] 'Therefore the poet must feign and imitate in order to represent, represent so as to move and teach, teach in order to persuade'.[23] The ancient slur persisted that rhetoric is an art of deceit, and poetry an art of lies.

In practice it was well understood that rhetoricians and poets must draw heavily upon logic and upon each other, and that the functions assigned to either art cannot be independently performed. Lively invention in whatever mode draws upon the forms of reasoning, 'certain witty questions and arguments', if only to 'delight the reader' with the ingenuity of the performance.[24] Contemporary pundits may have any or all of several senses in mind when they speak of poetic wit, not discriminating modes which can be distinguished only in theory.[25] Commentators on poetry follow the rhetoricians in taking wit for the means of inventiveness in the art. When they acknowledge a writer's wit they may have in mind his sheer adroitness in sophistical argument such as a training in dialectics fostered, that ebullition of 'a playing wit' which 'can praise the discretion of an ass, the comfortableness of being in debt, and the jolly commodity of being sick of the plague'.[26] But they more often mark his ingenuity in the devising of fictions which enshrine the truth:

true things are rather admired, if they be included in some witty fiction, like to pearls that delight more if they be deeper set in gold.[27]

Boccaccio found a rare mirroring of God's creation in this inventive power of wit. He defined the poet as one who 'by nature is excited by the force of wit, and as it were breathed upon by a certain divine spirit'. Poetry itself is 'a faculty which has its origin in the bosom of God . . . by whose work poets compose their fictions . . . That alone is pure poetry which we compose under veils and is unfamiliarly discovered and narrated'.[28]

Behind such a claim lurks the bold presumption that the creation itself amounts to a witty metaphor of God's being. Macrobius had suggested that a true heroic poem such as the *Aeneid* presents a micro-cosm of this universal conceit.[29] Yet the Renaissance commentators who propose such a lofty scope for wit are just as likely to speak of witty devices as enlivening a received truth. Croce observed that all critical thinking in the sixteenth and seventeenth centuries took for granted a quasi-Aristotelean separation of content from form, which makes art no more than the dress of a sense already given.[30] The Humanists questioned the arts of poetry and rhetoric precisely because they thought that truth needs no embellishment.[31] The English Humanists upheld Pico's claim that plain truth is more telling than witty eloquence. A common view of wit was that it serves to present established verities in arrestingly new ways.

Professed anti-Aristoteleans in the later sixteenth century did not disturb Aristotle's ordering of matter. The most aggressive of them, Peter Ramus, simply instituted a formal rearrangement of the academic disciplines, though the tendentiousness of his vaunted method won him a following far beyond the scope of the reform itself. Ramist method was taken for a counter-thrust against Aristotelean scholasticism and championed by Calvinist sympathisers. In more recent times it has been singled out as a forge of the metaphysical style.[32]

In Ramus's scheme the first two parts of traditional rhetoric, invention and disposition, were transferred from rhetoric to logic together with all the forms of proof and argument which they comprehended. Rhetoric thus lost its Aristotelean control over the processes of finding apt matter and disposing it in persuasive devices. It was left with the schemes and tropes, figures of words rather than the modes of thinking and argument. In effect rhetoric dwindled to the art of controlling the devices of fine speech and ornation.

Ramus insisted that logic and rhetoric are general arts in the sense that they pertain to all forms of thought and discourse. Thus every particular verbal art must draw upon them for the modes of reasoning and of ordering material. Ramists called in poetry among other verbal forms just to bear out this contention. They sought to exemplify logical relationships in places where readers are least likely to anticipate them, to show that all coherent discourse needs to be well ordered and to draw upon the categories and places. They made a war-cry of the traditional claim that orators and poets must be logicians in the basic processes of composition because logic provides the means of discovering and disposing material. Yet they were far from arguing that poetry should go in for syllogisms or tough processes of reasoning. On the contrary, they continued to treat poetry as an offshoot of rhetoric, taking it for an art which is allowed a laxity not permitted to logicians just because its particular business is fine speech and ornation. The function they specifically assign to the poet is delightful embellishment, the decoration of apt matter in rich colours, sweet sounds and the like, which carry the truth home to the reader by diverting him. Ramism confirms Puritan attitudes to rhetoric. It reduces poetry to an art of ornament:

A figure is a certain decking of speech, whereby the usual and simple fashion thereof is altered and changed to that which is more elegant and conceited.[33]

In Ramist manuals the function ascribed to figures of speech is just pleasing decoration.

Renaissance theories of discourse tend to look to ancient prescription. Macrobius, about A.D. 400, had formalised the assimilation of poetry to rhetoric as well as the presumption that poetry is an art of imitation. One of the dialoguists in his *Saturnalia* proposes that Virgil's *Aeneid* amounts to a manual for teaching the art of rhetoric. He claims and seeks to demonstrate that we may learn from Virgil all the modes of argument, pleading, and persuasion with their apt devices and styles, including the use of the places of argument and the ordering of a vast range of knowledge for use in these places. Virgil also teaches us the several kinds of eloquence and their appropriate styles, as well as the various means of evoking and expressing feelings, and the ornaments and flowers of language.[34]

Several dialoguists now bring in the central issue of the *Saturnalia*, which is Virgil's debt to his predecessors and contemporaries and to Homer above all. This discussion takes up most of Books 5 and 6. Successive speakers massively attest Virgil's re-use of passages from other poets and dramatists; and they pose the question whether this wholesale practice of borrowing is to be deprecated as theft or a plain confession of flagging invention.

Furius Albinus responds by distinguishing imitation from stealing. He says that Virgil was a master of imitation, which is not plagiarism but a positive artistic process of reordering and refashioning material to a new and brilliant end. This argument follows out Macrobius's own prefatory citation of the Horatian figure of the bees who take their material from here, there and everywhere but transform it all into honey.

Renaissance Humanists fastened upon the distinction Albinus makes here because imitation was inherent in their conception of language. From the Humanist view of the evolution of Roman civil life followed the idea that a language itself might come to its maturity, attain a consummate moment of refinement when its best users will afford an unsurpassable model of literary elegance. For writers in Latin the models are self-evidently Virgil in verse and Cicero in prose. Bembo fixed on Petrarch and Boccaccio as the models of the most refined vulgar style.

Bembo's *Prose della Volgar Lingua*, 1525, held up Petrarch's

Canzoniere for a matchless summation of love which succeeding poets could only strive to emulate. Bembo's own love poetry, as della Casa's, aimed at the utmost refinement of form and style within the set round of the Petrarchan attitudes. Following theorists showed more concern with the imitating of Petrarch's matter; and Giulio Camillo set out an elaborate system for the ingenious re-use of all Petrarch's attitudes and properties 'to the end that we have so many places stocked with as many conceits as will furnish the matter not just of plain erudition but of artifices adapted to the meaning in new ways, as well as all the words and things distinguished in their due order as may suffice for all human conceits'; 'If we wish to rework material already used, such as may come to hand . . . we shall see how to imitate the old writer in his universal meaning while nonetheless accommodating the artifice to our own particular end, in accomplishing which we shall aptly demonstrate our own skill'.[35]

Bembo and Camillo both assume the separation of matter from manner, meaning from style. The plain sense stands to be reapparelled in fresh figures and conceits, 'in which it seems that the true way and praise of poetising consists'.[36] Originality shows in the way a thing is said, the new use a poet makes of old matter. Giraldi Cintio ironically instances the work of one Mariano Buonincontro da Palermo who wrote 'the most beautiful sonnets in the world as far as the sounds and the rhymes went, which nonetheless said nothing whatever and were without feeling'.[37] Yet Cintio is at one with Bembo and his followers in confirming the true artistic stimulus of rivalry with the creator of one's chosen material and with those who have already made their own use of it:

Emulation always accompanies imitation, which is nothing else than a resolute desire to go beyond the writer whom one imitates.[38]

Camillo's system allowed poets the possibility of drawing on their author without reproducing him as, it was urged, the best of their predecessors had always done. Formally the system required a use of the places of logic, the ordering of properties and relationships in the minutely subdivided categories of the Aristotelean physics. In theory the poet takes an epithet or figure, breaks it down by reference to the places, and then builds it up again differently by drawing on other places or different aspects of the same place. The idea might still be Petrarch's in essence but the garb has changed; or to put it in Camillo's terms, the general substance remains constant and the particular artifice has been ingeniously varied to suit the fresh circumstances:

'But wishing to treat in the same tongue material which has already been used we shall be able to do it . . . And we shall show you how to imitate an old writer in his universal drift while nonetheless accommodating the artifice to our own particular end, in doing which you may aptly demonstrate your skill'.[39] To imitate without stealing some good figure which Lucretius has made it is only necessary to understand the art of Lucretius, 'which was to take arguments from the place of consequents'; for 'by taking matter from the same place I can form equal or better, and not in his words'.[40] Tasso sets out the full prescription magisterially: 'And new shall be the poem in which the texture of the intrigue is new, the resolutions are new, the episodes are new which lead up to them, however well known the material may be and previously treated by others'.[41]

Tasso's dictum undoubtedly bears upon his own poetic practice. Yet we may doubt whether poets ever actually plied Camillo's system, even though subsequent commentators cite Italian users and offer specific examples. Its significance is that it marks a shift of emphasis which now turns imitation to a wholly eclectic end, that of 'removing the iron and making all gold and silver', and of 'making of the perfect the most perfect by uniting in one the perfections of many'.[42] Paolo Beni praises Tasso for changing the copper of Homer and the silver of Virgil into fine gold.[43] Tasso himself persuasively argued that originality is better displayed in form than in matter,[44] putting a novel gloss on the old commonplace that poets seek glory as their proper due. Bembo's doctrine of imitation has opened a prospect which he himself might well have disrelished, that of showing originality by the ingenious reworking of a common motif. Du Bellay had commended the humble emulation of discipleship: 'Imitating the best Greek authors one transforms oneself into them, one devours them . . . and converts them to blood and nourishment'.[45] We now move on from that state of receptive pupillage to the confident assumption of rivalry and the struggle for advantage. A poet's acclaim will depend upon our recognising his model. Victory will be ours if we 'contrive it so that the material of others becomes our own property . . . so to say transforming it, now changing, now adding and sometimes omitting things'; as a piece wrought of another's metal is the glory of the workman and not of the owner of the metal.[46]

It is no great step to the belief that the poetic merit resides precisely in the ingenuity with which the given metal is handled, and the argument that without such reworking of known material 'one would not be exercised at all or have shown liveliness of wit in finding it, and therefore one would not merit praise'.[47] Tasso saw the opposite dangers besetting poets in the 1570s as the lure of the *arguzie* of the sophists, 'which stuff many compositions pleasing to the world', and the intemperate indulgence in 'the condiment of music'.[48] Poems which are all sophistical wit and poems which are nothing but euphony would be illegitimate offspring of imitation.

No less telling is the habit of thought Camillo's system assumes. Late Renaissance writers on poetry reiterate *ad nauseam* their axiom that figures are produced by reference to the places or topics 'from which not only arguments but almost all inventions of all artifices derive'.[49] The benefit ascribed to Camillo was the rediscovery of a technique neglected since Petrarch; he had 'shown it to be used by poets, particularly by Petrarch, in forming the topic of elocution, which was dug out of the same places from which arguments are drawn'.[50] Yet the profitable use of these 'places of argument such as poets ought to use'[51] could not be casual. It required a 'knowledge of the nature of things', which in practice meant a copious supply of commonplace matter and an adroitness in managing objects by their attributes: 'We conclude that to be a good and delightful poet one must above all know how to benefit by the nature of things . . . the properties, accidents, varieties, effects, likenesses, repugnancies of these things'.[52] The making of figures turns precisely on the exploitation of these likenesses and repugnancies in things, 'nor can he fitly find them who does not recognise the similitude of things in dissimilitude . . . whereby it appears that it properly belongs to philosophic wits to find them'.[53]

The tendency of a physics which treated objects as bundles of qualities divinely preordained is clear enough in the innumerable illustrations of figurative usage cited in such works as Camillo's *L'Idea del Theatro*, 1550. It is to concentrate attention on the manipulation of attributes ascribed by convention, and in particular on meaningful correspondence of attributes. Emblem and conceit, the paradigms of metaphorical use in the sixteenth century, are twin offspring of the mental habit of the time. Both emblems and conceits make attributes stand for ideas; both forms call for ingenuity in the way that a complex of meanings is packed into a figure, or teased out of it in an item by item materialisation of its properties.

Imitation proved a forcing ground of virtuosity, not to say extravagance. A curious outcome of the system was the mode of devout imitation which declared itself in the spiritualising of the manners of secular poetry and the use of the devices of amorous wit in pious causes. The love of Christ merits at least as vivid expression as the love of a woman:

> Out on thy ornaments of woven gold!
> Alas, long since for pleasures they were sold,
> Then weep forth pearls of tears to spangle thee . . . [54]

Convention approved a poetic repentance which simply redirected amorous passion to Christ, or moralised erotic pursuit as the evidence of misdirected zeal. Petrarch himself had concluded the *Canzoniere* in abject penitence for his lost years of secular passion – 'tanto error' – and a final rededication of his remaining powers to 'alto Dio' and 'miglior uso' (*Canzoniere* No. 364). Commentators had long made it their highest praise of the *Canzoniere* that Laura presented 'a universal idea of beauty and grace' who embodied 'all the perfections in common',[55] and personified chastity and reason.[56] The Council of Trent sponsored a systematic attempt to put literature in the service of God; and it was not merely policy but the thrust of imitation which suggested the exploitation of prevailing tastes to that end. The rewriting of Petrarch's text was already an approved test of wit. Poets vied with each other in elaborate feats of pious dexterity such as redirected to Christ all the lover's yearning for Laura and crowned the whole enterprise with the poems *In Morte*. Even before the prompting from Trento a commentator vented his distaste for an unrelieved diet of reprocessed Petrarch, 'Petrarch glossed, Petrarch souped up, Petrarch totally robbed, Petrarch temporal and Petrarch spiritual'.[57]

The outburst of witty piety which English poets promoted in the 1590s followed the impulse of this spiritualised Petrarchism. When Southwell told the love poets that he would 'weave a new web in their own loom'[58] he implicitly acknowledged his own debt to the Petrarchising Tansillo; and he urged the poets simply to redirect their ardours to a worthier end: 'Passions I allow, and Loves I approve, only I would wish that men would alter their object, and better their intent . . . Love is but the infancy of true Charity'.[59] Religious poets now took up the sonnet, traditional instrument of love, and drew on the devices and attitudes of contemporary love poetry:

> And if thou change the object of my love,
>   the wing'd affection which men Cupid call
>   may get his sight, and like an angel prove.[60]

By the last decades of the sixteenth century commentators grow strident in their warnings against excessive ingenuity. They denounce the deliberate obscurity of some who aim to be clever, but are chiefly scornful of conceited extravagance, as when a lover claims 'that his lady's hair outshone the sun in beauty',[61] that his passion dried up rivers and his sighs propelled ships,[62] or that the stars are the nails of heaven.[63] Tasso censures a number of poets including Dante for the vanity they display in the laboured extravagance of their conceits. He instances a poet who asserts that his mistress's eyes are arquebuses on wheels and her eyebrows Turkish arches, another who feigns that Charon has made a boat of the arrows launched at him by love and plies it on the river of the lover's tears, and another who speaks of the body as a 'carnal cloister' and 'carnal nest'.[64] Specific objections to conceits which smell of the lamp tend to ascribe this infelicity to a misuse of the places or categories. Critics warn of the darkness or absurdity which comes of 'transporting from afar',[65] making figures from 'categories too remote from each other'[66] and even 'from the contrary',[67] fetching material 'from arts or sciences far removed from the capacity and common use of the people':[68]

those conceits which are transported into poetry from the most intimate bosom of philosophy and the other sciences . . . do not bring so much of novelty with them as of difficulty, or so much of majesty as of obscurity and horror; and they are sooner abhorred by common men as enemies than admired or wondered at as strangers or pilgrims.[69]

The vehemence of such pleas for decorum suggests that poetic wit was running to extremes before the sixteenth century was out. Yet the conceits singled out for censure often come from much further back. The poetry which diverted the Italian courts in the 1480s and 1490s confirmed modes of wit that persisted as long as the Aristotelean logic itself supplied the categories of invention.

The scheme of places offered a prescription for ingenuity and was taken to open the way to a metaphysical endeavour of wit. A striving for wit was inherent in the practice of imitation, which fostered the use of the places for a reworking of established material. Wit claims metaphysical truth to the extent that it seizes upon the links between created things, coupling objects from distant categories of being and even different orders of being. In its capacity to hold unlike modes of existence in a single order a witty conceit may mirror God's creation. Critical discussion opened such possibilities of wit, and invites us to consider how far they are realised in the witty poetry which was written from the fifteenth century to the seventeenth century.

3

COURTLY CONCEITS

Conceited wit showed its character towards the end of the fifteenth century in the work of poets who made it their aim to exercise their hearers' minds with clever plays of metaphor and ingenious reasoning. What distinguishes these writers from poets who had juggled with metaphoric properties in passing – Cino da Pistoia, Petrarch himself – is that they make wit the whole end of their art. 'Language and style count for nothing. What scores is the farfetchedness of the conceits, the unexpectedness of the inferences, the liveliness of the antitheses'.[1] The assumptions then current about the writing of lyric poetry fostered this mode of poetic wit, and were systematised somewhat later in Giulio Camillo's elaborate projection from the Aristotelean categories.[2]

Camillo's formulation of his system in 1544 lends force to D'Ancona's much-disputed thesis that all the elements of the seventeenth-century style of conceited wit were already present long before 1600. D'Ancona characterises these earlier modes of wit as an 'anticipated Gongorism'. We must ask how far they anticipate Donne, and in what way the so-called 'line of wit' bears upon the character of metaphysical wit.[3] Like S. L. Bethell later[4] D'Ancona thinks that conceited wit came into Europe from Spain; and he finds it conspicuously displayed in the work of some lyric poets who enjoyed a European vogue in the early sixteenth century, notably the Spaniard Benedetto Cariteo (Gareth) and the Italians Antonio Tebaldeo and Serafino Ciminelli d'Aquila.[5] D'Ancona himself had no taste for conceited wit. He mocks the conceits and shows off their three perpetrators as mere fantastics who give poetry over to bizarre effects. D. L. Guss's claim that Donne was a Petrarchist in just this conceited mode would have seemed to him nothing more than an implied dismissal of Donne.[6]

These poets undoubtedly foster their own extravagance. Conceited hyperbole is the life of their style. The lover inundates the terrain in his wanderings, or fills a large river with his tears which relieves the thirsty beasts. The flames of his passion make a lantern for love, which guides lost travellers at night and even turns night into day; or they fry the birds in the air, set the trees alight as he passes, kindle the shepherds who come to drink at the fountain of his tears. He is so full of love's arrows that Cupid now carries him for a quiver. His lady makes the cockerels crow when she appears before dawn because they mistake her for the sun. Such seeming drolleries are not wholly wanton:

> Spesso questi arsi panni me dispoglio
> Et buttomi nel mar per troppo ardore . . .

The lover strips off his burning clothes and jumps into the sea to quench his flames, but the sea boils and ignites the rocks; so that even the rude elements are moved by his sufferings in the end while she alone remains obdurate against love:

> Che per domarte amor tenta ogni prova
> Forza è che un sasso al fin l'altro commova.

The conceit has been worked up into a consistent figurative action which is fantastic in itself and follows out a vast hyperbole yet vividly proclaims a marvel, that the lady he serves is at once irresistibly desirable and invincibly chaste.

Such plays upon common metaphors serve for occasional effects in a rich repertory of witty devices. This imitative mode of love poetry puts a premium upon ready invention. The poet sets himself the task of finding numberless ways of giving fresh life to a few set attitudes and figures. In fact nothing in the lover's situation ever changes, let alone develops, yet the attack and the witty devices shift all the time with conspicuous virtuosity. We might be offered a dozen poems on the same theme, each one attempting a fresh approach and a novel device. The lover extemporises upon the lady's mirror, her singing, her gloves, her comb, her ring, bracelets, ornaments, emblems. He finds any number of ingenious reasons for calling upon the moon, her window, sleep, night, the sun, his bed, her gown, her horse, the paper he writes on, a passing bird, the air itself, Apollo, Cupid, love, death, Charon.

The virtuosity is the more striking, and the more evident, in that the verse forms these poets work in are so restricting in themselves. Within the brief scope of the *strambotto* and the sonnet they contrive an ever-changing pageant of artifices and arguments. Their witty resource seems inexhaustible, and they show some artistry in the way they galvanise devices with all manner of ingenuities, surprising us with word-plays, bizarre epithets, extremes of paradox. Serafino develops a whole sequence of poems out of a play upon 'peregrinando', drawing a fresh line of conceits from each possible sense – wandering, pilgrimising, hawking, behaving strangely – and running the word itself through all its grammatical modes. The less likely the occasion the more striking the display of wit. They work up some unpromisingly humdrum incident into a hyperbolic conceit of praise, such as their lady's breaking her arm when she slips in the snow, suffering a nosebleed at a dance, receiving outlandish gifts, contemplating her own likeness in stone. They reanimate the tired old Petrarchan poses, renewing their force in vehement outbursts, strange anecdotes, vivid fictions and dialogues, comic impersonations, and revitalising them with every possible trick of wit.

These contrivances are never mechanically plied but take on a quick mental life because they are commonly put to work in a process of ingenious reasoning. Tebaldeo specialises in the conceited teasing out of some paradox of love and beauty. Why does Love make him love a woman who does not love him? Why should Cristoforo Romano seek to realise in marble a more perfect form of beauty than the lady already presents? A question is posed and weighed in all its intractableness, then suddenly answered with an ingeniously audacious conceit. Why were people so slow to put out the fire which destroyed her house? She cannot really wonder at their tardiness,

> che pigre fur le gente a le diffese
> Non per sua colpa, ma per tuo diffetto . . .

The reason he seeks is that her gaze set her rescuers on fire, so that they had to use the water upon their own breasts. But then why did the lover himself not run with the rest to rescue her and put out the fire? She herself is to blame because her lustre has reduced him to nothing but the fire of passion and the wind of sighs; hence he stayed behind so as not to cause her more harm by augmenting the flames he meant to extinguish.

In a much-anthologised sonnet Cariteo adroitly turns the tables on the lady whose scorn has destroyed and damned him:

> Voi, donna, ed io per segni manifesti
> andremo insieme a l'infernal tormento: . . .

The portents clearly promise that the lover and his mistress must go down to hell together, she for pride and he for his excessive ardour in daring to look upon heavenly sights. Yet in continuing to gaze fixedly upon her there he must increase her torments and his own content, so that he will remain the sole happy being among all those wretched creatures; for in having her perpetually before his eyes he will find a paradise in the midst of hell such as heaven itself could not promise him and the evil spirits may not mar. His true torment would be to lose sight of her face altogether.

Serafino, fledgling of the school, became its past master in the art of dramatising conceited argument. His inventive resourcefulness is extraordinary. The lover looks in vain for his heart amid the despoiled ruins of his own body, and discovers anew that love robs one of the best part of oneself. He intercepts his lacerated heart in full flight from a tormenting Jew to whom his own mind had delivered it, and urges it to return to seek redress, which it flatly refuses to do because that would be to go back to galley-service and its own destruction. He arrives before his time on the banks of the Styx and pleads with Charon for a passage, which Charon will not allow him because his flames might destroy the boat. He calls from his tomb upon a passer-by whom he urges to give him peace in the grave by cutting his mistress's image out of his heart, albeit at the risk of the traveller's own damnation. He expostulates with the sun, arguing that its proper business in its travels round the globe ought to be to reveal to the world the grievous error of loving. The burning lover cries out for relief upon Death, who arrives at the double only to assure him that nothing more can be done since his heart already dies every hour and then revives in its own flames like the phoenix. We cannot be surprised that the early editors garbled this intense little lyric, which calls for dramatic articulation throughout:

> Morte! Chi è la? Soccorri! Ecco che arrivo.
>   A che pur chiami? Ardo! Chi t'arde? Amore!
> Che poss'io far? Fammi di vita privo! . . .

'Death!' 'Who is there?' 'Help!' 'Here I come; why do you call me?' 'I burn!' 'Who burns you?' 'Love!' 'What can I do about it?' 'Deprive me of life.' 'But I kill you every hour.' 'Me? no!' 'Ask your heart!' 'My heart!' 'Who is it?' 'Are you dead?' 'Now dead, now alive!' 'What are you saying, alas, can a dead being be reborn?' 'Only I can, who, after death, little by little renew myself in flames like the phoenix.'

The incessant play of wit, always outgoing expectation, projects a life of the mind which is no less evident in the verve of the writing itself. The poems call for nimbleness in the reading. Serafino will carry an argument through quite unpredictably so that we can never just rest in the sense going forward but must keep alert to subtle shifts of direction, fresh applications of the device, incidental kicks of wit, sudden reversals and disclosures, startling paradoxes, clinching final strokes. He is adept at manoeuvres which lead us to expect a familiar outcome and then suddenly conclude quite differently in some irony or paradox which reverses the direction of the argument, or produces opposite effects from like causes, or unnaturally unites contraries:

> Se Salamandra in fiamma vive, e in foco,
> Non me stupisce quel che fa natura . . .

If the salamander lives in flame and fire I do not wonder at the things nature can do. Yet love, the enemy of nature, works still greater marvels, for she is made of ice and the lover is made of fire and yet she lives secure in the midst of his heart; in fact, the hotter his flames, the harder she gets: . . .

> Solo amor di natura aspro adversario,
> Che a suo dispetto unisce ogni contrario.

Thus love, bitter adversary of nature, has united opposites but without reconciling them; on the contrary it increases their incompatibility.

Serafino's way of slipping the carpet from under our feet works not so much to shock or disturb as to invite our admiration of the elegant dexterity of the performance. The lover steals her glove and she rages at him for the theft:

> A che minacci, a che tante ira e orgoglio,
> Per questa non farai ch'l furto renda.

He asks to be cited before Love himself to give his reason for it, and then duly puts it to the god that he was justified in taking her glove in reprisal for her theft of his heart. 'She took my heart, and I have taken her glove from her. I would like to know from you if a heart is worth so much.' These last-line coups can be quite subtly managed:

> Cor mio con chi stai tu? Ho tre patroni.
> Chi è il primo?

He interrogates his distracted heart which acknowledges no less than three masters, a blind deceitful boy, a deaf mother of confusion, and an envious unquiet woman who is constantly changing her dress. He leads us to take these tyrants for love, fortune and his mistress. But then the commiserating final couplet minimally adjusts the direction:

> Ahi come è miserabile tua sorte,
> Poi che servi ad amor, fortuna e morte.

The casual twist of the argument fulfils our expectation in a quite startling way. The mistress herself is death.

Whether or not their writing anticipated Gongorism – and Croce thought so little of it that he dismissed the question out of hand[7] – these poets initiated the modes of conceited wit which held in Europe for more than a hundred and fifty years. Tasso and Guarini are their heirs no less than Marino. What prompted this bizarre way of writing? The poetry cries out for its context. It certainly cannot be taken for the wantonness of wild men. Far from operating in the margins of their culture these poets served the most discerning patrons of their day, or any day. Theirs is a court art through and through. Cariteo and Serafino were professional court functionaries and entertainers, and Tebaldeo seems to have served so early on despite his clerical orders.[8] The careers of all three poets reflect their unstable times. Cariteo, a native of Barcelona, worked chiefly at the Aragonese Court of Naples whose glory he disconsolately outlived. Tebaldeo moved between Ferrara and Mantua, though he finished up as a priestly misanthrope in Rome. Serafino worked his way round the Italian courts passing freely between Naples and Rome, going on to Urbino, then crowning his career in the service of the d'Este sisters, Beatrice in Milan and Isabella in Mantua at the height of the brilliance of those two courts. Cesare Borgia snapped him up from the turmoil which followed the French invasion, and gave him a magnificent funeral when he died of fever in Rome at the age of 35.

In contemporary accounts of court life we hear much of the activities of these poets who preside and perform at court festivities, devise ceremonial entertainments, sing to their own lute accompaniment and the like. They acquired great repute and the European courts vied for their services, hoarding copies of their poems as collectors' items.[9] In the service of Cardinal Ascanio Sforza at Rome Serafino was the compeer of Josquin des Prés and Pinturicchio; and his fame at Milan rivalled that of his colleague Leonardo da Vinci. When he died in 1500 the untimely event prompted the first ever collection of funeral tributes by the celebrities of the day,[10] as well as several Lives and Memoirs and a rush of editions of his poems.[11]

The work of all three poets bears the character of its performance at court. Their witty strokes exploit local occasions and invite dramatic enactment. Serafino's first editor, in 1502, acclaims the all-round excellence of his accomplishment, 'his profound memory, admired wit, lucid and ardent style, the gravity of the sentences, perfection of the music, the singular grace in every act and in reciting above all else'.[12] They play upon the circumstances of their own recitals or cast a lover's lament in the form of his altercation with some hidden power, love or death or Charon or whoever. The very mode of hyperbole, whose unrelieved excesses drew objections even then,[13] is set by a bond of patronage which could be aptly represented as the endless devotion of the lover to his irresistible yet unattainable mistress whom he celebrates for her unique combination of those contradictory merits – 'Che se è pur ghiaccio il volto, il cor tutto arde' (Serafino, *Strambotto* No. 169).

The captions of the poems in the 1503 edition of Serafino's verse show just how these Renaissance *jongleurs* sought to transform into lively art the casual traffic of court life. 'Upon a labyrinth which the Marchesa of Mantua wore as her impresa'; 'To the Duchess of Urbino for a marble Cupid'; 'For the S. Berat. Dall'Anghillara who by chance wounded his beloved in the finger'; 'Upon a medal of the Marchesana'; 'To a shirt which was given to him'; 'Upon a picture sent to the Duchess of Urbino'; 'Upon a falcon of King Ferrante'; 'For an artificial fly worn by the Duchess of Urbino'. 'Attached to the collar of Ascanio's dog'; 'The two following sonnets were sent to the Countess of Lacerra with a bird, at the instance of S. don F. d'Arag.'; 'Upon certain gloves'; 'To Cecilia Galerana' (the mistress of Lodovico il Moro, painted by Leonardo); 'For a bracelet which was given to him'; 'For a pomegranate given to him by Laura Schiappa of Verona'. Such occasions repeatedly make starting points for a virtuoso exhibition of conceit-spinning.

Serafino was renowned above all for his quick inventiveness in recitation, an effect he evidently cultivated since his apologist assures us that his poems were never delivered extempore in fact: 'He did not improvise his compositions despite his quickness of wit, saying that a sudden extemporaneousness rarely merited success or praise'.[14] These contemporary witnesses discover a more studied brilliance of invention in the use the poets made of their literary sources, which they do not so much imitate as conspicuously exploit. Cariteo's vaunted possession of a manuscript collection of the Provençal poets was taken to open a rich mine of exotic conceits to him, which he augmented so freely from the ancient writers that his modern editor sometimes lists as many as a dozen sources for a single short poem. Serafino flaunted his borrowings much as he advertised the motifs which set him going. His contemporary biographer, sometime secretary to Beatrice d'Este, evokes the principle of imitation set out by Macrobius in the *Saturnalia* to justify this witty piracy, proclaiming that the poet 'rather merits praise for the redisposition than blame for the thefts.'[15] Colocci admiringly tracks Serafino's brilliant pillaging of the known estate of lyric poetry, pointing out how he transforms the things he takes from the Greek Anthologists, the Roman poets, the troubadours, the Sicilians and the *dolce stil novisti*, Dante, Petrarch, the Renaissance neo-Latinists, 'and innumerable other poets living and dead'.[16] These early sixteenth-century commentators are at pains to prove that imitation is the spur of wit.

For all their resourcefulness the poets themselves found only limited scope for their wit. Serafino had no adequate language for motives which fall beyond the round of court diversions, even the solemn promptings of the Court itself. All he can manage by way of mourning the calamitous death of Beatrice d'Este, which devastated the Milanese Court, is a series of spiritless attempts to accommodate Petrarch's *In Morte* motif to his own conceited idiom. Love has lost his kingdom by her death, and remains doubly blinded; her death deprives the world of love and leaves it a desert, robbed of all its glory and pomp; love addresses the wayfarer from her tomb, advising him to succumb to death as love itself has done now that its powers have all died with her:

> Però morir volsi io, poi che caduta
> Era mia gloria, or che ben stulto dico
> Colui che per viltà morte refiuta.

This juggling with the old counters falls so far short of the occasion because it has no roots in felt experience. The lack of an inner life is what trivialises all this courtly art and denies it the possibility of development. It also precludes a metaphysical consequence in the conceits.

If metaphysical wit were merely a style of writing then the standard characterisations of Serafino and the rest might prompt us to take them for proto-metaphysical poets, as D. L. Guss does.[17] L. De Marchi long ago spoke of their wittifying of lyric poetry ('Questo processo di acutizzazione') which turned sonnets into epigrams, *canzone* into drama, and set these poets upon a hunt for the strange and unexpected effect.[18] De Marchi finds in Wyatt an English representative of this mode of wit and the initiator of a line of wit in English poetry. Yet for all his imitations of Serafino, and all his courtly address, Wyatt's wit has more in common with Donne's wit than with the hyperbolic mode of the Italian courts.

Wyatt gives his Petrarchism an ironic twist, as when he proves that his mistress's cruelty thwarts itself and so serves to keep him alive:

> But if that you will have my death
>   And that you would no nother,
> Then shortly for to stop my breath
>   Withdraw the one or other,
>   For this your cruelness
>   Doth let itself, doubtless,
>   And that is reason why
>   No man alive nor I
>   Of double death can die.
>   'At last withdraw your cruelty'

Moreover his rehearsal of Petrarchan attitudes only serves to set off the wit itself, on which all his poetry turns. He is a witty poet through and through in his own cavilling manner. He would sooner she maintain her obduracy towards him than break her faith:

> And if ye were to me as ye are not
> I would be loath to see you so unkind.
> But since your faith must needs be so by kind,
> Though I hate it, I pray you leave it not.
>   'To rail or jest'

A proposition is made to prove its own converse in that the conduct he complains of ultimately works to his advantage. What undoes him mends him:

> Your feigning ways as yet forget them not
> But like rewards let other lovers have,
> That is to say, for service true and fast,
> Too long delays and changing at the last.

This mode of witty love poetry is quite unlike that of the Italian court poets. The wit follows out a different order of relationships in which celebratory hyperbole has no place at all, and irony and cool argument are more to the point than admiring awe. This lover hits back at the lady who uses newfangledness and dismisses him once she has had her pleasure of him:

> But since that I so kindly am served
> I would fain know what she hath deserved.
>   'They flee from me'

The poems play out a public ritual of beguilement, betrayal and ingenious threat in which a poet needs to know how to hold his own:

> If this be under mist
> And not well plainly wist,
> Understand me who list
> For I reck not a bean;
> I wot what I do mean.
>   'Me list no more to sing'

Wyatt evokes a harsher world than Serafino and the rest inhabit, in which a wary scepticism about people's motives becomes a condition of survival. 'Trust therefore first, and after prove'; 'And as I find / So will I trust'; 'Hereafter comes not yet'. This lover has his eyes open to the world he lives in and recognises, without being put down, how faith is mocked. Her feigned tears and faked indispositions will not succeed in making common sport of him:

> But as ye list, feign, flatter, or gloze.
> Ye shall not win if I do lose.
>
> Prate and paint and spare not;
> Ye know I can me wreck.
> And if so be ye care not,
> Be sure I do not reck . . .
> By God and by this cross
> If I have the mock
> Ye shall have the loss.
>   'To wet your eye withouten tear'

Wyatt's stand of sturdy independence, his mockery of his own attachment, gives his writing an abrasive vigour. Yet his wit is tempered by his control of movement and form. Far from dramatising his own sufferings he holds an elegant poise, exploiting the lyric pattern to catch nuances of tone and tauten the movement of his thought:

> What should I say
> Since faith is dead
> And truth away
> From you is fled?
> Should I be led
> With doubleness?
> Nay, nay, mistress!

Even the slightest of refrain movements tends to be argumentatively based, turning the tables on his tormentor with urbane cogency. She has furthered him by hindering him, made a gap where she intended a stile, smiled where she meant to frown:

> Lord! how thyself thou didst beguile
> That in thy cares wouldst me have lapped!
> But spite of thy hap, hap hath well happed.
>   'In faith I wot not well what to say'

A seemingly simple lyric progression will follow out a sequence of reasoning which completes a process of thought:

> It was my choice, it was no chance
> That brought my heart in other's hold . . .

Since he placed his heart in bondage by choice then it is right that she should accept it; if she refuses it and denies him even one happy hour then right has no force; if right has no force then love goes by chance and fancy; though fancy drew him to love yet love needs a firmer knot:

> It lasteth not that stands by change.
> Fancy doth change, Fortune is frail.
> Both these to please, the ways is strange.
> Therefore, methinks, best to prevail,
> There is no way that is so just
> As truth to lead, though t'other fail,
>   And thereto trust.

The ground of Wyatt's reasoning is always legalistic, even toughly contractual. He takes love for a compact or bargain in which justice ought to prevail though it rarely does, and defection merits a rejoinder. A broken promise begets a countering promise:

> But since to change thou dost delight
> And that thy faith hath ta'en his flight,
> As thou deserv'st I shall thee quit
> I promise thee, I promise thee.
>   'Thy promise was to love me best'

Indeed without such a contract of love the lover may have no claim upon her; but then neither can he complain if another lover benefits by his pain:

> I have no wrong where I can claim no right.
> Naught ta'en me fro where I nothing have had.
>   'Th'answer' that ye made to me, my dear'

Justice requires love for love, his proven faith ought to prompt her answering regard, 'Which is my just reward'. Such even measure is too much to expect. Simple devotion is all too likely to come off badly,

and then the lover's sole redress lies in the power of his wit to wish
some exquisitely apt return upon her for her arrogant rejection of love:

> May chance thee lie withered and old
> The winter nights that are so cold,
> Plaining in vain unto the moon.
> Thy wishes then dare not be told.
> Care then who list for I have done.
>
> 'My lute awake'

This quickness of a sceptical intelligence is what brings Wyatt's love
poetry closest to Donne's and Carew's. The lover anticipates Donne's
shrewd grasp of his own dilemma:

> For if I thought it were not so,
> Though it were so, it grieved me not;
> Unto my thought it were as though
>   I hearkened though I hear it not.
> At that I see I cannot wink
> Nor from my thought so let it go
> I would it were not as I think;
>   I would I thought it were not.
>
> 'Deem as ye list'

Nonetheless Wyatt is not a Carew, let alone a Donne or a Marvell. His
contractual expectation of love draws him into witty quibbling, yet his
intellectual sleights quite lack the metaphysical sentience which gives
urgency to the wit of the seventeenth-century poets.

4

INTELLIGIBLE IMAGES

When Jean-François Champollion announced his decipherment of the hieroglyphic section of the Rosetta Stone, in September 1822, he resolved a doubt which had perplexed the European academies for more than three centuries. The event had its bearing upon wit. For the sixteenth-century dalliance with Egyptian hieroglyphics bred an elaborate system of witty image-making which was sustained by a metaphysical theory of wit. This theory has entered our modern discussions of wit, via Croce.[1] Mario Praz argued that metaphysical wit derived from the same 'phase of taste' as the mode of the emblem.[2] J. A. Mazzeo and S. L. Bethell make the still untested claim that seventeenth-century expositions of the *impresa* offer a key to metaphysical poetry, if not to sacramental truth.[3] What light the theory of the hieroglyph really throws upon metaphysical wit is a question which remains to be resolved.

In 1505 Aldus Manutius published at Venice a little book in Greek whose translated title is *The Hieroglyphics of Horapollo of the Nile*. Aldus thus brought to European attention an annotated anthology of Egyptian hieroglyphics which had been first gathered together in the fifth century A.D. and translated into Greek some time later. This collection purports to represent an antiquarian attempt to salvage the fast-disappearing sign-language of the old Egyptian priesthood; but it may well strike us now as an inconsiderable little volume in itself, scarcely less dull than quaint. A modern reader might wonder why Aldus bothered to publish it at all.

Yet the recovery of so ancient a system proved a momentous event. The publication sponsored a cult. It fed current presumptions about the way to true knowledge and focused the interests of savants upon bizarre pictorial forms, cryptographic collocations of objects and properties which might yield arcane interpretations. We can scarcely encounter these curiosities as Aldus's readers seem to have received them:

HOW THEY DENOTE A WATCHFUL PERSON

ιθ'. Πῶς ἐγρηγορότα γράφουσιν.

To denote a *watchful person*, or even a *guard*, they portray the HEAD OF A LION, because the lion, when awake, closes his eyes, but when asleep, keeps them open, which is a sign of watching. Wherefore at the gates of the temples they have symbolically assumed lions as guardians.

HOW AN AMULET

χδ'. Πῶς φυλαχτήριον.

When they would denote an *amulet*, they portray TWO HUMAN HEADS, one of a male looking inwards, the other of a female looking outwards, (for they say that no demon will interfere with any person thus guarded); for without inscriptions they protect themselves with two heads.[4]

These humdrum forms were allowed the force of talismans and taken for signs of universal truth, even reverenced as the ark of the holy spirit: 'they are called mysteries, that is to say secret, hidden sacraments . . . holding within themselves some occult divinity'.[5]

They were invested with such qualities precisely because they are intelligible images whose essential appeal is to the mind: 'so we take care to put all our study in the inner meaning and not in the external form'.[6] The condition is insistently made, and has Neoplatonic point. In this mode of art the eye simply mediates a conceit to the under-standing, working in the opposite direction from those organs which make the mind a slave to passion. For sixteenth-century theorists these hieroglyphs represented a singularly pure artistic endeavour because they simply signified as pointers beyond themselves, visual represen-tatives of ideas which show us in their own nature the way from earth to light.[7] The physical representation has merit only in so far as it stands for a meaning and sustains some ingenious device, 'representing metaphorically the inward concept'[8] by a kind of visual wit. Hence it might be infinitely reproduced without losing quality, an apt offspring of the new era of printing and the woodcut and a witness in itself of the power of the mind to transcend its particular embodiment.

Champollion's paper demystified the hieroglyph. It demonstrated that the Egyptian cryptograms on the Rosetta Stone are not soundless symbols at all but an alphabetic language from which the Coptic languages partly derived, and of which the royal decree in Greek at the bottom section of the stone is a straight translation. Yet his announcement, decisive in itself, did not have the devastating effect of Casaubon's exposure of the Hermetic writings in 1614. For the cult of the hieroglyph was by then long defunct. It had ossified in Italy and France by the middle of the seventeenth century when Tesauro, Picinelli, Menestrier and other rhetoricians of wit codified all the symbolic forms in their monumental treatises.[9] Menestrier dismissed as dreadful gibberish – 'un épouvantable galimathias' – the sixteenth-century claim that the *impresa* might embody divine secrets.[10] What was earlier taken for an entry into universal truth had become no more than a theory of metaphor, or a device of rhetoric 'useful to orators, preachers, academics and poets'.[11] By 1822 the idea that Egyptian hieroglyphs are the occult embodiment of sacred mysteries had long been moribund and waited only to be authoritatively discredited. It had grown from a total misconception.

Yet the delusion itself was fruitful and followed out an influential vision of our place in the creation. For Aldus's publication prompted an outpouring of manuals of esoteric symbolism which enable us to see why these bizarre devices were taken up with such fervour and even sustained a faith. They combined the status of a proto-science with the appeal of magic. The adepts who marshalled them discover nothing less than a universe entirely made up of divine hieroglyphs which express the ordered working of God's creation. Our mastery of nature's powers is made to depend upon our capacity to read these enigmatic signals aright, and imitate them in hieroglyphs of our own devising which themselves encode the hidden relationships in nature. Such devices are taken for readings in the Book of Creation, revelations of hidden truth which might even work spiritual ends.

This occultism was formulated by G. B. Valeriano in 1556. He speaks of God's language of hieroglyphs and says that God communicated in hieroglyphs with Adam and the men before the Flood.[12] Luca Contile of the Academy of Pavia adds that the first two *imprese* were the tree of the forbidden fruit and the rainbow after the universal deluge.[13] G. A. Palazzi of Urbino cites among other divinely instituted *imprese* the Ark, the emblems of the Evangelists, the dove, the lamb, the pelican.[14] These commentators assumed in common that the pristine knowledge of men was hieroglyphically rather than discursively acquired, by which they understood that the first men intuitively read their universe for direct intimations of God's purposes and truths, which were thus revealed to them at a stroke. Noah and his successors, 'because of their purity conversed with celestial intelligences'; they 'imitated God who was the first inventor of Imprese' and discovered in the creation about them 'the likeness of the eternal beatitude'.[15]

What follows for such zealots is that we ourselves must try to take the same way to truth despite all the impediments which accumulate as we move further from the Fall. They offer us the authoritative examples of St Eucherius of Lyon and St Bonaventura, who showed us how God's Book of Creatures may disclose his providential design to us;[16] and they propose just the itinerary which Henry Vaughan pursued a hundred years later when he translated Eucherius on the divine hieroglyphs in nature[17] and declared himself a primitive Silurian, if only by regeneration.[18] Then they show how the Old Testament itself, the history of early men, is full of such divine hieroglyphs in which St Augustine, St Jerome and their successors were able to discover an intimate prefiguring of Christ's own career as well as the ascent of the fragmented soul towards loving oneness with God.[19] In effect these mid-sixteenth-century theorists already bring together a world of symbolic forms, which comprehends not only scriptural examples but the allegorised genealogies of the gods, ancient epigraphy, the Cabala, the ceremonies of civil and domestic life from rituals and pageants to gifts, gardens and liveries. Nothing is excluded which might be symbolically understood.[20]

Aldus's little anthology had its remarkable effect because people were already disposed to seek such hieroglyphic evidences of occult providence, even to expect that universal truth might disclose itself cryptically in enigmas which only mirror the order of creation itself. The impeccable antiquity of the hieroglyphs simply confirmed their manifest claims to preserve ancient wisdom. Commentaries multiplied around each distinct kind of symbolic use.

The fashion took its impetus from something more than a general Humanist enthusiasm for the recovery of lost antiquity. It answered a real need, appeasing the old yearning to reclaim the knowledge Adam possessed which has long since faded from our degenerate minds:

Egyptian characters were used by the first people of the world before they established them between themselves in the customary hieroglyphics . . . The characters together with the sciences were . . . rediscovered and taught by Adam our first parent. Nonetheless the animals, in whom resided the particular similitudes of divine secrets, served solely for priestly purposes and not for the common written use.[21]

This knowledge now proves to have been miraculously preserved, and restored to us at least in part. We may take the hieroglyphs which have come down to us for nothing less than 'divine characters', signs of the perfection of that universal nature which is 'minister of divine providence'.[22] So the commentators wrangled as fancifully over the provenance of hieroglyphs as over the hermetic writings. Some held that the Egyptian priests inherited these devices from Noah, who received them from Adam's offspring or from Moses. Some supposed that Prometheus brought them down to the Egyptians and that Pythagoras, or Noah himself, took them from Egypt to Italy. Such speculations burgeoned revealingly just because the lineage mattered. Hieroglyphs confirmed religious conviction. The cult flourished vigorously in the train of the Council of Trent, and its devotees often display a counter-reforming exclusivism. Their ardour grows out of the quite specific sense of a loss which may be repaired only by the initiate in occult researches.

The academic theorists of the *impresa* defiantly proclaim the metaphysical agency of wit. They educe the character of the *impresa* from the constitution of the creation itself. G. P. Valeriano finds a prescription for hieroglyphs in the Homeric chain of gold which links all created things with each other and connects them all to God.[23] Valeriano and Ripa evoke a creation which manifests its order hieroglyphically, epitomising for our instruction the providential disposition of created things.[24] Whitney tellingly attributes the disclosure of the system to Aristotle, who discovered it by 'searching the secrets, natures and qualities of all creatures'.[25] Contile speaks of the making of *imprese* as a restoring of lost wisdom 'by means of the likenesses that all things have with other things' ('per similitudine c'hanno tutte le cose con le cose').[26] Bargagli finds the operating cause of the *impresa* in the 'wit or intellect disposed outside itself and apt to recognise the fittingness, the similitudes, the conformities that are found between things':

It being the case that there is not a thing in the world . . . which has not one or more compatibilities or conformities with one or another thing, however diverse; and these more or less like, among themselves. Whence the *ingegno* is more praised and of greater prize that understands how to make and rediscover more links between these or more conforming parts, and knows very well when it has found these how to avail itself of them and to express its conceits, reducing them in the form that has been shown at this time, according to our understanding, to be that of the true and legitimate *impresa*.[27]

These accounts assume that the creation is ordered in a universal network of correspondences between the qualities of things which stand in unlike categories of being. A chain of gold may fitly present this universal bond itself just because gold is the most refined and precious of material substances. Such qualitative kinships operate across the categories of being from the lowest forms of existence to the highest, linking sensible properties with moral and spiritual qualities in an ascending scale of value. To transmute a base element into gold would be to make a general advance up the scale of being corresponding to the ascent from touch to sight, sense to spirit, beasts to angels, lower angelic orders to the seraphim.

Farra and Contile rework Pico's arguments for the dignity of man into an assertion of our focal standing at the hub of a universe of correspondences. The economy of the little world of man exactly replicates the economy of created nature and the order of creation itself. Man is 'truly a divine creature' who is 'naturally called a little world, in which all the things of the grand world are contained with a stupendous bond'.[28] Yoking a mortal with an immortal nature we are collocated in the middle of the universe and by our own choice or divine grace have it within us to assume an earthly or a heavenly aspect, 'by which it may well be discovered in what manner man is linked with and embraces by similitude all things, earthly and divine'.[29] The rediscovery of the links may be more than an academic exercise. In reassembling the scattered pieces into a whole picture we restore our bond of sympathy with other created things which may give us some power to control them. Farra's derivation of the modern academies from 'the Magia of Zoroaster and Zamolside'[30] conflates the making of *imprese* with the art of magic. It opens to the academicians the prospect of an affective part in the universal interchange of love whose sponsor is the thrice-great Hermes himself, 'firstborn of the sempiternal Jove'.[31]

The search for occult knowledge becomes at once spiritual and practical, amounting to an attempt to control the forces of nature both within and beyond ourselves. In effect the end must be the recovery of man's lost powers rather than the discovery of something new. We grope for an apprehension which men once shared intuitively with the angels but have long forfeited, the obscured or occulted signs of truth which are still there to be read even though our decaying faculties cannot spontaneously comprehend them. The sceptical thought that the natural order itself may be decaying had not taken hold of the theorists of the hieroglyph.

These theorists looked only to recover the mysterious truths which were obscured in consequence of the Fall and are now normally concealed from us. Their preoccupation with hidden mysteries led them to take obscurity itself for a mark of truth. The more enigmatic the sign the more it will resist any but an initiate intellect, and the more likely it is to hold the truth. 'Divine things must be held occult', says Valeriano,[32] who adds that the Egyptian priests kept their wisdom and mysteries arcane, hiding divine secrets under hieroglyphic figures; and we should do the same. 'One must keep silent concerning secrets',[33] as the Egyptians preserved their sacred mysteries against the vulgar by wrapping them up in enigmas.[34] The need for secrecy is the greater if such signs do indeed have magical properties, powers which may be rightly used only by one who is spiritually fit to make the discovery having recovered in himself so much of the wisdom which mankind lost at the Fall.[35] The right interpretation of them calls for 'minds elevated to high and almost divine affairs' which 'for their purity might converse with celestial intelligences', and will prove themselves 'so much more praiseworthy' as the task is 'more difficult and fatiguing'.[36]

Such ideas bear on more than hieroglyphics. On this understanding the process of making or reading hieroglyphs is not essentially different from the processes of natural investigation or natural magic, as they were then understood:

Natural magic therefore is that which contemplates the powers of all natural and celestial things, and searching curiously into their sympathy doth produce occult powers in nature unto public view, so coupling inferior things as allurements to the gifts of superior things by their mutual application that from thence arise wonderful miracles, not so much by art as by nature, to which art becomes an assistant whilst it works these things.[37]

The theorists themselves speak only of their contemplative pursuit of truth as it contrasted with the active way. *Intus Non Extra* was the motto of the Brescian Academy.[38] This contemplative quest is purely intellectual and works through intelligible signs, whereas the active venture seeks to exploit the properties and virtues of things to the end of manipulating nature.

Sixteenth-century theorists of the hieroglyph took such activities for several modes of the search for an arcane wisdom, which may be gained only by an elite band of regenerates who have purified their intellects: 'On an unused path, by means of intellectual cognition, I prepare myself to rise above the steep and eminent summit of the true and unshadowed honour'.[39] Thus the maker or interpreter of hieroglyphic devices is no less a spiritual hero than the magician or the alchemist: 'Christ, who was the fulfilment of the Prophets, occulted a great part of the divine secrets under the obscurity of his parables'.[40] They take him for a modern magus who is capable of seeing beyond the appearance of disorder and actually reaffirming the lost correspondence of things:

For that gift of Nature which is called wit consists precisely in conjoining by means of shrewd apprehensions objects which in fact appear disconnected, retracing in these the occult vestiges of friendship between the same contrariety, the unobvious unity of special likenesses in the highest unlikeness, some knot, some relationship, bond, kinship, some confederation, where others would never have suspected it.[41]

When the discovery of truth consists in establishing links between things seemingly discrete and unlike each other then sheer mental agility may mark a purifying of vision. Spiritual heroism calls for nimble wits.

The hieroglyphs which do the rounds of the treatises suggest that there was not much spiritual heroism about. To turn from theory to practice is to mark a certain bathos; as when della Porta and Cornelius Agrippa find confirmation in simple magnetic experiments of their marvellous vision of a universe of correspondences held in harmony by the force of divine love.[42] The devices themselves scarcely open occult mysteries to us. One of Alciati's most celebrated emblems depicts a plump baby whose right hand is pulled towards the earth by a large stone which is tied around it while its left hand is lifted towards the clouds by a pair of wings. The verse simply points to the ambiguous status of a being who is simultaneously lifted by feathers and pulled down by a heavy weight; while the motto incongruously proclaims a moral commonplace, 'Paupertatem summus ingeniis obesse, ne provehantur'.[43]

Sambuco shows 'the difference between physics and metaphysics' with a crowded emblem in a frame, which centres on the figure of a multi-breasted and leg-swathed Nature. This figure stands like a mummy in a cloud-crossed landscape with her left hand pulled down

to earth by a large dangling rose and her right hand borne up towards
the clouds by some flying wings. A crescent moon to the right of her
head counterbalances a bird of prey which is perched on her left
shoulder. To the front and left of the figure, alongside the rose, a
round shrine surmounted by the globe of the world sits squarely on
the earth. Behind her and higher, on her right, a temple crowned by
an astrolabe hangs among the clouds. An eighteen-line poem in Latin
points the double disposition of nature which offsets time with
eternity, matter with spirit, the temple of Diana with the temple of
God.[44] Labia offers the bizarre device of a fish-bishop, who stands
upright in the sea between the flying motto *Ex Sion Species Decoris
Eius* and the supporting maxim in Italian 'That a bishop must match
the tenor of his life to his lofty name'. Labia himself explains the
device at length, recounting the tales of sailors who had sighted such
marine bishops and in one case actually taken up a specimen of the
order from the Polish seas, clad in its full pontificals. This curious catch
was carried as a present to the king, whom it gave to understand by
gestures that it wished to be thrown back into the sea so that it might
resume its ministry to its scaly flock in that vast diocese. The motto
indicates that all a bishop's 'excellence and beauty comes from that
religious Zion which is the Church itself'.[45]

Without doubt some theorists would have taken such serviceable
specimens for mere moral emblems, examples of an inferior form
which is apt for common understanding only. The mode of the hieroglyph which prompted the loftiest claims, and furthered an exclusive
cult, was the *impresa*. Strictly, *imprese* had developed independently of
Horapollo and could not claim ancient authority at all. They were the
product of the courtly ritual of chivalry and came into being as
heraldic signs, the personal insignia of a knight. Sixteenth-century
manuals of chivalry explicitly codify them as a modern form which
may have owed something to imperial Rome. Gabriele Simeoni
derives them from Roman medals.[46] Giovio, Ruscelli, Tasso and
Fraunce all point out that the *impresa* cannot have derived from the
ancient Egyptian signs but grew out of the chivalric exigencies of the
recent European wars.[47] Nonetheless the form was developed as an art.
Military *imprese* were marshalled and categorised, precisely legislated
for and evaluated in keen comparisons. The pundits of this form claim
no hermetic intent. Their concern is to give chivalric ceremony a
learned grounding in devices which figure the 'filosofia del cavaliere'[48]
and offer an ideal register of the place of the noble orders in the body
politic. This heraldic office of the *impresa* persisted as long as chivalry
itself survived.

The *impresa* went esoteric when the mode was taken up by the learned academies which mushroomed in France and Italy in the later sixteenth century. Hundreds of these academies emerged,[49] many of them professing occult ends. The academicians took themselves for the heirs of the magi. Farra of Pavia traced their direct descent from the magus Zoroaster, and 'all those magicians and sages of antiquity'.[50] They attached huge importance to the choice of an *impresa* which might serve for their occult sign and cryptically justify their solitary spiritual endeavour.

The academies took titles which proclaimed their rarefied aspirations and were defined in the institutional *impresa*: *Occulti, Affidati, Stellati*. They truly spawned *imprese* since each member then proposed his own device which amplified or played upon the idea thus espoused. The *Affidati* of Pavia took the *impresa* of the *stellini*, little stars, guides along the ascent to divine love. The academicians themselves took titles in keeping, *Il Chiuso, L'Arcano, Il Solingo, L'Offuscato, Il Sommerso, Il Sepolto*. They themselves commissioned the publication of collections of their *imprese* with highflown exegeses which make up a manifesto of the aims of the Academy itself.

These defiantly arcane publications simply take the *impresa* for a mode of the sacred hieroglyph. They claim extraordinary powers for their own devices which are now hailed as revelations of divine mysteries, channels of occult virtue, signatures of providence. Taking their cue from Valeriano, and feeding upon each other, the academic expositors urge the extreme case for the sacred origin of the hieroglyph and the metaphysical scope of the *impresa*. They challenge us to try the claim upon the devices which they celebrate, such as the crab and butterfly of Augustus Caesar with its motto *Festina lente*, the salamander of Francois I with the motto *Nutrisco et extinguo*, the porcupine of Louis XII with its curious motto *Cominus et eminus*. This *impresa* of the porcupine was generally acknowledged to be the supreme specimen of the art:

It scarcely fulfils the expectations which the sustained praises of it arouse.[51] We might judge that the meaning commonly assigned to it, as to all of these regal devices, has more to do with secular power than with spiritual mystery.

The manifesto of the occult Academy of Brescia is typical of its bizarre kind. It was compiled by Bartolomeo Arnigio, who explains that the Academy devotes itself to 'Keeping awake and pure that divine particle which Blessed God has occulted in the penetralia of our bodies in the manner of a ray of fire'.[52] Hence it has elected for its *impresa* the antique image of a Silenus, an artificial rather than a natural form which the ancients depicted with a hollowed body such as might 'preserve closed up some most beautiful idea of a God or Goddess'. Within the sensual husk the divine image thus occults itself in its entire perfection, untarnished by contact with air and mud. The motto for this *impresa*, *Intus non extra*, intimates that the academicians devote their entire study to the inner idea rather than the outward appearance. Arnigio discovers no less than seven distinct meanings in the *impresa* of the Silenus, which all grow out of the linked ideas that the truth must be kept dark and that the divine spirit may conceal itself in a 'grotesque and concupiscent body of sense'.

One of the academicians of the *Occulti*, who is evidently Arnigio himself, takes the style of *Il Solingo*, which he justifies in his *impresa* of the ibex. We are to understand by this *impresa* that, as the ibex climbs up the Alps alone and dwells in parts remote and unfrequented, so Solingo wraps himself up in his own thoughts and gets above the things of this vile world so as to lose himself in divine speculation. Arnigio finds it a merit of this device that it proclaims its bearer's commitment to an ascent which the 'blind and foolish' world leaves unused and very few may attempt yet whose reward in the world is only calumny. Arnigio sustains for several pages his exposition of the *impresa*, ingeniously canvassing every conceivable scriptural and mythological application of a solitary ascent to truth and especially celebrating the elevation of a divine madness, such as Bacchus himself seeks when he goes up hills in order to be made drunk with the nectar of God's mysteries.[53]

What seems patent in all these commentaries is that the expositors themselves read and evaluate their *imprese* not as magic signs but as witty metaphors or cryptogramic conceits. They make no bones about the primacy of wit; indeed the work of wit is essential to their understanding of the quest to recover occult truth:

Man's particular virtue is to know how to discern the likenesses and conformities between things which are diverse in themselves. [His wit] stands on its own in the equal midst of all things, of whatever kind they may be, and acquires more virtue from that host of correspondences as the difficulty of distinguishing them increases and it needs more acuteness and clarity to dig them out.[54]

Their practical demonstration of the working of *imprese* calls for no such occult or metaphysical provisions as even so chaste an account evokes. Nor are all the commentators out-and-out occultists. For Aresi, Domenichi, Simeone, Ammirato, as for Paradin's English translator, an *impresa* is simply a metaphor.[55] We make an *impresa* by discovering or creating some sensible image which will proclaim a moral truth. Arnigio shows how the creator of an *impresa* must work his way through the properties of an animal or object, which need not be the characteristics the thing naturally possesses but may be those attributed to it by various authors. From these he will make a choice of those features which are relevant to his purpose, seeking to accommodate them to the subject or sponsor of the *impresa* and using every correspondence he can discover.[56] Bargagli cites the device of the porcupine to show how we must 'consider the similarity in unlike things'; and he speaks of 'the most velocitous discourse, and as it were syllogism of the intellect' which is involved in 'compounding the likeness of the recognised nature of the porcupine with the quality of this King who carried such an animal for his *impresa*'.[57] Man's creative power to exploit the likenesses and conformity between things which are diverse in themselves shows up the more strikingly as our wit finds more difficulty in making these relationships.[58]

Wit, by penetrating into the true nature of things, permits us to see and make the essential links or couplings between apparently disparate objects. What these accounts propose to us is a creation which providentially coheres throughout by witty correspondence and is intelligible to agile wits. On this understanding we arrive at our knowledge of it by canvassing the range of correspondences between objects which are qualitatively ordered; and the outcome of that process may be realised in intelligible images 'which are made to signify a different thing from that which is seen with the eye'.[59] Such images, we are told, present themselves as similitudes and work by a relation of properties across the general categories of matter, playing upon the correspondences between things in terms of such defining characteristics as their form, substance, attributes, material cause, formal cause, efficient cause, or whatever.

The entire elaborate system of occult correspondences turns out to be nothing more than a projection from the Categories of Aristotle, which is taken for a map of the universe and a revelation of the hidden order of created being itself. Even such formal academicians as Palazzi and Bargagli directly refer us for the means of making images to Cicero's rhetorical ordering of Aristotle's *Analytics*, in the *Topics* and the *De Inventione*.[60]

The academic understanding is that we know and control our universe by means of the coupling of things in different categories of being, according to the degree of their possession of qualities or properties in common or the unlikeness or contrariness of the qualities. We show our recovery of a lost apprehension in our capacity to perceive and relate the properties of things across the categories of matter, as it were by repossessing ourselves of correspondences which are already occultly there. A true act of restored perception will entail the yoking of things seemingly yet not finally unlike, and might produce quite radical couplings as the objects thus related by their particular properties seem more generally incongruous or lie in more distant categories of being. We might couple a low object with a high one, or represent an exalted spiritual state with a gross material object; and the incongruity would convey its own intimation of the distance between spirit and sense.[61]

The making of witty *imprese* calls for the correlation by like properties and qualities of objects from quite distant categories of being, to an end which may be enigmatic and even arcane. Precepts and examples by the score show us just how this process is to be carried through, all of them drawing upon the methods of persuasion recommended in the textbooks of rhetoric. Ripa instructs us in the method of coupling unlike elements, such as fortitude and a column which is to present that virtue, making use of all the correspondences of properties he can discover as well as the points of unlikeness, contrariety, repugnance and so on.[62]

These accounts of the actual making and reading of *imprese* leave no doubt that such processes call for quick wits rather than spiritual elevation, and are unlikely to yield metaphysical truth: 'For the most part they are nothing other than similitudes and comparisons'.[63] They belong to Rhetoric, 'which is an art of knowing how to lie'.[64] The rules of the game as Bargagli, Tasso and others set them out keep us wholly in the realm of rhetorical effect.[65] We discover similitudes in diverse things by our acuteness in perceiving like qualities and quick dexterity in coupling them; and the more distant the objects related the better. The coupling itself is to be squared in that at least two terms on either side should be exactly matched up. The more such relationships we discover in a single stroke, and the more things the reader thus learns at a stroke, the better the effect.

The aim is always to arouse wonder and the overall effect should be marvellous. The more difficult and rare the device the better, and the more praiseworthy becomes the capacity to grasp it. There will be no merit or novelty in a device which is intelligible to everyone and grows out of evident resemblances; the whole art lies in exhibiting something while still keeping it hidden 'so that it fits the capacity of purged intellects to penetrate it'.[66] Nonetheless decorum must be observed; and obscurity, darkness, enigma are appropriate only to the forms which embody sacred mysteries. The motto of the *impresa* should be brief, ambiguous, and singular, and should complement the device in such a way that the two elements together amount to a kind of syllogism; yet the formal effect will be that of enthymeme, a 'sophistical cavillation' whose end is truth.[67] Later rhetoricians of wit, such as Tesauro, simply take over these requirements.[68]

These rules curiously transform into a hermetic endeavour the Aristotelean process of making metaphor. Even the incongruity between the crude representation and the complex meaning discovered in it is taken for a positive virtue, showing us how far the spirit outgoes the gross body. A hieroglyph becomes a sensible cipher for a spiritual perception. The image is strictly intelligible in that its meaning does not dwell in the particular sensible embodiment but may be fully realised in all manner of reproductions, as each kind realises its form in particular objects. Printing itself presents a neoplatonic emblem. It remains to be seen how far such a conception of wit may bear upon the practice of poets who take another view of the relation of the spirit to the body.

5

ARTS OF INGENUITY

Seventeenth-century theorists in Europe canonised wit. Croce unearthed a body of theorising which formalised the cult of the witty conceit. He mustered some six treatises in Italian and one in Spanish to witness the critical principles of the time.[1] The titles of these works indicate their scope and appeared as follows:

M. Pellegrini, *Delle Acutezze, che Altrementi Spiriti, Vivezze, e Concetti, Volgarmente si Appellano*, Genoa, 1639; and *I Fonti dell'Ingegno Ridotti ad Arte*, Bologna, 1650.

P. F. Minozzi, *Gli Sfogamenti d'Ingegno*, Venice, 1641.[2]

B. Gracián, *Agudeza y Arte de Ingenio en que se Explican Todos los Modos y Diferencias de Conceptos*, Madrid, 1642 and (much augmented) Huesca, 1648.

Sforza Pallavicino, *Del Bene*, Rome, 1644; and *Trattato dello Stile e del Dialogo*, Rome, 1662.[3]

E. Tesauro, *Il Canocchiale Aristotelico*, Turin, 1670 and, with two sections added, Bologna, 1675.

Only Gracián's and Tesauro's treatises seem to have made any mark. Tesauro's *Il Canocchiale* was republished in the augmented version in Venice, 1682, and in a Latin translation of that version in Cologne, 1714. Gracián's *Agudeza* ran to three editions in its first seven years, and fifteen editions in all down to 1773. A modern edition was published in Madrid in 1942 and reprinted in 1957.

Mario Praz found that the treatises of Gracián, Tesauro and Sforza Pallivicino simply bear out the thinking of the times, which brings the entire universe 'under a mode of wit'.[4] J. A. Mazzeo and S. L. Bethell followed up the lead Croce and Praz gave, but they reversed Croce's estimate of the theories themselves while nonetheless relying heavily on his account of them.[5]

Croce himself parades these theorists as stalking-horses in an aesthetic debate with his own times about the function of style in art.

He finds them stuck in a false separation of form from content which leads them to take style for mere decoration and wit for no more than the ingenious embellishment of received commonplaces. He dismisses as a settled fallacy the assumption that style is a rhetorical extra, a view which denies the essential oneness of form and content and belies the true end of art. Yet he also detects some sign of a truer judgment overriding the Aristotelean preconceptions. He takes Gracián's pronouncement that the end of *agudeza* is neither truth nor the ornation of words to imply that wit must be judged by its own criterion of beauty, as a harmonious concordance between extreme terms. Still more tendentiously he finds an inkling of an aesthetic of pure beauty in Sforza Pallavicino's categorising of poetry as a mode of First Apprehension, that order of discourse which does not require that statements be true or false. He makes an aesthetic hero of the obscure rhetorician Pellegrini, claiming that Pellegrini alone recognised the error of the distinction between the naked sense and its dress, and discovering in his remark that the wit should be subordinate to the argument nothing less than a foreshadowing of 'the modern theory of literary form' which supposes that the form is not an ornament but the meaning itself, and its own end.

Mazzeo and Bethell discover claims to universal truth where Croce found so little to redeem the crass repetition of ancient error. They independently contend that these seventeenth-century *trattatisti* develop a full-blown theory of metaphysical wit, or actually provide a theoretical prescription for the wit of metaphysical poetry. Mazzeo assumes that the treatises themselves were intended to serve as guidebooks for poets. He compounds Croce's recasting of Sforza Pallavicino by claiming that First Apprehension actually prescribes for the discovery of truth. In Tesauro and Pellegrini he finds theoretical justification of the assumption that wit deals in occult mysteries. Wit relates things from different logical categories so as to recover the primal correspondences between the various orders of being in the universe.

Bethell transforms Croce's readings of Gracián and Tesauro into a prospectus for a sacramental quest. He attributes to those theorists the apprehension that wit is the godlike faculty in man which discovers a harmonious yet surprising order in the universe. The function of wit is to reveal the beauty of a divinely ordered creation by discovering the links between things such as make up a universal system of correspondences. Wit may be distinguished from Dialectics in that its end is not logical correctness but the discovery of beauty; in fact its specific means is the logical fallacy, which opens a surer way than the syllogism to the beauty of nature itself. Bethell attributes to Tesauro this distinction between logical processes and wit though he draws upon Gracián too for the idea that the witty use of logical fallacy may reveal a mystery, disclosing an order beyond the reach of the correct processes of logical reasoning. One such use of a formally fallacious mode of reasoning would be that which is entailed in the attempt to read the creation as a divine hieroglyph. Another might be the creation of conceits which run counter to ordinary expectation, and actually set aside the encumbrance of contingent circumstance so as to seize upon the divine truths which lie hidden amid the squalor and obscenities of the everyday world. 'Without getting in the way of truth'; 'jewels among the mud': Bethell adapts some phrases in Tesauro to sum up an art such as Donne's, which makes much of cavilling logic and mingles supernatural mysteries with baser matter and even obscenities. He claims that this conception of wit is not new in European thinking but goes back to those Church Fathers who had their literary roots in Alexandria, and whose manner was brought to bear upon seventeenth-century poetry by the Jesuit revival of patristic preaching.

Bethell supposed that the English metaphysical poets really do explore metaphysical states and aim at sacred truth. A successful conceit offers us 'the clearest proof of the omnipresent activity of God'. His uncompromising persuasion that wit seeks to mirror the order of the universe set him against the subjectivism of the 1930s critics, who took Donne's radical incongruities for the expression of inner states. He scouted Johnsonian detractors of the metaphysical poets for whom metaphysical conceits at best make a fantastic flourish upon the humble sense. Following Rosamund Tuve[6] he distinguished the strictly functional wit of the metaphysical poets from the ornamental wit of the Elizabethans. Nonetheless he repudiated Tuve's purely logical differentiation of wit on the ground that a witty conceit is a wholly different device from a geometrical theorem.

To turn to the treatises themselves is to come right down to earth. Their bearing upon metaphysical poetry is scarcely obvious. Pellegrini is a rigid Aristotelean whose *Acutezza* is no more than a handbook of smart sayings and jokes; and his *Fonti* is a *copia* of conversational wit which recommends the use of the formal categories of matter to engender witty devices. Minozzi's *Gli Sfogamenti d'Ingegno*, of which very few copies survive, simply includes among its celebrations of some northern Italian cities a praise of the pungent and witty style of the Bolognese writers, which makes them so superior to the ancients. Sforza Pallavicino's *Del Bene* is a moral essay, taking in a general characterisation of poetry which the author followed up in his *Trattato* with a systematic exposition of literary imitation and poetic embellishment. Tesauro describes his vast *Canocchiale Aristotelico* – 'The Aristotelean Spyglass' – as a treatise of elocution 'which teaches good speech'; but it effectively amounts to an attempt at a comprehensive codification of wit which categorises the working of wit in all its verbal and pictorial forms, chiefly by way of synthesising the notable discussions of witty examples from the mid-sixteenth century to his own day.

Gracián's *Agudeza* is the one work which outlasted its age, partly because it remained the only major study of poetic wit. Its reputation has swung as violently as Donne's. J. H. Wiffen in 1823 judged it to teach 'an art of writing . . . founded on the most absurd principles and supported by good and bad specimens, jumbled together in the most discordant manner'.[7] Menéndez y Pelayo allowed that it is simply 'a rhetoric of the conceit', which errs in reducing all the qualities of style to one quality only. But he discovered in it 'a highly original attempt to substitute for the purely formal rhetoric of the schools . . . another ideological rhetoric in which the style reflects the quality of the thought, and might give body to the most intricate conceits of the mind'.[8] Croce brusquely punctured Pelayo's claim: 'But in truth Gracián's work is rather an enthusiastic recommendation and anthology of *secentismo* preciosity than a work of true and proper theory . . . it shines neither in originality nor in coherence'.[9] Only in the aftermath of the new rage for metaphysical poetry did the *Agudeza* re-emerge as a serious study of wit. Mazzeo put Grácian in the vanguard of a critical revolution which supplanted the idea of imitating nature with an ideal of self-contained symmetry. Bethell found that he prescribes for the contemplation of the hidden order in nature.

These seventeenth-century commentators all assume that *acutezza*, or *agudeza*, is an indispensable constituent of literary worth. They define this quality in various ways but they concur that without it a discourse lacks life. Their one truly radical step is to propose a new pantheon of the writers who excelled in wit, and to disparage the primitive insipidity of such as Dante, Petrarch and Boccaccio, who supposedly lacked it.[10] Several of them declare that the great days of style began only with the development of *acutezza* in the sixteenth century and the emergence of the conceited poets. Minozzi insists that modern writers in general far outdo the ancients just because we value wit and they neglected it; so that we should now invent our own conceits instead of imitating theirs.[11] Tesauro found much wit in the ancients, yet he claims that it was the conceited preaching of Musso in the sixteenth century which inaugurated the great age of Italian sermon-style.[12] Gracián actually champions ancient writers on the ground that they had more soul and ingenious vivacity than the moderns, because they threw everything into their conceits instead of playing with words or artifices of style.[13] He himself draws on Martial almost as often as on Góngora to exemplify the modes of wit. Yet his very conception of wit promotes radical conceits, and the poets whom he singles out as *culto* for their exquisite ingenuity of wit are Góngora, Marino and Guarini.

The new literary taste is reflected in the theorising only to the extent that these treatises devote so much zeal to the ordering of wit and witty writing. In their critical thinking all the commentators look back to ancient precepts and the categories of the Renaissance rhetoricians, frequently assimilating entire passages from earlier writers. Tesauro's title proclaims the Aristotelean basis of his work; and his scheme becomes a hold-all of Renaissance literary attitudes. Their common starting point is the presumption that poetry is an art of feigning which serves the ends of rhetoric. Croce remarked that they cannot get beyond the limited conception of style and wit which we find in the sixteenth-century rhetoricians just because they all take for granted the Aristotelean separation of form from matter. When Sforza Pallavicino announced in 1662 that poetry is an art of imitation which needs to be distinguished from copying or robbery he confirmed the Petrarchan axiom that the poet shows his individual quality in the way he presents the thought; and he conducted his entire discussion within the terms of the old Humanist controversy over ornation, backing up the Ciceronians against the champions of a plain style, Barbaro against Pico, Poliziano against Cortese, Bembo against all the detractors of imitation. Gracián's basic assumption is that wit aspires to put the truth in its most striking form. When he speaks of 'gilding the truth' he means that beauty lies in the ingenious elegance of the way in which the truth is presented: 'The *ingenio* is not content with truth alone, as is the judgment, since it also aspires to beauty. It would count for little in architecture to assure firmness without attending to the ornate'.[14] He makes it clear that the beauty he refers to here is a grace of the understanding and not just of the eyes or ears; it is what gives truth that intellectual pungency which implants it in the mind.

The grandiose claims all come down to the witty exploiting of properties across the Aristotelean categories. Pallavicino cites Euclidean geometry as an instance of the purely logical use of the categories which wit needs to go beyond; whereas he takes poetry itself for a mode of rhetorical discourse which has its own extra-logical ends and means.[15] For all their hermetic flourishes Tesauro, Pellegrini, and Pallavicino share the effective understanding that *acutezza* is specifically not discovery or rediscovery but artifice. They agree with Gracián that all forms of wit arise from the artificial likenesses or unlikenesses between properties in different categories of being, an effect which is distinguished from a rhetorical trope by some special circumstance in the correspondence and may be heightened still more by suspense and surprise. Tesauro defines *argutezza* as the product of art, meaning that it occurs in relationships which are not existentially given in the order of nature but must be artificially contrived as even nature, the angels and God himself contrive them.[16] He limits the scope of *argutezza* to devices which are formed by the second and third operations of the intellect, those which go beyond simple metaphor as metaphor itself goes beyond the plain and proper names of things.[17] Only such complex contrivances may truly be called *ingegnosi* and merit the name of perfect *argutezza*; and he claims that their making calls for a double capacity, requiring not just perspicacity in perceiving the links but also adroitness in exploiting them.[18] Thus the operation is not limited by the actuality of correspondences in nature but may be free and even arbitrary, constrained only by the normal rhetorical obligations of aptness and decorum.[19]

Gracián finds that there are three basic modes of *agudeza*, which follow out distinct ways of using likenesses or unlikenesses between properties in different categories of matter.[20] The first mode is correlation, which we use when we exploit the degree of likeness between things in different categories so as to produce similitudes and parities, disparities, confrontations of corresponding properties, effects of proportion, disproportion, correspondence and the like. The second mode is contrariety, which we use when we exploit the degree of unlikeness between things in different categories to set off contraries and contrarieties, counterbalances, harmonies in dissonance, conditional exaggerations. The third mode is surprise, which we use when we exploit some unexpected likeness or unlikeness between things in different categories so as to bring about surprising paradoxes, sudden reversals, perplexities and resolutions.

Gracián adds that the *agudeza* is the more striking as the objects are less like each other and come from more distant categories.[21] Indeed he defines the conceit as a dexterous correlation between intelligible extremes.[22] A conceit consists in a vividly direct confrontation of unlike objects which throws up meaningful points of likeness or repugnance between them. A conceited similitude is a similitude lifted beyond a mere rhetorical trope or figure by its 'soul of subtlety', which may be infused into it by 'some form of mystery, contrariety, correspondence, improportion, sentence etc.'; and for this reason it takes the first place in the order of wit. We judge conceits by the extremeness of the terms, the number of points of correlation made in one stroke between contrary and distant things, the difficulty of the coupling, the extent to which the effect surpasses previous uses and the reader's expectation. Conceits contrived by a seemingly impossible coupling are best of all. Guarini's comparison of love with the sea is a superlative conceit because it turns upon a radical correspondence of cause and effect, which is grounded in the myth that Venus is the sea's daughter.[23]

Yet Gracián plainly finds little savour in forms of simple correspondence. His taste is for more pungent meat; in fact his favoured effects of wit always involve some mode of contrariety and he prizes contraposition above all. This preoccupation with effects of contrariety and contraposition is a chief reason for the notorious disorder of the treatise, given that his poetic illustrations themselves almost always resist his schematising. He continually brings chaos to his exposition of the modes of wit by darting off after every stray effect of counterposed terms until his scheme of wit itself lies in ruins. The *Agudeza* might fairly be taken for an elaborate assertion of the primacy of contraposition over all the other modes of wit.

Gracián uses his poetic specimens to exemplify the modes of *agudeza*, categorising them by their management of the conceit. His concern with them is aridly formal. Lope de Vega's beautifully controlled conceit of the Old Testament and the New Testament as two capes, St Joseph's and St Martin's, is commended simply as an example of an absolute correspondence which is founded in an exact conformity between the subject and the terms: 'He proposes the confrontation by way of question, forms an artificial competition, and gives the reason of the excess with exaggeration; and though the style is not very highlighted this is made good with the power of conceit, which is the principal part'.[24]

Gracián favours unexpected correspondences which carry some strangeness between the terms, such as Bartolomé Leonardo's conceit of death as a club-blow which refines coarse cloth to fine wool,[25] or Salinas y Azpilcuela's conceit of the crucifying of St Andrew as the tuning of an instrument to celestial pitch.[26] He singles out 'the divine Ledesma' for his sustained feats of correspondence, as in the depicting of Loyola as a blacksmith who forges souls upon his anvil,[27] and his representation of a martyr's death by a stone in the chest as the taking of a medicinal tablet which will cure all worldly ills.[28] Such sustained correspondences call for unusual ingenuity, requiring that 'one looks for some correlation between the topics which fall within some circumstance or predicate common to all of them'. F. A. Fuser brings it off notably when he renders Longinus's piercing of Christ's side with a spear as the striking of a stone upon a flint which ignites the tinder of the cross and sparks forth the fire of love as a beacon to the whole world.[29] Gracián commends this laboured piece just because it is so elaborately contrived. He finds it 'full of highlighted manners for the plurality of the conceits and the singularity of each one, though more for the bond and composition which holds all these together'. Góngora's magnificent 'Arbol de cuyos ramos fortunados' wins no higher praise than that for its extended play upon the name of the poet's patron, Mora, a mulberry tree.[30] Gracián's repeated eulogising of this poem solely addresses the felicity with which the play is managed, the 'harmony and correlation . . . between the terms themselves [and] the subject'. He judges that the poem shows how a play of correspondences becomes 'perfect when one succeeds in uniting the conceits and making a body bound with some device'.[31]

Gracián finds more promise of wit in contrariety and contradiction than in straight correspondence, and most wit of all in the forms of contraposition. He repeatedly speaks of the coupling of opposites as a condition of poetic vitality: 'Contrariety is the grand foundation of all subtlety';[32] 'This contrariety gives soul to the similitude, which in itself would be dead';[33] 'To unite by the force of discourse two contradictory extremes is an exceptional argument of subtlety';[34] 'The subtlety increases in pace with the contrariety of the two correlates'.[35] Any number of his examples confirm the tastes of the times. Marino, 'Fattor fatto fattura' – 'The maker becomes the thing made'; Góngora, 'Burning in dead waters live flames'; Luis de León, 'And my joy exchanged for infinite pain', 'Found for paradise a wild prison', 'Drank for fresh water burning fire'. Ausonius Gallus's epigram on Dido of Carthage pops up several times for its neat *discordia concors* – 'a very concordant dissonance between the contrarieties':[36] 'Her first husband perished and she fled; her second husband fled and she perished'.

Conceits of contraposition are to be worked up from disparities between terms in distant categories, by opposition between extremes, correlations of contraries, dissonances by disproportion, artificial discordances: 'The improportion and dissonance of the extremes themselves serve to found the conceited dissimilitude, and that contraposition is the more effective for being very artificial'.[37] The special circumstances, which give a foothold to *agudeza* and make a disparity conceited and highlighted beyond the scope of a plain figure of rhetoric, 'can be taken from one or other of the adjuncts of the matched subject, whether of causes, effects, properties, contingencies or any other special occurrence'; and he gives examples in quantity, place, time, effects.[38] One may found a conceit of contraposition and disproportion in disparity, as did Bartolomé Leonardo when he wrote on the death of the inventor of life,[39] or in the counterbalancing of proportion and disproportion, such as the same author contrives in his sonnet on St Lawrence, 'Qual cisne . . . '.[40] This poem works up into an extended conceit the apparent contradiction of St Lawrence's singing under torture and in the fire, setting off his pains against his joy, his dying against his revival to new life which 'gives a living sepulchre to a dead corpse'.

Martial shows the mordancy of a well-placed contraposition in his epigram on Lavinia entering her bath behind a boy – a Penelope goes in, a Helen emerges.[41] Counterposed terms may produce stark paradox, as in the opening of Juan de Valdés's poem upon Leander – 'Gazing upon the light, most blind with the light'.[42] Or the poet may seize upon some likeness within the opposing elements, as Andrés does when he plays off against each other the martyring of St Lawrence in fire and St Orentius in ice so as to bring out the common factor in two such unlike manners of death.[43] Góngora looms large in Gracián's pantheon of wit because he perfected this mode: 'the triumph of his great wit consisted in ingenious contraproportions . . . His works are woven with this subtlety'.[44] Gracián cites some well-known examples from Góngora, including the notorious effects in *Angélica e Medoro*.[45] Gracián singles out Marino for the mastery of contraposition he shows in such poems as his sonnet on Christ's passion which is built upon this device:[46]

> Qui per altri labar di sangue tinse
> Sue pure membra il gran Figliol di Dio,
> qui con l'humor che di sue neve uscio
> del paterno furor le fiamme estinse . . .

Christ's blood sets off his purity, his virgin snow quenches the flames of wrath; a crown of honour stands against the crown of thorns, the food of glory against pure gall, the opened heart against the wounded side, life against death. Gracián's comment on Marino's supplication to the Virgin as 'Stella di Dio', which startlingly makes a new Leander of the sinful poet, well brings out his purely rhetorical conception of wit. The poet 'links a nominal correspondence to an agreeable similitude, a mysterious allusion, and an erudite application. With even more ingenuity than holiness he founds the similitude of a defeated Leander upon the name Maria, which is star of the sea, and makes an extreme contraposition to conclude'.[47]

Gracián appraises such effects for their cleverness, showing greatest enthusiasm for the most radical feats of contrariety. He particularly approves sleights of transposition or transmutation, in which opposing extremes get converted to one another or work to confirm the same end. Guarini's 'Una farfalla cupida, e vagante' effects a simple transformation, the lover's heart dying as a butterfly but rising again as a phoenix.[48] In Marino's 'Piaga dolce d'amore' the wound in the lover's side becomes the mouth of an eloquent heart, the drops of his blood turn to amorous tongues.[49] Marino's mastery of these witty reversals is acknowledged in his presentation as the Italian Góngora. His conclusion of a moral sonnet sets up a drastic expectation which it suddenly reverses in a manner 'not less sweet than ingenious'.[50] 'Ecco del mondo rio' – this wicked world conceals thorns under the roses, snakes in the grass, endless cares in its insidious beguilements:

> Volgeti a quel signor, che en croce esangue,
> vela il riso nel pianto, e che ripose
> vita nel suo morir, gloria nel sangue.

The terms are cross-transferred, the seeming pleasures of the world turning to effective evils, the apparent miseries of Christ becoming real glories.

The difficulty of the linking is one of Tesauro's touchstones of wit. He too judges that the wit gets better as it makes more points of relation between things in more distant categories; and he adds that all such effects are much enhanced when they are carried off with speed, brevity, surprise so as to produce some quite novel outcome. Celerity and velocity are his continual watchwords.[51] Pellegrini finds that even witty sayings depend upon the artificial linking of diverse things in one remark, and have most effect when the terms are distant or extreme, or sharply counterposed.[52]

All these theorists agree that the process of linking the properties of objects in different categories is metaphorical, and that wit itself works as metaphor. When Pellegrini speaks of *acutezza* as a mode of the third operation of the intellect he means that it conjoins diverse things through a third term and works metaphorically in the manner of an enthymeme, whereas the second operation simply announces, predicating one thing of another by a simple verb.[53] He is far from claiming, as Mazzeo and Bethell suppose him to claim, that this use of the places of logic draws upon a universal system of spiritual sympathies or that witty metaphors are hieroglyphs of hidden mysteries. None of these seventeenth-century theorists takes the logician or the poet for a magus, or attributes talismanic force to the syllogism or the witty metaphor. The correspondences Gracián speaks of are logical constructs, not the occult sympathies between things in unlike categories such as natural magic strove to exploit, 'so coupling inferior things as allurements to the gifts of superior things, that by their mutual application . . . from thence arise wonderful miracles'.[54] All the modes of suspense and surprise which Gracián rehearses work by the management of metaphorical properties and effects; indeed, Gracián shows himself altogether more interested in ways of giving striking expression to the truth than in processes of argument. Tesauro finds that *argutezza* is doubly metaphorical in that it brings together several things in one stroke and affirms things which are not literally true. He adapts Aristotle's explanation of the pleasure we take in assertions which we know to be strictly false, arguing that we doubly enjoy the ingenuity of a device which teaches us several things at once.[55]

Poetic fabling dwindles down to the pleasing deceit of metaphor. Yet the process of making metaphors is not reprehensible for it does not work to deceive. The aim of *acutezza* is not literal truth but verisimilitude which, as Pellegrini argues, may have truth in another sense than the literal.[56] Pallavicino makes poetry a mode of First Apprehension in order to distinguish it from forms of discourse in which statements are true or false. He poses this distinction not out of a wish to set poetry apart from truth in a pure aesthetic category of beauty but because poetry appeals to the senses rather than the judgment, and aims at likeness to truth rather than truth itself.[57] Poets tell marvellous lies to the end of making the truth manifest.[58]

In Chapters 7 and 8 of the *Canocchiale* Tesauro draws out a thoroughgoing Aristotelean theory of metaphor, by whose terms he exhaustively orders the body of ideas which had emerged in the sixteenth-century discussions of metaphorical wit and of the *impresa*.

Since his subject is wit he sets out to distinguish witty exercises of metaphor and thinking from processes which are not witty, such as the syllogistic modes of logic, whatever value these processes may have in themselves. His presumption is that within the limits of decorum a metaphor becomes the more witty and conceited the more radical it is, in that its terms have been taken from more distant categories and hence are less like each other. Terms which stand too close, and are thus too much like each other, yield only tame conceits which have no wit in them. Tesauro admits no other mode of wit than the conceit or radical metaphor.

Tesauro's account of the working of witty devices curiously mingles practical instruction with analysis, and takes over whole passages from the sixteenth-century commentators on Aristotle's *Poetics* and on emblematic devices. He advises that a conceit should preferably be squared, by which he means that it should have four active terms, as does Aristotle's own coupling of the cup of Bacchus with the shield of Mars. Such a yoking of several unlike terms at once is essential to the effect for the pleasure of a witty metaphor lies precisely in our recognising, and hence learning, several new relationships in a single perception.[59] A witty conceit will follow the modes of the syllogism but differs from a syllogism in that it cannot be logically valid; it asserts what is not literally true by a process which would be sophistical in logic. The nub of Tesauro's argument is this premise that a witty conceit presents itself to us as a kind of avowed lie, or what he calls an urbane cavillation. He speaks of it as simulating for the sake of its own kind of truth a process of logic which is deliberately and openly false. A man is not literally a lion though there may be point in our speaking of him so.[60] A witty conceit is necessarily fallacious because it deliberately goes beyond the proper reference of the terms to make an application of them which is recognised to be other than the proper one. We speak properly of the root of a plant because the term 'root' properly belongs to this relationship. We speak conceitedly of the root of a problem because the term 'root' is here metaphorically applied where it does not strictly belong.

Such a mode of reasoning will remind us that these accounts of wit depend upon assumptions which we may not share. Tesauro thinks of metaphor as any application of a term which goes beyond the plain and proper use.[61] True *argutezza* is distinguished by its radical use of the categories in that it correlates the properties of things in distinct and distant orders of being; and the entire field of *argutezza* may be disposed in three ascending orders of metaphor. A stroke of *argutezza* may be a simple metaphor, or a continued figure, or an urbane cavillation. Simple metaphor is the general basis of all metaphoric use, verbal and representational alike; and Tesauro finds that there are eight basic species of metaphor. These are proportion or similitude; attribution; equivocality; hipotiposis (putting things before the reader's eyes); hyperbole; laconism; opposition (opposing a supposed adversary); and deception (surprising turns, feints, reversals and the like). Only metaphors of proportion and attribution are defined by their direct coupling of properties, and they have primacy over the rest just because they turn upon the common possession of integral properties. Tesauro allows that the other species make a mixed bag of rhetorical manoeuvres and stylistic devices; but he says that all eight species may work as *argutezza* when they put one thing for another by exploiting the categories.[62]

This 'strange mode of division', as Croce terms it,[63] purports to be a scheme for use. Tesauro shows how to take each species of metaphor through the categories to produce, on a given subject, simple metaphors of deception, metaphors of hipotiposis in the category of visible quality, metaphors of hyperbole in the category of consequence, metaphors of attribution in the category of instrumental circumstance, and so on to the limit of permutation. He draws up rules for producing conceits of various orders on a given theme, and systematises them in a series of 'practical theorems to make witty conceits'. He shows how these theorems may be supplied from a categorical index of witty material which we compile by making emblems of things we encounter as we go about our daily affairs, take walks, and look around us; and he trawls specimen terms through such an index to demonstrate its use, discovering thousands of ways of denoting the same thing and filling pages with ingenious circumlocutions for the simple terms 'Rome' and 'dwarf'.[64]

Gracián praises the ingenious orator who culled from great writers so many ways of speaking of the sun; and he lists nearly a score of these hyperbolic epithets. The sun is the king of light (Virgil), honour and splendour of the heavens (Horace), mirror of day (Ovid), fount of light (Lucan), lamp of the world (Silius Italicus), rose torch (Vida), coachman of day (Boethius), dance-leader of the stars (St Gregory Nazianzen), resplendent eye of heaven (St Basil), and so forth. Gracián gives an extract from a sermon by Padre Francisco de Borja in which all these terms are run into a continuous discourse in praise of the king. The sun is most illustrious because among so many noble descendants it is father of the stars; among courtiers the mirror of day and of its age;

among titles and lords the prince of brightness; among great men the giant of splendour.[65]

Tesauro shows how to vary a common metaphor, taking *Love is a fire* as his specimen. He exemplifies the making of continued figures, suggesting ways of prolonging to the length of an entire apologue or allegory the simple metaphor of the rose as queen of flowers. Such demonstrations propose a limited ideal of wit; and in all this remorseless categorising Tesauro shows himself preoccupied with clever periphrasis, novel ways of varying the plain and 'proper' use such as will strike the beholder with the ingenious individuality and sheer rareness of the stroke. Calling a nightingale a winged organ or an organ without pipes, and an organ itself a nightingale without feathers, are strokes of *argutezza* he several times singles out for praise on precisely such grounds. He continually seeks to engage writers in an all-out search for extravagantly novel epithets, straining to accumulate more and more such locutions by way of example. This taste for ingenious variation seems to be typical of the times. Pallavicino evidently has such processes in mind when he takes up Marino's claim that imitation need not be robbery or copying but may be novel and individual, producing surprise and wonder at the ingenious reworking of the thought.[66] Gracián distinguishes the roundabout manner of feigned artifice from the naked directness of plain truth.[67] His star examples repeatedly come before us by way of bearing out his assumption that the business of the witty poet is to point the truth, not least the great Christian paradoxes.

Several of these commentators take metaphor for pleasing deceit in a more formal sense. They understand the agreeable feignings of metaphor to include or reach perfection in the simulation of formal reasoning. Witty argument has its place in all Renaissance schemes of discourse. Even the conceit-hunting Gracián makes movements of ponderation his third mode of *agudeza* and describes his examples in terms of argument; though the effects he seeks seem calculated just to heighten the surprise of a clinching contraposition or paradox.[68] The poet raises a doubt or difficulty, holds the reader in suspense for an answer, and then ingeniously resolves the uncertainty with a surprising outcome. The most effective kind of initial difficulty is that based on contrariety and flat contradiction, which 'doubles the artifice' of less rigorous oppositions of terms. Uniting two contradictory extremes is 'an utmost argument of subtlety . . . the subtlety increases in pace with the contrariety of the two correlates'.[69] The reason that one gives in response has to be ingenious in itself and needs to resolve the discord, answer the question or whatever. The reason should be subtle, may be exaggerated, and must be extraordinary; when the reason given is contrary to what was anticipated it acquires much pleasure for its unexpectedness and for the difficulty. He instances Lope de Vega's great sonnet on the death of Absolon, 'Suspense està Absolón entre las ramas', which sets up a crowd of correspondences and then powerfully resolves them at a stroke, finally intertwining Absolon's vain aspirations with the bizarre manner of his end – his hope and ambition scattered with his hairs to the wind and to the sky, hostage to the vain occasion which holds him suspended between earth and heaven.

One may similarly heighten surprise, he says, by simulating such stratagems of debate as the raising of objections, counter-arguments and the like, appearing to escape from impossible difficulties, suddenly turning back on oneself and even reversing the apparent direction of the argument. Such examples of these devices as Guarini's beautiful poem 'Il ciel chiuso in bel volto',[70] and Góngora's 'O claro honor del liquido elemento'[71] show that he had other effects than conceited paralogisms in mind. When he quotes some prodigy of conceited cavilling, such as Marino's 'Figlia di Dio'[72] or Guarini's madrigals 'Pendeva a debil filo'[73] and 'Occhi stelle mortali',[74] he disregards the logical juggling, describing the wit wholly in terms of the deployment of correspondences and contrarieties of properties from distant categories.

Other commentators discriminate more precisely the part logic plays in wit. Pellegrini says that all metaphor is implicitly enthymeme, and that *acutezza* not only works by enthymeme but imitates the processes of sophistical logic. Yet it has no more than the appearance of logic, and its ends remain those of metaphor in that it aims at pleasing dissimulation rather than at correct reasoning. Pellegrini is emphatic that the force of the formal enthymeme should be brought out in order that the ingenious show of logic may excite wonder in itself; the writer aims to dazzle his beholders by the quickness and dexterity with which difficulties are overcome and distant things related, by the rarity and novelty of the effects, and by the vivacity of the *ingegno* thus displayed.[75]

Pallavicino says that the aim of the conceit is to delight through the marvellous, an end which is greatly furthered by surprising strokes such as surpass expectation; and he finds that ingenious sophisms play a large part in this process. He argues that false effects better befit poetry than does fidelity to fact, and an imitator is the more praiseworthy the more convincingly he deceives, as long as the deceit is recognised and prompts admiration. Poetic fables and similitudes are all forms of pseudo-proof. In fact paralogisms give particular pleasure, such as the ingenious sophistries we find in Marino's conceits. These paralogical effects are much heightened by surprise, he says. Their life depends upon the sudden adroitness of the twists, turns, reversals of the argument, the brief pungency of the stroke, even the difficulty thus posed. In some circumstances these effects are enhanced by enigma, the sheer cryptic terseness of the stroke of *acutezza*.[76]

A singularity of Tesauro's scheme of wit is that it led him to make chop-logic the paradigm form of *argutezza*. Urbane cavillation is his third and highest operation of the intellect.[77] He equates it with the logical enthymeme and makes its ingenious use the specific distinction of the *arguto* writer. The perfect stroke of *argutezza*, in whatever mode, will be found to reduce itself to the form of an enthymeme, not because its perpetrator is a skilled logician but because metaphor itself takes that logical force: 'To devise witty urbane fallacies it is not necessary to know logic but one must be able to make a simple metaphor'.[78] Tesauro follows Pellegrini and Pallavicino in altogether distinguishing this *arguto* use of enthymeme from the fallacies of logic. Such a use is based not in the sophistical modes of Dialectics but in the eight species of metaphor. Rhetoric, Dialectics, and the urbane cavillation propose different ends 'in that just as Rhetoric looks to popular persuasion, and Dialectics to scholarly instruction, so the urbane cavillation has the scope of cheering the spirits of its hearers by some pleasurable stroke without the constraint of truth [*senza ingombro del vero*]; but the dialectical cavillation sets its aim to corrupt the understanding of disputants with falsity, as if by sleight of hand'.[79]

An urbane cavillation is a metaphor by definition, a kind of lie which consists in predicating something of a character or object which it does not properly possess. Indeed a reasoning process founded in metaphor will of necessity be a cavillation or 'lie', as we see when we set it out formally:

> Achilles has courage.
> A lion has courage.
> Therefore Achilles is a lion.

He makes a like cavillation of his supreme example of *argutezza*, Louis XII's *impresa* of the porcupine, with its motto *Cominus et eminus*:

> The porcupine hurts its enemies near and far off.
> King Louis hurts his enemies near and far off.
> Therefore King Louis is a porcupine.

He indicates that this cavillation or 'lie' consists precisely in identifying King Louis with the porcupine in respect of the one attribute they have in common. To know how to lie in such a manner is the unique praise of *argutezza*. Yet like the fables of the gods, which have always been recognised for lies, this cavillation aims to please and not to deceive. It would be a confusion of categories to call it sophistical for it belongs not to Dialectics but to the category of ingenious and pleasing effects. In a word, such strokes of wit fall under the urbane mode precisely because they serve civil ends and not sophistry.

Tesauro makes no bones about his rhetorical design. He finds that urbane cavillations serve the general ends of all *argutezza* which are the honest, the useful and the just; they fall into one or another of the three categories of *arguti* conceits, the adductive, the deductive and the reflective; and in common with every other tool of rhetoric their proper work is to persuade in the service of the three kinds of discourse, Demonstrative, Deliberative and Judicial.[80] Even in Tesauro's wit-dazzled eyes these devices amount to no more than a means to praise or blame, to counsel for or against, to accuse or excuse; and they further such ends in the manner of all other rhetorical tropes by a show of rational argument, by moral suasion, or by arousing feeling.

The *Short Treatise of Conceits for Preaching* which Tesauro added to the *Canocchiale* in 1675 easily adapts the forms of lapidary *argutezza* to pulpit oratory, bringing out the urbane cavillation as the most effective kind of preaching device. These modes of sermon-wit differ from the secular modes only in the material they handle. The matter of sacred *argutezza* will be drawn from figural exegesis of the Scriptures, hieroglyphic readings in the Book of Creation and the like. Otherwise they simply call for an especially strict exercise of decorum so that they do not aspire to replace true and sound reasons in sermons, or impede their development, but serve for embroidery in the fabric of the discourse.

Tesauro sternly warns preachers against the too-lavish use of *argutezze*, which would be to fill their sermons with confetti as he thinks.[81] Pellegrini had given a like warning;[82] and a question arose between these theorists and Minozzi whether a writer might actually overdo the use of wit in prose discourse. It was the difference between these two views which prompted Croce to take this debate for a preliminary joust in a battle of aesthetic principles, Minozzi assuming that wit is the indispensable life of all good writing and the others supposing it to be no more than an incidental embellishment which might easily become an end in itself and swamp the main argument.[83]

What they are clearly not doing is debating the character of meta-physical conceits, as J. A. Mazzeo claims.[84]

Tesauro shows by means of his Practical Theorems how to make urbane enthymemes on a given theme from any of the species of simple metaphor. He gives twelve specimen methods in fact, finding the wittiest use of the mode in such historical conceits as the courtly sleight attributed to one Carlo Emanuele:

> The bridge trembles under the king
> because under the king everything trembles.

He explains that the *argutezza* here compounds a double metaphor of proportion and of equivocation, passing us from physical tremor to moral awe and playing upon properties which are 'in one instant acutely observed and velocitously conjoined'.[85] He shows how to draw a witty enthymeme from a metaphor of proportion and a metaphor of attribution on a given theme, producing enthymemes by the handful from Martial's hapless conceit of the bee dead in amber. He varies this theme wittily and conceitedly 'through all the eight kinds of metaphor' and 'through the three modes of Rhetoric, Demonstrative, Deliberative, and Judicial', then uses it to 'animate an urbane enthymeme of the pathetic form . . . the rational form . . . the moral form'.[86] When he rates the urbane cavillation so highly he has just such conceited forms of the enthymeme in mind.

All these theorists allow one constraint upon the dexterities of wit. Decorum of circumstances must curb merely arbitrary or extravagant coupling of things from distant categories. Wit might be free of all such control in one mode of discourse only, that which draws its effects from the class of *ridicoli* and aims solely to divert. The need to make people laugh excuses such deliberate transgressions of propriety as the capricious coupling of things to make absurd conceits; and Tesauro remarks that the dross of the burlesquery will heighten the effect of the wit. He justifies this commonplace with an argument which gives colour to S. L. Bethell's conviction that Tesauro grounds wit in the divine creativity itself:

Now you should not hold it in disgust to philosophise over disgusting matters, so that you may gather as if from the mud the gems of a noble art . . . On the contrary, the human mind participates in the Divine, which dwells with the same divinity in the swamps and in the stars, and from the most sordid of them fabricated the most divine of bodily creatures.[87]

Yet Tesauro simply repeats an academic commonplace when he discovers a way to occult truth in the most humdrum rhetorical manoeuvres. His own examples of witty incongruity seem bathetically unilluminating, such as that religion is the *cloaca* of humility, and the academy is a tavern of the muses. All he effectively means by the figure of the gems in the mud is that the sludge sets off the brilliance.

Tesauro's treatise culminates in an account of symbolic wit which simply orders the common lore. Tesauro distinguishes symbolic forms of wit from lapidary forms just in that the symbolic devices are presented visually. Even then they work as metaphor by putting one thing for another, and may belong to any of the eight species of metaphor. Tesauro makes this visual wit depend still more directly than verbal wit upon a qualitative hierarchy of fixed orders or characters, such as a scale of nobility. He is chiefly interested in that form of symbolic *argutezza* which most subtly expressed nice discriminations of status, the heroic *impresa*. He takes this form to present the highest and most inclusive mode of symbolic *argutezza* and of the whole art of persuasion, measuring other forms of wit by the ways in which they fall short of the consummate excellence of this one. Thus the emblem is a popular form which must be more apparent in its witty signification, so that it necessarily lacks several merits of the *impresa* and falls well short of that perfection.

The heroic *impresa* is preeminently witty because it has the double task of expressing a civic endeavour while remaining individually apt. It is at once public and private, shaped by the requirements of chivalric ceremony yet cryptically denoting the particular virtues of its bearer and no one else. The successful *impresa* will be manifest to all but understood only by the few who can recognise its personal aptness. Tesauro takes account of the *imprese* of the academies, allowing that those institutions first put the cult on a learned footing and perpetuated it when it had ceased to be of civil consequence. He finds that academic *imprese* should be more erudite, occult and complex than heroic *imprese*, having the double task of individuating at one stroke the academy itself and a particular member of it.

Tesauro then rehearses the rules for the making of the heroic *impresa*, incongruously glossing rhetorical prescriptions with hermetic flourishes. He says that the *impresa* is essentially a mixed device, comprising both figure and motto. The figure will ideally take the form of a metaphor of proportion, though most figures work by simple attribution. Metaphors of description are also effective in *imprese*, and so are devices of contraposition such as the witty juxtapositions of contrary images, the drawing out of contrary effects from like causes and so on.

When he speaks of putting one thing for another he has in mind the representation of a man's qualities by something categorically distinct from itself in virtue of some shared symbolic properties. The process will be witty in proportion to the degree of likeness in unlikeness, which means in practice that the wittiest effects relate most properties across categories lying furthest apart and differing from each other most radically. Tesauro shows how the search for an apt symbolic image gets progressively harder as we individuate the subject, passing from immaculate virginity to steadfastness under duress, and then to St Agnes's endurance of the fire. Many white things stand for purity; rather few white things stand for virgin purity; only flax stands for St Agnes. Tesauro makes it clear that it is precisely the sensible unlikeness between the subject and the symbol, St Agnes and flax, which confirms the wit of the device.

Tesauro draws out three theses for the composition of the most perfect *impresa*. Such a nonpareil will be a metaphor, which teaches us about several objects at once; it will be a metaphor of proportion; and it will have the form of an argument. He adds that the motto of the *impresa* may be drawn from any of the eight species of metaphor but must always be conjoined with laconism; which is to say that it must be brief and succinct. The conjunction of the figure with the motto comprises the *impresa*, which will remain incomplete or unintelligible if either stands alone. Figure and motto together present an urbane cavillation and will be capable of expression in the form of a fallacious syllogism, though the effect remains wholly metaphorical since the end is not deceit. Tesauro finds that this compound form is governed by rules which Giovio drew up and other theorists have augmented. These rules require among other things that the human body be excluded from the figure of the *impresa*, that the action should be one and noble, that a natural figure be preferred to an ugly one, that the motto should be in verse and taken from some classical author. The prescriptive force Tesauro allows such conditions shows them for what they had become, the self-imposed hazards of an esoteric game. They serve to multiply difficulties, to make the task harder, and the attainment of perfection, so artificially defined, still less likely. Yet they are not altogether arbitrary. For one thing the exclusion of the human body from the figure of the *impresa* is necessary to the character of a witty metaphor, which represents a man by an object in a different category of being.

Tesauro is particularly concerned to accommodate the *impresa* to the general ends of rhetoric: 'Every *impresa* is a rhetorical argument founded in the verisimilar'.[88] The most perfect *impresa* always looks to some rhetorical end, falling under one or other of the three formal modes of rhetoric and availing itself of the appropriate means of praise or blame, counsel, accusation or defence. This form calls for a particularly stringent exercise of decorum because of the double obligation of the *impresa* to conform to the general laws of rhetoric while epitomising a unique personal character in a quite particular set of circumstances.

Tesauro's rules hyper-refine the formulations of the sixteenth-century academicians.[89] His essential requirement is just theirs, namely that the *impresa* should be squared to its subject and individuated by this squaring; it will express its subject in that the two terms of the device will match the terms of the subject so as to tell us something about him. Yet he insistently brings out the need for multiple reference. The *impresa* will merit greater praise as it signifies the more attributes of its bearer, his dynasty, prowess, status, office, fame, history, domestic and personal circumstances. Best of all will be that device which conveys to the understander the very essence of its bearer's status. By the figure of the porcupine we apprehend King Louis's power to impale alike his domestic adversaries and his foreign foes. Tesauro simply confirms the prestige of this *impresa* of the *histrice* when he makes it his sublime and consummate example of the art, the very touchstone of wit; and he bears out longstanding judgment in his demonstration that it obeys all the rules of the form, offering no less than eleven distinct points of excellence. Thus it presents a coupling of two intelligible forms so as to produce a third mixed form. It is pointedly ambiguous in that it may be taken in several ways. It is marvellous in its effect, and prompts us to marvel at it. It is not simply an enigma, though its meaning cannot be discerned without effort. It is made by the coupling of things which are not so obscure, distant, or learned as to be more appropriate in a sacred or an academic *impresa* than in the device of a soldier. It is intelligible to some but not to all. It expresses the philosophy of a knight, and is individual and personal to him. Its figure and motto together amount to a syllogism. Figure and motto make a knot of body and soul, mirroring man's little world. The motto is brief yet concise; it is indispensable to the meaning yet it forms a kind of syllogism in itself.

For all his mechanical schematising Tesauro puts wit unequivocally in the service of meaning. He belies Croce's characterisation of the seventeenth-century theorists as pedlars of an art of frills. Croce makes aunt sallies of Tesauro, Gracián and the rest when he accuses them of taking wit for mere ornation; yet he does expose an ambiguity in the way they understand form. They speak of gilding the truth and embellishing a plain sense while continuing to think of wit as the architecture of a discourse, the form we impart to the rude material which gives it grace and point. Their practical assumption is that wit is not just a superadded flourish but a pungent way of bringing out the sense. They waver uncertainly between incompatible expectations of wit because their critical judgment pulls against their rhetorical pre-conceptions. The separation of meaning from witty presentation is built into the Aristotelean scheme.

Bethall takes fundamental issue with Croce's account of Gracián and Tesauro. He justly points out that Croce misjudges Gracián's argument when he finds a recipe for extraneous flourishes in the comparison of wit with architecture. Yet the treatises do not bear out Bethell's counterclaim that Gracián and Tesauro conceive of wit as a means of apprehending metaphysical truth. They are emphatically clear that wit is a mode of metaphor, which we hit upon not by spiritual intuition or revelation but by artificial contrivance. When Gracian speaks of witty mystery all he has in mind is a rhetorical device in his third class of wit, that mode in which we heighten the effect by posing a problem, creating suspense and the like. Above all, the links between things which wit discovers are nothing more than the unexpectedly like properties of objects in different categories of matter such as enable the poet to produce ingenious metaphors. To claim that witty strokes work as gems in the mud, or escape the restraint of truth, is not to allow them a significance beyond nature but simply to sum up the rhetorical commonplaces that genuine wit will shine through the coarsest material, and that poetic inventiveness need not be tied by literal fact: 'As Rhetoric regards popular persuasion so the urbane cavillation has for scope a cheering the mind with plausibleness, without the encumbrance of truth'.[90]

Bethell's discussion tells us more about his own expectation of the English metaphysical poets than about the theories of Tesauro and Gracián, which he so urgently canvasses for a means to grace. His valiant attempts to read some of Donne's love poems in terms of the categories of wit prescribed in Tesauro's treatise only show up the aridity of those rhetorical prescriptions. He hunts down supposed logical fallacies in the poems, unmindful that Tesauro specifically distinguishes between false logic and cavillations. This tendentiousness does matter. In importing a sacramental intent into these continental rhetorics he contrives to blur the crucial distinction between metaphorical wit and metaphysical wit, and to beg the question of the provenance of English metaphysical wit.

These seventeenth-century treatises emerged far too late to shape English metaphysical poetry, whatever light they throw on wit. They are illuminating because they make explicit the assumptions about knowledge and metaphor which followed from the Aristotelean account of matter, and show these longstanding assumptions still holding the stage in Italy as late as the 1680s. Their conception of wit is grounded in a physics which set an absolute distinction between essence and attributes, and differentiated things by their essential kinds in qualitative categories. Wit enters when we distinguish the 'proper' or essential reference of a term from its metaphorical applications, and think of metaphor itself as a linking by like properties of things in distant categories of being. Such a system of wit can have only a limited bearing upon the practice of poets who effectively deny any distinction between essential form and accidental embodiment.

All these theorists take wit for a tool of rhetoric. They all expect to find a logical or argumentative structure in good discourse, and a certain agility in the processes of reasoning. Metaphor itself is to be persuasively deployed, however it may be savoured for its own ingenuity. Gracián codifies poetic conceits according to their rhetorical modes. Tesauro's system amounts to a rhetoric of witty metaphor which accommodates the forms of wit to a general scheme of mental operations and meaning, and resolves that 'Every perfect *artugezza*, being a persuasive oration, necessarily reduces itself to one of the three kinds of causes, Demonstrative, Deliberative, or Judicial'. Tesauro concludes that 'persuasion is the universal end of all *argutezze*, as of all the other enthymemes'.[91] These mid-seventeenth-century theorists laboriously exemplify a way of looking at literary effects and at visual images which was fast becoming outmoded. Their very conception of discourse resists the radically revised ideas of human nature and of matter which had gained ground in Europe in the wake of the .Reformation. Yet their comprehensive codifying of a long tradition of witty writing does serve to mark off conceited wit from wit which is truly metaphysical.

6

METAPHORICAL WIT

The funeral epigrams which Michelangelo wrote for the death of the young nephew of his friend Luigi del Riccio have been dismissed much as Johnson dismissed the metaphysical poets. Commentators have followed J. A. Symonds, who speaks of their 'laboured philosophical conceits . . . strange blending of artificial conceits with spontaneous feeling', and judges that they exhibit 'too much of scholastic trifling and too little of the accent of strong feeling'.[1]

The cavilling manner of the epigrams themselves, not to say Michelangelo's self-deprecating asides to del Riccio, may seem to bear out Symonds's assumption that the sequence was not seriously meant:

> Se fussin, perch'i'viva un'altra volta,
> Gil altru' pianti a quest'ossa carne e sangue,
> Saria spietato per pietà chi langue
> Per rilegar lor l'alma, in ciel discolta.

If the tears of others could put flesh and blood on my bones to make me live again then anyone who weeps for pity would lack pity; for he would retie my soul to my body, from which it is free in heaven.

Yet Michelangelo's habitual disparagement of his poetic skill tends to mask a profoundly serious concern. The sequence rings the changes round some seemingly extravagant conceits which the poet offers tentatively enough by way of lamenting the loss of so brilliant a youth, whose beauty is shadowed in the funeral effigy which Michelangelo himself had carved for the boy's tomb. The epigrams variously claim that the youth's pure spirit survives, not only in those who loved him but in a heavenly realm of transcendent beauty; and that nature itself is diminished by the withdrawal from the world of such a vitalising power of virtue and beauty.

These conceits are brought to life as consolations in a range of dramatic personifications and ingenious arguments. Some take the form of logical demonstration, advancing a proposition and defending or denying it by a quibble, as when he argues the independent existence of the soul by the shock which the boy's apparition (the bust/his ghost) might give to the living, which it could not do if we were persuaded that the entire being died with the body. Many epigrams offer a conceited proof of some paradox, such as that the brevity of the boy's life only confirms the immortality of his soul, or that his death actually increases the love people feel for him and the benefit his existence affords them.

To take such dexterities for witty trifling would be to sell Michelangelo short, not to say wit itself. The conceits are poignant with the sense of a brief vitality. They invoke a stark confrontation of intense being and mortality, living beauty and decay:

> Per sempre a morte, e prima a voi fui dato
> Sol per un'ora . . .

I am given to death forever, and first was given to you only for an hour; and I wore my beauty with such delight, and then left so much misery behind me, that it were better I had never been born.

The wit sustains a tension between the evidence of our brevity or nothingness and the conviction of a kind of immortality. Not all our being dies, and beauty itself endures. All these conceited consolations further a metaphysical endeavour, proving the immortality of essential, or spiritual, beauty. Like his Florentine mentors Michelangelo puts the idea at issue because he celebrates an embodied beauty whose outward aspect only mirrored the beauty of the soul, which itself reflects the eternal beauty:

> Qui sol per tempo convien posi e dorma,
> Per render bello el mio terrestre velo;
> Ché più grazia o beltà non have 'l cielo
> Ch'alla natura fusse esempro e norma.

Here just for a time it befits me to rest and sleep so as to render up my earthly veil in all its beauty; for heaven has no greater grace or beauty than this, which might serve as an example and a norm to nature.

The conceits take the strain of the struggle to reconcile a temperamental commitment to personal beauty with the presumption that our individual element dies and is forgotten whereas our spiritual element returns to its source, the one eternal author of all beauty. 'Dal ciel fu la beltá mia diva e 'ntera . . . ' – 'My divine and perfect beauty came from heaven, and only my mortal body from my father'; or as a later Platonist put it, 'The One remains, the many change and pass'.

Michelangelo's metaphysical wit really does rehearse the problem of the Many and the One, and in that endeavour works counter to the wit of such poets as Donne and Vaughan who take blessedness for the fulfilment of individual being. The conceits which eternalise our love of beauty serve an opposite end from the wit which discovers the presence of grace in nature.

The minute dissection of love that goes forward in the mid-century *Dialoghi d'Amore* poses problems and sifts relationships which are often expressly metaphysical. The participants debate such formal questions as the nature of a lover's dependence upon his mistress and the extent of her dependence upon his love and praise; the relation of desire to love and of sensible attraction to intellectual admiration; the distance between erotic love and spiritual love, or between earthly beauty and heavenly beauty. Some of them ponder the bond between mutual lovers as it is tried in parting and bodily absence, or in the aftermath of sexual fruition.

Maurice Scève (?1500–64) is just one lyricist who picks up meta-physical issues from these discussions, prompting the claim that he is an early metaphysical poet.[2] He draws upon Speroni's *Dialogo di Amore* (1542) for some subtly managed conceits in the long *Delie* sequence (1544), arguing the lover's involvement in his mistress's being, and the interdependence of body and soul in love. 'Asses plus long, qu'un Siecle Platonique . . . ': the months of his absence from her were far longer than a Platonic cycle. But when he sees her tranquil brow again – 'the exalted lodging of all honesty, where the empiry of wisdom is sustained' – then he believes dreams to be prophets:

> Car en *mon corps*: mon Ame, tu revins,
> Sentant ses mains, mains celestement blanches,
> Avec leurs bras mortellement divins
> L'un coronner mon col, l'aultre mes hanches.
>
> No. 367

The conceit builds upon the ambiguous status of a mistress who is at once divine and sensual. A syntactical ambiguity (tacitly revised in De Mourgues's account of the poem) plays off one possible effect of her nature against another: 'Car en *mon corps*: mon Ame . . . ': 'For you return to my body, and my soul'; 'For you, my Soul, return to my body'. Her return ministers to his mind and his senses; one hand crowns his head, the other his haunches. The Platonic cycle comes to an end, the lover is brought to life again by the reuniting of his body with his soul, his dreams are answered in the spirit and the flesh; yet he is also left in unresolvable dilemma, seeking a consummation of spirit and sense together.

Scève calls upon the relationship of soul and body to bring out the lover's dependence upon his mistress:

> La blanche aurore a peine finyssoit
> D'orner son chef d'or luisant, et de roses,
> Quand mon Esprit, qui du tout perissoit
> Au fons confus de tant diverses choses,
> Revint a moy soubz les Custodes closes
> Pour plus me rendre envers Mort invincible.
>   Mais toy, qui as (toy seule) le possible
> De donner heur a ma fatalité,
> Tu me seras la Myrrhe incorruptible
> Contre les vers de la mortalité.
>
>   No. 378

The lady's power to bestow death or immortality upon her lover is argued from the play upon spirit. The return of his wandering soul to revive his dying body with the dawn is also his mistress's return to him, in that she resumes her power over his life then after the ruinous distractions of sleep. Hence she must hold the means of preserving him from death, for he cannot die while body and soul remain at one and his being retains such an incorruptible balm against the worms of our mortality. And what then, we might ask? There is only his hope of keeping her favour by such a vivid proof of his devoted reliance upon her. The conceit remains a conceit, serving a wholly Petrarchan end.

In the lyrics of Guarini and Tasso such theorems of love form part of a formidable armoury of resources which give life to the writing. Guarini's sheer inventive fertility makes his lyrics a conspectus of the motifs of the love poetry of the sixteenth and seventeenth centuries, including Donne's. These neat little madrigals and sonnets regularly take the form of proof. He finds innumerable ways of arguing such propositions as the lover's dependence upon his mistress, and the dependence of her beauty upon his celebration of it; the oneness of mutual lovers; the necessity of bodily fruition; the lovers' encompassment of all the world's riches in one embrace; the lover's continued presence in his absence.

His lyrics themselves are distinguished for the pithy management of such conceits, like the elegant working out of a proof in geometry. Gracian frequently uses them for examples of particular modes of wit, and especially praises a sonnet in which the lover 'excuses himself because he cannot sing the beauties of his lady':

> Il ciel chiuso in bel volto, e il sol diviso
> In due stelle mi prega Amor ch'io cante,
> Dov'ei soleva, invitto e trionfante,
> Nel seggio star della sua gloria assiso . . .

Heaven closed in a beautiful face and the sun divided in two stars Love begged me to sing where, invincible and triumphant, he was accustomed to stay seated in the stronghold of his glory.

But that eternal Love, which saw that an earthly love was unworthy of her beautiful face, wished for himself those holy beauties and enclosed Paradise in a little cell. Whereby I, full of stupor, form voice and words imperfectly, and under the heavy weight fail in thought as well as in rhymes and verses.

Nor let it be a little thing that of so clear a sun, which a thousand holy rays converted to heaven, just one of them should shine to the world in my pages.

The poem sparkles with ingenuities of figure and form which help work out a high and complex conceit in celebration of the dead lady's paradisal beauty. It intricately plays off one effect of her heavenly beauty against another, the poet's love for her against 'quell'eterna Amor', taking us through a process by which he is finally enabled to write the present poem after the lady's death dashed his early hopes and paralysed his powers. Gracián esteems the poem particularly for its spirited style and witty substance – 'que es bizarro en el estilo, y agudeza en la sustancia'. He singles out its exemplary use of contrariety, how one 'postpones the contrariety in which the reply [reparo] is founded until the reason is given' (Discourse viii). In fact Gracián's critical categories never can cope with the qualities of the poems he praises, and reduce to a mere formula-piece this truly beautiful invention.

Tasso's lyrics too work out their witty devices, but they carry them off in a fervour of idealising admiration which often shades into sheer voluptuousness. Tasso solicits his mistress's love with the argument that between them they comprise the four elements; and he maintains the claim in a series of conceited teasers, 'Se . . . Se . . . Se . . . Se . . . ':

> Se'l vostro volto è d'un'aria gentile
> E i bei vostri occhi son due fiamme ardenti . . .

If she is air and sweet fire, and he is bitter water, ash and earth, why does their coming together produce such war between them? The more natural prospect would be that her fate and his destiny should draw them together so that they make one whole being; and then 'Oh che vita felice e gloriosa!'. The sheer ardour of the writing gives some substance to the conceit, such as these conceited proofs commonly lack. Gabriel de Trellon's neat elaboration of a like idea simply operates at the level of a cold device – 'Madame, vous et mois, faisons un autre monde! . . . ' (published 1599); though it does spring a metaphysical masterstroke:

> Votre esprit commandant ce petit univers
> De L'Esprit le plus grand ne doit être divers,
> Qui assemble le corps, les étreint et les serre . . .

One of Tasso's most ravishing sonnets memorably celebrates his lady's beauty by lamenting that it puts him in irresolvable self-conflict, at once drawing his soul up to a realm of pure spirit and luring his humanity down to a delicious imprisonment in sense:

> L'alma vaga di luce e di bellezza
>   Ardite spiega al ciel l'ale amorose,
>   Ma sí le fa l'umanità gravose
>   Che le dechina a quel ch'in terra apprezza; . . .

His soul remains feeding among the pearls and roses which Love spreads in her beautiful face, a voluntary prisoner to those delights among so many shining gifts of heaven. The hyperbolic praise of her beauty is set off against the elaborate Neoplatonic conceit not so much to point the contradictions of an aspiring love as to celebrate her attractive power. She is the object of both impulses here in fact, the heavenly aspiration and the sensuous desire; and the contradiction is in the lover not in her.

The divided impulse of love breeds ambiguity, which sustains itself in paradox, irony, contradiction. Sidney uses the scope of the sonnet sequence to work out the condition at length:

> Then some good body tell me how I do,
>   Whose presence, absence, absence presence is;
>   Blessed in my curse, and cursed in my bliss.
>   *Astrophil and Stella* No. 60

Astrophil and Stella is a brilliant *tour de force* which humanises its virtuosity in an inward drama of love. The sequence presents itself as the life of a mind caught up in inescapable contradiction, the struggles of a consciousness trapped between the conflicting imperatives of its own nature. Sidney repeatedly works out some ambiguous urge which leads him to an irresolvable dilemma or self-frustrating paradox. He allows that the pursuit of a heavenly beauty truly surpasses sensual love, yet cannot stop himself desiring Stella's body; he perceives a Platonic idea of virtue realised in Stella's form, which nonetheless inflames his desire for her embodied beauty; Stella's lofty conception of true love altogether contradicts her lover's impulse of love, so that she may come to love him in his way only if she ceases to love him in hers – 'Dear, love me not, that you may love me more' (No. 62).

Sonnets so dynamically conceived offer a complex intellectual life because they dramatise the frustrated vitality of an intelligence which well recognises how it continually traps itself. This vivid play of mind is elegantly articulated. Sidney's wit depends upon his formal mastery, such as he shows in his dramatic deployment of ideas and reasoning processes across the entire movement of a poem. Yet Sidney does not truly reason in verse, let alone raise metaphysical issues. His sonnets never work out a conceited argument. They vividly realise a predicament which reason in the end cannot touch:

> So strangely (alas) thy works in me prevail,
> That in my woes for thee thou art my joy,
> And in my joys for thee my only annoy.
>
> No. 108

Even such idealising aspirations as they express are not carried through or seriously pondered. They serve to locate the terms of a conflict between virtue and desire, a self-struggle which is essentially moral.

By the 1590s in England conceited wit was being cultivated for its own sake. The sonnet sequences which follow the fashion of wit set by Sidney tend to be externally conceived, displaying a crude zest for the bizarre and the shocking, a frantic search for ever more extreme metaphorical terms in which to profess one's love:

> How often hath my pen, mine heart's solicitor,
> Instructed thee in breviat of my case?
> While fancy-pleading eyes (thy beauty's visitor)
> Have patterned to my quill an angel's face.
>
> *Zepheria* No. 20

Entire sonnets turn upon the ingenious if not obscene expression of the lover's case or his mistress's beauties in the particular jargon of some profession or activity, law, cosmology, geography, games, architecture, mercantile practice, music, university regulations and so on.

Cultivated grotesqueries of metaphor and absurdities of diction abound. A mistress's hands are conduit pipes, and her eyes eat hearts; her brow is the bowling place for Cupid's eye, and also a pompous gallery and the sole hierarchy of the lover's soul; her face is the empiric globe, her eyebrows are 'love's true-love knots' and 'lily-lozenges', her voice is the organ-pipe of angels' choir, her beauty is conducted through love's sluice to her rosy face. These sonnets of the 1590s present the crudest and most mechanical form of conceited wit, which no one would dream of calling metaphysical. Yet the violent yoking of heterogeneous ideas is the entire point of their endeavour.

No doubt Marino had more elegant effects in mind when he proclaimed that art should astonish and prompt wonder with out-of-the-way conceits and the strangeness of novelty– 'la novità della inventione . . . la bizarria de' concetti':[3] 'Poetry calls for singularity'.[4] A character in his *La Sampogna* urges the *peregrino* spirit to turn aside from the signposted path of trite and common discourse and pursue a new course, following out novel thoughts – 'Ingegnati pur dunque', 'Stir your wits then!'. Marino himself never says anything directly but outgoes even Tasso in extremes of stylistic ingenuity:

> Rosa riso d'amor, del ciel fattura,
> rosa del sangue mio fatta vermiglia,
> pregio del mondo e fregio di natura,
> de la terra e del sol vergine figlia . . .
> *L'Adone* iii, 156

Rose, smile of love, creature of heaven; rose made vermilion with my blood; prize of the world and embellishment of nature; sole virgin daughter of the earth and the sun . . .

Venus's eulogy of the rose which has pricked her varies conceited epithets through three *ottava* stanzas and culminates in an elaborate parallel between the rose and the sun, which runs for another two stanzas:

> Tu sei con tue bellezze uniche e sole
> splendor di queste piagge, egli di quelle . . .

You with your beauties are unique and sole splendour of these slopes, he of those. He in his circle, you in your stalk/axis; you a sun in earth and he a rose in heaven . . . He with your insignia, with your spoils, will dress the dawn in its rising; you will unfold in your locks and in the leaves his golden and flaming livery . . .

De Sanctis took these stanzas for a paradigm of baroque poetry.[5] Anything less like Donne's wit can scarcely be imagined. This is an art of conspicuous artifice, a show of virtuoso excess in which the ceaseless varying of the performance becomes an end it itself and every circumstance promises a prodigy. The mother who falls transfixed by the sword which has stabbed her baby becomes a cross for her own son – 'al figliuol crocifisso è fatta croce' (*La Strage degli Innocenti*, ii, 58). Quite humble events are wrought into exotic feats. A comb running through a woman's hair is exquisitely described as an ivory boat passing through the golden waves in which the poet would love to be shipwrecked and drowned; a lady washing her legs prompts him to wish himself a new Alcides or Samson to embrace those columns and bring on his own sweet ruin; an oyster presents the lover's situation in the turbulent sea of love, at the mercy of his octopus-mistress who may yet engulf him in an ardent agony.

Marino's art fulfils itself in the play of inventive wit upon a set subject. The celebrated poem on Raphael's *Ecce Homo* puts a series of questions which bring out the distance between the picture of the hapless Christ and the true image of the son of God:

> È questo oimè, del tuo celeste figlio
> L'imago o Rè del Ciel?

Then the last tercet turns the contradiction back upon the beholder himself:

> Questo Sol ti sia specchio, anima errante,
> Di novo Dio fè l'huomo. Ahi fù ben'empio,
> L'huom ch'a Dio tolse d' huomo forma, e sembiante.

Erring soul, let this be a sole mirror to you/let this sun be a mirror to you. God made man a new God. Ah, man was indeed wicked who took from God the likeness of man.

Gracián's high praise of this play of wit does not take us far: 'These are the agreeable proportions and disproportions of discourse, concordance and discordance of the conceit; foundation and root of almost all wit, and to which one may reduce all conceitful artifice, because they either begin or end in this harmony of correlated subjects' (Discourse v). In fact the sonnet gets its life from a double contraposition. It sets off the hurt that a human hand has done to Christ's human form against the new life another hand has given that body. Then the ingenious contraposition of 'Dio' and 'huomo' suddenly reverses our understanding of the event. This is the death of

God made man, not of a man who is also God. Marino's apprehension of the divide between God and humanity, the divine spirit and the human body, leads him to a quite different conception of wit from the understanding which shapes English metaphysical poetry. His entire art depends for its effect upon our awareness of the distance between the artifice and its object. There is nothing remotely metaphysical about the wit which ornates his poems.

Góngora's poetry also offers a sumptuous show of prodigies, which it displays in lavish hyperbole:[6]

> Purpúreas rosas sobre Galatea
> la Alba entre lilios cándidos deshoja: . . .

The dawn sheds upon Galatea purple roses amongst white lilies; Love doubts which is most her colour, whether purple snowed over or red snow. The Eritrean pearl is a vain rival of her brow. The blind god frets, and finding his own splendour outgone leaves it to hang in gold at the mother-of-pearl of her ears.

> *Fabula de polifemo y galatea*, 105–12

Yet Góngora's conceits do more than indulge a luxuriant fancy. They animate a creation full of wonders, which multiply themselves quite naturally in a universal interplay of love and beauty. The luxuries themselves are heaped up to an end which is expressly unvoluptuous. These conceits hold an equipoise between the opposing virtues of lilies and roses, snow and passion, such as tempers love itself. Hyperboles tend to enlarge quite complex moral characters:

> Ven, Himeneo, donde entre arreboles
> de honesto rosicler, previene el día
> – aurora de sus ojos soberanos –
> virgen tan bella, que hacer podría
> tórrida la Noruega con dos soles,
> y blanca le Etíopia con dos manos.

Come Hymen, where among red clouds of pure roses a virgin forestalls the day – aurora of her own sovereign eyes – [one] so beautiful that she could bake Norway with her two suns and whiten Ethiopia with her two hands.

> *Soledad* i, 780–5

This virgin's beauty actually resides in a universal counterpoise of qualities, the all-cooling snow of her hands regulating the solar power of her eyes.

Such extremes and superlatives evoke a world of superbeings whose primal harmony with nature is confirmed in the conceits, to the point of self-parody at times. Polifemo's eye is 'near-rival of the daystar'; and the mightiest pine is no more to him than a light baton or a shepherd's crook (*Polifemo Galatea*, 49–56). The wit is not casual, or transparent. Góngora cultivates occult effects, dislocating syntax and narrative so as to hold back the key to some elaborate play, exploiting surprise and novelty to the end of a sudden disclosure. The more commonplace the subject the more bizarrely hermetic become the conceits which develop it. A simple incident from Ariosto, Angelica's falling in love with her desperately wounded enemy Medoro, affords an opportunity for a brilliant series of juggling feats with the Petrarchan properties:

> Del palafrén se derriba,
> no porque al moro conoce,
> sino por ver que la hierba
> tanta sangre paga en flores . . .

She gets down from her palfrey, not because she knows the Moor but because she sees that the grass pays for so much blood in flowers. She wipes his face, and her hand feels Love who hides himself behind the roses whose colours death is violating. He hid behind the roses so that their harpoons might work the diamond of Cathay with that noble blood.

Góngora's conceits repoint Ariosto's narrative, ironically playing off this drastic state against an innocent idyll of love. Wild flowers and roses turn to blood and bloody pallor, armed Cupid becomes a lurking viper or a jewelsmith whose points cut deep, compassion reveals itself in a prodigy, 'un mal vivo con dos almas / y una ciega con dos soles'. The conventional conceit of coupled hearts and minds now ironically proves itself in this drastic transformation of hatred into love, which only their dire extremity has brought about. Love's miracles appear in the monstrous spectacle of a near-corpse with two souls, and a blind woman with two suns.

Góngora's notorious device of ingenious periphrasis is more than a casual sleight of wit or a surrealist extravagance. The conceited cross-transference of attributes continually sets off natural harmony against artificial simulations of it. Birds are feathered organs, plumed lyres, 'sweet bells of sonorous feather'; streams curl their foam into ears to hear nature's music, and a boat running with the surge becomes a musical instrument whose strings are the oars. In the sea-pastoral idyll of the *Soledades* nature's processes succour man. When the shipwrecked youth spreads out his sea-drenched clothes on the sand the sun 'scarcely licking them with its sweet tongue of tempered fire slowly assails them, and with smooth style, the least wave sucks from the least thread' (*Soledad* i, 34–41).

The continual posing of stylistic enigmas is calculated. The poet justifies it with a claim which amounts to something more than the customary defence of dark conceits. The delight of penetrating a difficulty leads the mind to the truth which lies hidden behind it – 'debajo de las sombras de la obscuridad'. The reader's struggle with the obscurity of the writing becomes a pattern of the search for truth, which always conceals itself under shadows and ultimately draws us back to the source of all truth: 'the end of the understanding is the seizing of the truth, which will not satisfy us if it is not the primal truth, conforming with that sentence of St Augustine, "Inquietum est cor nostrum, donec requiescat in te"'.[7]

He had reason to claim that his conceits aim at primal truth. They are always turning back upon their own extravagance to express a yearning for simplicity and permanence. They mark the distance between innocent being and our present state, playing off natural life against artifice, organic processes against machinery, simplicity against a corrupting sophistication, bright hope against the world's destructiveness and the ruin people bring upon themselves. No heaven-threatening modern artifice offers such shelter to the wayfarer as the humble country cottage, 'where innocence rather than steel guards the goatherd better than his pipe [guards] the herd' (*Soledad* i, 88–100). The bold conceit which opens *Soledad* ii invites astonishment for its bizarreness, as R. O. Jones notes.[8] Yet it actually figures a fatal transformation. A stream descending to the sea becomes a moth fluttering into the flame, but a moth whose wings are waves:

> Entrase el mar por un arroyo breve . . .

The sea enters by a brief rivulet, which with thirsty pace to receive it precipitates itself from its natal rock and drinks not only much salt in a little glass but its own ruin, and solicits its end, crystalline butterfly – not winged but wavy – in the lamp of Thetis.

> *Soledad* ii, 1–8

The stream's eager self-precipitation into the ocean follows a self-destructive urge which expresses itself in an abandonment to turbulence and change.

Góngora's most admired poem develops the image of a flowing river:

¡Oh claro honor del liquido elemento . . .

O lucent honour of the liquid element, sweet brook of running silver whose water spreads through the grass with gentle sound at a slow pace – since she for whom I feel myself freeze and burn admires herself in you, love portrays the snow and the scarlet of her face in your tranquil and white stream.

Go on as you do, do not slacken the wavy rein on the crystal bit with which you control the swift current; for it is not right that the great lord of the wet trident should gather confusedly so much beauty in his deep breast.

The image of reflection contrasts the pure tranquillity of the stream's motion with the turbulent self-conflicts of love which her beauty provokes in the lover. In urging that the tranquil flow should continue unimpeded by such passions he seeks to preserve her beautiful image from the erotic perturbations which would submerge it; for she will all too easily fall prey to 'the great lord of the wet trident', who confounds such beauty by gathering it into his deep bosom. The Petrarchan ardours threaten the element which reflects them with the prospect of a fatal change from simple innocence to corrupting sexuality.

Flux and stasis contest the ground of Góngora's moral landscape. The wit of his celebratory poems works to hold some stable quality against the chaos of our shifting lives. His habitual stance of praise, as of mourning, assumes a perpetual menace to our security such as only a heroic self-transformation may resist:

Arbol de cuyos ramos fortunados
las nobles moras son quinas reales . . .

Tree, of whose fortunate branches the noble Moors are royal barks, tinged in the blood of loyal captains, not unhappy lovers; in the fields of the Tagus most gilded, and most honouring its crystal [waters], you rise equal with the sublime palms and raise yourself above the laurels. A silkworm, may I feed myself on your leaves; a small bird, may your branches sustain me; and may I shelter myself, a pilgrim, in your shade.

I will spin out your memory among the people, I will sing, hushing the fame of others, and will devote my life to your temple.

'Mora', a mulberry tree, as well as the family tree of a line descended from the Moors; 'quinas', the cinchona tree which yields healing quinine, but also the royal arms of Portugal to which this nobleman owes native fealty: the plays sustain the conceit. The poem confirms its own wit, as itself drawing out the silk thread and the bird-song which Mora's patronage fosters.

Góngora's endless inventiveness in the game of coining names, heaping up epithets which then take on a figurative life of their own, is quite solemnly exercised in the honouring of a royal tomb:

> Máquina funeral, que desta vida
> nos decís la mudanza estando queda,
> pira, no de aromática arboleda,
> si a más gloriosa fénix construida; . . .

The tomb becomes a funeral-machine, a phoenix-pyre, a lightship, and finally the oyster-shell of a pearl – 'margarita' – which has emerged from obscurity into glorious light. The conceited epithets discover in the tomb itself a still point of stability, guidance and renewal amid the shifting tumults of the world. They culminate in the play on the name of the dead queen herself, which produces such a bizarrely powerful image of rebirth and glorious new life.

This poet will seize wittily upon a name as the ground of a funeral hyperbole. Góngora's beautiful little madrigal for the tomb of Donna Maria de Lira turns upon the claim that the mute lyre may still have its voice, which he justifies by casting the poem itself in the metrical form of a *lira*:

> La bella Lira muda yace ahora
> debajo deste mármol que, sin duda
> le ha convocado muda,
> como solía canora: . . .

The beautiful Lira lies here mute under this marble, which without doubt she has silently convoked, as she used to do melodiously. So the Tagus gilds the sands, the illustrious stones – refined monument to this instrument of the Muses.

Inscripción para el Sepulcro de Dona Maria de Lira, natural de Toledo

The poem works to justify the huge conceit that this Lira has retained even in death the musical power to move the stone which covers her body, arguing that her renewed harmony of being better fits her than Orpheus to be an instrument of the Muses. Her voice has been transformed by death rather than silenced.

Radical transformation is the impulse of Góngora's wit. A tomb is metamorphosed into a beacon and a pearl, a dead woman into a universal principle of harmony, mourning itself into celebration. The death of a young prince must be mourned, as the untimely slaughter of a unfledged bird – 'Ave real de plumas tan desnuda . . . ' (*En la muerte de un cabellero mozo*). Yet death itself is a transforming agent. The

boy has been carried off not by some fabulous deity 'whose talons . . .
are a keen scythe', but by a divine force which amends his very
immaturity. It is neither a Ganymede nor a winged spirit but the transfigured boy himself who now sings sacred songs to Jupiter in heaven.

The sudden turn-about which Gracián so admired in Góngora's
beautiful sonnet *Al Nacimento de Cristo* proves the character of this
poet's witty vision. This meditation on the birth of Christ opens
startlingly enough with a picture of Christ on the cross, and then
works its way to a brilliant reversal which affirms Christ's birth to be
a greater wonder than his crucifixion:

> Pender de un leño, traspasado el pecho
> y de espinas clavadas ambas sienes . . .

To hang upon a wood, the breast transfixed and both temples nailed with
thorns; to give your mortal pains in hostage of our glory – this was indeed a
heroic feat. Yet it was still greater to be born in such a strait, where – so as to
show us for our own good how far you descend, and from whence you came
– a crèche needs no roof.

It was no greater deed [than that], O my great God, to have conquered in
weak age with strong breast the frozen offence of time (for it cost more to
sweat blood than to grow cold) – just because there is a more immense
distance from God to man than from man to death.

Christ's birth in human meanness was a more truly heroic feat than his
dying for us on the cross precisely because the distance from God to
man is so much greater than the distance from man to death.

From human nature to God, from blood and mire to jewels:
Góngora's art offers the prospect not just of embellishing nature but of
changing it. Yet the startling conclusion of 'Pender de un leño' shows
us why his wit can never be metaphysical in the manner of Donne or
Herbert. The wit works not at all to hold together unlike orders of
being as Christ's double nature coupled them. It simply measures the
distance between one order of being and another.

The pious poets whom Gracián singles out for their wit make wit
their means of spanning the gulf between God and man, the secular
world and an absolute state of blessedness. They bring out the paradoxes, ironies, contradictions inherent in the Christian conception of
an incarnation and atonement; and they wittily transform secular
circumstances into divine testimony.

Gracián praises the witty gravity of Fray Luis de León (Discourses v
and xxxviii) without showing interest in that poet's truly metaphysical
vision. León (?1527–91) is a metaphysical poet in the manner of Dante

or Michelangelo. He catches a double apprehension of our state, playing off the world and the universe as we see them against the divine
harmony of the creation as it truly is. Leon values nothing in our
mortal existence save the shadows of celestial joys. He takes the
heavens at night for a window upon eternity in a world which is
otherwise just a dark prison of the soul:

> ¿Es más que un breve punto
> el bajo y torpo suelo, comparado
> con ese gran trasunto
> do vive mejorado
> lo que es, lo que será, lo que ha pasado?

Is it more than a brief point, the low and heavy earth, compared with that
great image [of its maker] where all that is, will be, and has passed lives
perfected? Whoever beholds the great concert of these eternal splendours,
their settled movement, their various paces which are yet concordant and
equal in proportion . . . who is he that can look upon this and prize the meanness of the earth, and not groan and sigh to break through that [wall] which
imprisons his soul and exiles it from these blessings?

Noche serena: a Diego Olarte

Leon conveys the wonder of earthly beauties, such as the beauty of
music, while always measuring the distance between them and the
heavenly reality which they shadow or echo, and straining for the
transformation of the momentary joy into an eternal bliss. He values
music highly as an echo of the eternal harmony which helps the soul
recover 'the lost memory of its first high origin'. His great ode to
Francisco Salinas, Professor of Music in the University of Salamanca,
is built upon the vast Pythagorean conceit that the creation is God's
instrument on which God makes harmonies that sustain the universe.
Divine music bridges the gap between our present state and eternal
being, reawakening the sleeping soul so that 'It passes beyond all the
air until it attains the highest sphere, and there it hears another kind of
music which does not perish and is the prime origin of all music'.
Petrarchan paradoxes burgeon in what seems a quite un-Petrarchan
cause simply as a means of expressing the double nature of the
transition we ourselves might make from one state of being to the
other, which is agonising and yet inexpressibly sweet. Death itself is a
'happy swoon', a 'sweet oblivion' which 'gives life'; and he longs to
remain in its repose 'without ever being restored to this low and vile
sense'. The contrast with Vaughan is striking in a poet of comparable
stature. Luis de León is a transcendentalist who takes the world for a

poor shadow of eternal being which he longs to exchange for the substance. Vaughan sees eternal being in the natural creation itself, and his wit is integral to that vision.

One of Gracián's prime exemplars of pious wit, Alonso de Ledesma (1551–1632), directly exploits the apparent incongruity of the sensible metaphor with its spiritual subject, grounding his art in the ingenious management of metaphor. Ledesma's three series of *Conceptos espirituales* (1600, 1606, 1612) amount to some six hundred short poems and make a staggering display of virtuosity. These poems put the circumstances of Christ's career or of other objects of devotion 'in the metaphor of . . . ', which appears to be what Ledesma understands by his term 'conceit'. His titles indicate the strange endeavour. *To the divinity and humanity of Christ; in the metaphor of a clothmaker. To the Sacrament; in the metaphor of a hunt. A pastoral colloquy to the most Holy Sacrament; in the metaphor of rustic games. To the tears that Christ wept upon the Cross; in the metaphor of heart disease. To the most holy sacrament; in the metaphor of shooting at a target. To the glorious St Lucy when her eyes were pulled out for God; in the metaphor of a washerwoman. To the conversion which Blessed Father Ignatius brought about in the lake with a dishonest sinner; in the metaphor of an anvil.* Gracián highly praises the subtlety of the correspondence between Loyola's feat and an anvil, though he characteristically shows no concern with the point of the game. The opening lines propose the device: 'Vulcano cojo . . . ', 'Crippled Vulcan, Biscayan smith, if you wish to melt the frozen iron of a stubborn and obstinate sinner, pull out your forge in the midst of the way . . . '. Loyola's oratory becomes the bellows to rekindle the burnt-out coal, and his zeal will be the forge of love to which the sinner must be drawn with the tongs of obedience. The sinner is to be fashioned anew with a judicious application of the fire of Jesus's name, and the hammer and the anvil of his own conscience; and then Loyola himself will be the 'hyssop placed in water', to temper the reforged steel.

These devices often get their kick from a bizarre coupling of elements. The birth of Christ seems oddly rendered in the metaphor of a plague:

> Una pesta tan cruel
> venís Doctor a curar?

Yet the conceit is not radically worked out, because the terms as he takes them are not really so far apart after all. Christ is a doctor who comes to cure a plague with a precious antidote, and is stoned and killed for his pains.

Such conceited plays of metaphor which give dramatic life to an icon recall the manner of the witty Petrarchans, and have effects much like theirs. St Sebastian is celebrated at length in some *Redondillas*, 'in the metaphor of a fletcher'. Love, rather than some enemy, shoots arrows of fire which inflame body and soul. Sebastian accumulates so many feathers in his body that he flies like a bird up to its nest in heaven, or like Icarus seeking a secure port. When he has reached the sum of riches his divine effigy will be deposited there, like an Aztec god, to be an image of feathers. This continual manipulation of metaphor can be quite arbitrary, directed just to drawing out the properties of the icon in the liveliest possible way. A poem of ten lines appraises the holy sacrament 'in the metaphor of ports':

> En Sancta Maria del puerto
> hazen liga Dios, y el hombre,
> cuya armada de gran nombre
> la Fee nos ha descubierto . . .

In the port of Santa Maria God is bound to man, whose navy of great fame has been revealed to us by Faith. In Vera Cruz/On the true Cross he was killed, its Captain, for my good, and now they see him rise where he will defend us, he who stays in the port of Ostia/Host and also that of Cadiz/Chalice . . .

The doctrine of the incarnation, atonement and eucharist is cleverly run through a Spanish maritime muster by means of the double-references of the place names themselves – port, Santa Maria, the Armada, Vera Cruz, Cadiz, and so on. Yet it all remains just an ingenious game. There is no implication that these places actually embody or re-enact the divine events, no sudden apprehension that these events are simultaneously present in the temporal circumstances. The relationship between the two orders of occurrence remains purely metaphoric in that the ports provide a metaphor for Christ's redeeming sacrifice rather than an embodiment of it in another mode of being. The whole work of the wit here is to bring out the meaning of the sacred truths by ingeniously discovering a secular parallel for them. There is no concern to demonstrate an essential relationship between spiritual and secular being, much less a spiritual presence in secular life.

The play of wit just occasionally throws up a closer congruence of the terms. Ledesma's best known poem, the *Romance: To St Stephen: in the metaphor of a lapidary*, discovers a relationship which is more than arbitrary between a martyr's death and the lapidarist's art:

Estevan un lapidario
muerto por recoger piedras,
y no de las Orientales,
sino de las desta tierra . . .

Stephen, a lapidary, killed for collecting stones, and not the Oriental kind but those of this earth.

Today you carry them to the Court of Heaven for greater profit, because any stone Stephen takes there he is bound to sell.

Down here they take him for a madman, seeing the price, because he barters rough badly worked rocks and hard pebbly stones.

Yet he well knows what he is buying, for we see him turn them into beautiful fine rubies, and plump bright pearls . . .

And he does not fashion them with irons/flaws [hierros/yerros], for this artificer professed neither to take iron/error in his hand nor to hang it from his shop. He works them only with blood because it is important for their hardness; and so he burnishes rough and rude things into smooth and polished jewels. And because it is a laborious work it needs so much spirit that he dies (for the God of heaven) as he imparts it to them.

The stones of St Stephen's martyrdom become jewels which heaven will help him to carry and sell. They appear so rough and badly worked that the world disprizes them; yet the connoisseur who knows how to look at them sees that they are of the finest quality, highlighted from heaven, vivified with the lapidary's vital spirits, worked with his life-blood, which gives them firmness and permanence as well as polish. The wit of this poem does work to offer us a double view, a simultaneous vision of events in two apparently distinct orders of being which turn out to be the same order. The rough stones actually become the jewels, refined into great beauty by the martyr's squalid and painful death. We are offered together the ugly circumstances of the martyrdom as the world sees them, and their true nature as they are spiritually transformed. The effect of the wit here is expressly to follow out this sacred transformation, imitating the work of grace which makes a martyrdom the means of transmuting base matter into glory. The martyr's blood transforms into jewels the stones which spill it; and wit works to translate the one state into the other. It is precisely not the case that the stones are already jewels in some way, or have a material and a spiritual nature simultaneously. Base matter must be transformed into a higher condition. Stones become jewels only when they are reworked with a martyr's blood.

The idea of a spiritual transformation of secular events gave scope to a true metaphysical wit, of a kind. We find it powerfully at work in some of the religious poets whom Gracián most esteems, though he himself is too preoccupied with formal categories to attend to the vision they articulate. He praises the poems of B. Leonardo de Argensola for their handling of the forms of logic and argument. Argensola's 'A Cristo nuestro señor, orando en el huerto' is a meditation upon Christ's agony in the garden which Argensola sets out as the formal posing of a question with several alternative answers. The design precisely exemplifies Gracián's third form of wit, the formal question and response. Here the question arises from the paradox of Christ's show of human apprehensiveness in the garden:

> Qué estratagema hazéis, guerrero mío?
> Mas antes ¿qué inefable sacramento? . . .

Is it the sweat of fear which opens Christ's veins in the garden? Or is it blood which oozes forth now in anticipation of his impending wounds? It is neither of these causes in fact, 'sino como se os viene ante los ojos / mi culpa'. Christ burns with anger at the poet's sins, whose continuance only heightens his agony. The picture of the poet before Christ's eyes devastatingly responds to the picture of Christ before the poet's eyes.

Gracián singles out this sudden reversal at the end, which so aptly retorts upon the poet himself by discovering a different cause for the effect he describes (Discourse xvii). Yet the poem turns upon a metaphysical apprehension in that it attributes Christ's sweating in the garden not to his own fear but to our misdeeds. This is a striking though not radical effect of metaphysical wit, since the relation of our sins to Christ's suffering is the received Christian understanding. But it does catch the metaphysical shock of the discovery of a direct spiritual incitement of the physical event, and of the timeless consequences of a contingent action.

Extremes of conceited paradox become all but interchangeable between poets of secular passion and poets of pious ardour. Both states suppose a contradictoriness in our experience which may be resolved by a transforming grace; poets of either kind express their devotion in an all-out striving to be witty. Death which renews life, the loss of self which finds self, wounds which soothe and heal – these lovers' contradictions become the common testimony of the late sixteenth-century devout poets.

Juan de Arguijo (1565–1623) finds in Narcissus a type of the lover who madly brings about his own undoing in the fire of his self-love and then discovers renewed hope and growth in death: 'and now that he is converted into a purple flower the water that was the agent of his death makes him grow, and seeks to give him life' (*Narciso*). St John of the Cross makes explicit the spiritual thrust of such conceits. He commits himself to an impassioned love affair with Christ which he works out wittily in the very terms of erotic ardour. His heart is Christ's secret beloved, which longs for its night of passion and an ecstatic intermingling of the lovers:

> ¡Oh noche que guiaste,
> oh, noche amable más que la alborada,
> oh, noche que juntase
> Amado con Amada,
> Amada en el Amado transformada!

Oh night that was the guide, oh night more pleasant than the dawn, oh night that joined lover with beloved, the beloved transformed into the lover!

Canción de la subida del Monte Carmelo

He celebrates a love which heals by wounding, a wound which is inexpressibly sweet, a white soft hand which administers delicious death and transforms death into life. What alleviates his pain gives him grief, what offers him hope gives him more grief, so that his only remedy must be death – 'I live and do not live in myself, and my hope is such that I die because I do not die' (*Coplas del alma que pena por ver a Dios*). Love's paradox will be resolved in a final transformation, when the lover is made one with the beloved and 'I die because I do not die' becomes 'I live because I do not die'. The contradictions of our experience here may not be transcended, but they will certainly be transformed in the all-fulfilling union with the beloved.

The English recusant poet William Alabaster (1567/8–1640) continually strives to be witty in pious meditation, determinedly discovering paradoxes, bizarre correspondences, startling metamorphoses in the quest for grace and in the sacramental processes themselves. He seeks to draw out the contradictions and incongruities which are inherent in the Christian doctrine of grace. Petrarchan-style plays of metaphor and paradox are his stock-in-trade. Sins dry him out, or drown the world; Satan scorches him and freezes him; his tears make brooks, and Christ's loving tears cool us and warm us at the same time; grace rains down upon dry ground and withered fruit; Christ's body is our bread, or our vine, or a merciful pen, and his blood is the wine or the ink; Christ on the cross is a vine whose fruit flows freely for our good, infusing heaven into the spirit and creating the more thirst the more it satisfies:

O drink to thirst, and thirst to drink that treasure,
Where the only danger is to keep a measure.
                    No. 32, *Upon the Crucifix* (2)

Alabaster's essential concern is the difference between the appearance of things in the material world and the spiritual actuality. He
conveys this difference by wit because he continually offers a double
view of events and conditions, playing off the unregenerate or
material state against the regenerate or transfigured state, or working a
transformation from the one state to the other. To seek to rise may be
to fall, to go downwards may be to ascend; his soul must 'Sink down
. . . Into the anguish of thy sins', as Christ descended into hell, before
it may hope to rise to heaven; and he labours the paradox vigorously:

> And upwards, downwards by humility,
> Since man fell upwards, down by Satan's train,
> Look for no fairer way unto thy crown,
> Than that Christ went up, by going down.
>   No. 22, 'Sink down, my soul!'

For all his artistic crudity Alabaster is more than a juggler with a
metaphor who merely tricks out Christian attitudes. He has a metaphysical case to make, which he proves in the figure of transformation.
The wit is his means of rehearsing a transformation of nature into
grace, or a transplantation which will bring that change about:

> For as the rain that driveth from the skies,
> Is rain above but hail in lower place,
> So tears that trickle from repentant eyes
> Are tears with us, but turned in heaven to grace.
>   No. 13, 'My soul within the bed
>   of heaven doth grow'

His aim seems to be simple enough, just to bring home to himself the
wonder of grace by elaborating some metaphor which dramatically
points the scope of God's sacrifice for man. The entire operation of
the wit supposes an absolute gulf between nature and grace, which
only Christ's will may bridge. He asks what ferryman will convey his
desires safely across the dangerous brook which divides this world
from the next, and implores Christ to remove the brook itself, somewhat inconsequentially producing the same effect from opposite
causes:

> Dry it with thy love, or drown it with my tears.
>   No. 4, 'What blessed ferryman'

He hits on some quite bizarre figures as he strains to show how Christ affords God a hold upon nature and our humanity:

> Jesu, the handle of the world's great ball,
> By which the finger of omnipotence
> Took hold of us . . .
> No. 54, 'Two, yet but one'

Alabaster comes nearest Herbert when he meditates the double character of Christ's crucifixion, or the fusion of contraries in it which makes it simultaneously bitter and sweet. Yet he can do little more with this prodigy than to spell out his divided responses to it in the figure of a written confession of sin, which he invites Christ to expunge and overgo. His grief becomes his means of acknowledging his responsibility for Christ's suffering:

> My tongue shall be my pen, mine eyes shall rain
> Tears for my ink, the place where I was cured
> Shall be my book, where, having all abjured,
> And calling heavens to record in that plain,
> Thus plainly will I write: no sin like mine.
> No. 24, *The Sponge*

In fact the witty figure takes over the poem, and itself becomes the centre of interest as he follows it out so remorselessly. Christ's Passion is a 'tart sponge' which may blot out that record, and replace it with an opposite sense:

> then be thy spirit the quill,
> Thy blood the ink, and with compassion
> Write thus upon my soul: thy Jesu still.

The wit has some power in the way it works out the contrary directions of the crucifixion itself so that the one inscription precisely responds to the other, the sestet counters the octave. Yet the forced play of figure works to elaborate a devotional commonplace rather than to articulate a spiritual condition. In making the vinegary sponge of Christ's Passion the very means to erase our sins he risks a bathos which is inherent in his conception of a witty metamorphosis. As it appears, a transformed sponge works just like any other sponge to wipe the board clean.

He struggles wittily with his central metaphysical concern when he develops the traditional emblem of a ring to define God's relation to his creation, marking the reunion of end and beginning, God and man:

> So God and man became one person.
> Thus nature's circle as a ring doth run.
>   No. 63, 'The first beginning of creation'

Christ seals the bond between God and nature, the infinite and the finite, the One and many, divinity and humanity:

> So stands two rings upon one diamond,
> The knot of both and either, where are met,
> Finite and infinite, more and one . . .

The figure is not arbitrarily taken up, as Alabaster's figures so often are, but its incoherent development betrays a schematic understanding of wit. The emblem of the ring does not realise an apprehension of Christ's double nature but is conventionally brought in to carry a weight of definition which it is quite unable to sustain in itself. Alabaster cannot convey the difference between the one state of being and the other, or the transformation which Christ must bring about so that two such unlike conditions may couple. When the French poet Jean la Ceppéde uses the figure of the ring to define the relation of Christ's humanity to his divinity his wit at least serves the spiritual need.   ·   •

La Ceppéde (1550–1622) systematically exploits the modes of sacred transformation in his *Théorèmes . . . sur le Sacré Mystère de la Redemption* (Part 1, 1613; Part 2, 1621/2), an endeavour which has prompted the emphatic claim that he too is a metaphysical poet.[9] He discovers parallels with Christ's career in mythology, ancient history, natural history and the like, which show the ancient wonders not only fully realised but wholly transformed in Christ. As the phoenix goes to its self-appointed doom on a pyre of fragrant wood, so Christ endures his death upon his wood, 'Qui parfume le Ciel d'une odeur tres-parfaicte'. Then he rises again as a far mightier phoenix:

> Sur l'azuré lambris des voutes estoillées
> Eslevera son bois de rayons éclatant.
>   Part 2, Book 1, No. 35

The fulfilment of types in their antitypes is one of this poet's recurrent proofs. He follows out thus far at least the mode of the *Vexilla Regis*, that Good Friday announcement of the blessed sacrament which he himself notably put into French.[10] His *Théorèmes* in Part 1, Book 3 work a series of such sacred transformations of Christ's cross, starting from the premise that the cross is the nothing from

which Christ made everything – 'D'un rien créer ce Tout' (1, 3, 29);
or it is an instrument of cruelty which Christ makes holy:

> L'autel des vieux parfums dans Solyme encensé,
> Fair or' d'une voirie un Temple venerable,
> Où de Verbe incarné d'Hypostase adorable,
> S'offre tres-odorante à son Pere offensé . . .
>
> 1, 3, 23

The cross perfects all the Old Testament salves. It is the new pole on
which the serpent is raised to cure the venomous bite; the new winepress 'Pour noyer dans son vin nos lethales Viperes' (1, 3, 23); the new
Jacob's ladder which sustains the man-God who enables us to enjoy
the good which was only promised to our fathers – 'Nous fait joüir
des biens qu'il promit à nos Peres' (1, 3, 23); the staff which became
Jacob's boat in the river of Jordan; Goliath's sword which was fated to
help David rather than its master; the strong trident which enabled
the Israelites to cross the Red Sea; the wood with which 'ce bon
Capitaine' honeyed the gall of the bitter fountain; the landmark for all
mariners who tack towards their port in the promised land. The
engine of shameful execution becomes the means of saving the world;
that ancient scandal is abolished, the nectar of Christ's blood outgoes
absinthe and moly. Christ's cross confronts Satan's tree, green wood
opposes dry wood, good counters evil. On this dry wood grace over-
takes truth, justice is reconciled with mercy.

Truth succeeds to the shadow of figures, the old law gives place to
Christ's new decrees. Yet many of la Ceppéde's types have an
authentic life of their own, as when he parallels Moses' rod with
Longinus's spear, the one striking healing water from the rock in the
arid desert as the other broached nectar from Christ's side which gives
the world eternal life:

> Ce doux Nectar attraine un cristal blanchissant
> Dont se forms en l'Eglise une sainte Piscine
> Où se vuide le pus, qui nous suit en naissant.
>
> 1, 3, 95

How do the types relate to their antitype, and what does the antitype
owe to its types? Does Christ's godhead transcend his humanity, or
does it comprehend his human nature? The relation of humanity to
divinity, flesh to spirit, is central to la Ceppéde's endeavour. In the
earlier part of the sequence he repeatedly seeks to define these
relationships in witty conceits; and he strikingly returns to re-examine

them in the part published nine years later. The poems in Part 1 hold a distance between Christ and his own humanity. Christ wears human flesh as a garment, a red robe of suffering which will also enfold our red sins. Christ takes the image of man, concealing his godhead under the shell of mortality, 'Dieu se cachant de luy sous l'écorce mortele' (1, 2, 71). The red garment of flesh will be transformed into a robe of glory, the shell will fall away to reveal the god. God manifests himself in his work by clamant signs – 'Par des signes bruyant mysterieuse-ment' – for his being is not consubstantial with bodies:

> Non pourtant qu'l s'unisse hypostatiquement
> A ces corps (le seul Verbe a faict céte accointance)
> Ils luy servent icy d'enseigne seulement.
> Il resoud quand il veut leur visible existance.
>
> 2, 4, 6

Devout poets are not always so helpfully aware of the assumptions which shape their work. La Ceppéde categorically attests that God does not unite himself hypostatically with the sensible phenomena in which he chooses to manifest himself. These bodies are just circum-stantial signs, which God simply annuls when they have served his purpose. As God embodies his powers in sensible objects in order that he may be apprehended by men at all so the poet himself subtly finds sensible figures for pure spiritual ideas:

> Non pas pour déchifrer ce que n'ont pas compris
> Les cerveaux mieux timbrés . . .
> Mais bien pour enseigner au peuple moins scavant,
> Comme en forme de langue, et de flamme, et de vent
> Vous estez descendu sur la trouppe fidele.
>
> 2, 4, 1

He sees his poetic task not as a decipherment or an exploration but as the embodying of abstract truth, which his wit brings to vivid life.

In the 1621/2 sequence la Ceppéde returns to redefine the relation of Christ's divinity to his humanity, proposing a bond which his earlier conceits had seemed to refuse. Sonnet 2, 1, 11 works out in the figure of a precious ring the 'just unity' of soul and body which follows from the close union of divinity and man in Christ. This poem decisively revises the clear-cut understanding of the poems published nine years earlier. The elaboration of the figure works to define a full union of divinity and humanity in Christ. Christ's final victory over death and Satan 'truly witnesses that the close union of the divinity to this man is without end; that without doubt he entirely embraces holy humanity':

> La mort a bien dissoult céte juste unité
> Qui de l'Ame et du corps par un noeud delectable
> Fit un tout, tout parfaict; Mais Dieu demeure stable,
> Avec et l'un et l'autre en toute eternité.

Christ's godhead stands to his humanity as the soul to the body, or the jewel to the ring in which it is mounted. Death has untied the knot and dismembered the ring, yet the eternal goldsmith holds both the jewel and its setting and will finally reunite them; and meanwhile the Word sustains both parts of our nature:

> Il est joinct à ce corps dedans la sepulture,
> Et descent joinct à l'Ame aux antres de Pluton.

La Ceppéde's wit does not sustain this apprehension of a fusion of god-head and manhood in Christ, or assume a present union of body and soul in our nature. Yet in this sonnet it does work to couple unlike orders of being and to promise their eternal bond.

These ponderings of Christ's nature hold in question the status of our lives in the body, as well as the work of wit. They are made urgent by a heightened concern with flux and relativeness such as Montaigne expresses and defines. Has our being any permanence or value beyond its momentary ardour? Are we more than the creatures of time and change? The attempt to apprehend our lives in a double perspective, as at once fleeting and enduring, calls for a mode of wit which might appropriately be termed metaphysical.

Such an attempt partly justifies A. Boase's insistence that Jean de Sponde is a metaphysical poet in the manner of Donne and Herbert; though Boase himself does not look beyond formal affinities.[11] De Sponde (1557–94) is a poet of strikingly imaginative vision and intensity who does have qualities in common with the English metaphysical poets. The dominant impulse of his poetry is the struggle to oppose some order against the sheer flux of being, and the ephemeralness of our experience in the world. His love poems express together, and with equal fervour, an atomic apprehension of being and a yearning for stability.

De Sponde's *Sonnet d'Amour* iii turns upon the vast conceit of a double perspective of our place in the cosmos, as of love. To look down on the earth from space would be to see it as just one insignificant atom which is lost in a cloud; whereas the firmament viewed from the earth seems infinitely great, and of incomprehensible grandeur. So then with his love, which leads his eye upwards to 'ce grand ciel d'Amour', while others' loves simply drop them back in the atomic world of the Epicureans – 'Leur amour tout de terre, et le mien tout celeste'. Yet the poem finds no way of reconciling the two prospects. It allows no such traffic between them as we find in Vaughan's *The World*; nor does it hold up to ordinary lovers an exemplary mode of love, as Donne so often does. It spectacularly poses an atomic universe of sense against an eternal heaven of mind or spirit, setting earthly love on an opposite course from celestial love.

De Sponde seeks exotic ways of playing off ephemeralness against stability, vividly complicating the Platonic figure of soaring and sinking. 'Si j'avois comme vous, mignardes colombelles . . . '. If his body had wings like the doves' to fly to the bliss of its desire he would be content to shackle his soul; but he deceives himself to think that such flight might be the mode of constant love:

> Mais quoy? je le souhaite, et me trompe d'autant.
> Ferois-je bien vollar un amour si constant
> D'un monde tout rempli de vos aisles ensemble?
> *Sonnet d'Amour* vii

Augustine returns upon Plato. De Sponde meets his Platonic aspiration with the conceit that constancy is heavy, drawing him to a centre in a world of light whirling things without focus.

A ritual lament for his sorrows in love quite startlingly opens a contrast between heavenly constancy and an earthly and unstable passion. His astonishment that all-devouring time does not also devour his troubles leads him to the apprehension that the beautiful flame of his love is not hostage to time at all, having no other quality than that of a soul 'Qui court vers l'eternité' (*Chanson: Un bien qu'en desire tant*). Seeking a principle of stability amid the tumult of our experience he hits on the miraculous counterpoise of winds and water which keeps the earth steady, and the balance of the elements in our own constitution which sustains the body unshaken. Thus his extreme love may hold steady between the contrary gusts of light impulses which blow incessantly from all sides, keeping 'Sa constance au milieu de ces legeretez' (*Sonnet d'Amour* i). The conceit is arresting in the way it wittily holds unlike elements in question together, the conservation of the world, the bodily constitution, his love. What gives the wit point and urgency is the keen sense of radical instability it expresses, the apprehension of an ever-shifting condition of being in which only a very few constants may be miraculously discovered and held on to. Like some English poets of the seventeenth century de Sponde does seem to have been shaken by the prospect of an Epicurean – or a Montaignean – universe. He is continually pre-occupied with the witness of constant flux we see all about us, which impels faith itself to seek its centre in another order of being altogether.

In common with Donne's love poetry and Rochester's, de Sponde's poems convey a haunted sense of present being. Their commitment to the impulse of the moment is intensified by the close prospect of death and disintegration, the random dispersal of our bodies in a universe of ever-shifting atoms. His *Sonnet de la Mort* i offers an extraordinary vision of human lives carried on unthinkingly amidst the very remains of the dead, and the degeneration of our own bodies:

> Vous qui r'amoncelez vos tresors, des tresors
> De ceux dont par la mort la vie fust ravie: . . .

The poem addresses mortal beings who take their lives from mortals, heap up treasures snatched from the dead, live in the houses of the dead, and yet shut their eyes to death. It turns the *memento mori* around so as to excuse our reluctance to recognise our condition, paradoxi-cally taking our forgetfulness of death for a premonition of eternal life. *Sonnet de la Mort* ii confronts life dramatically with death, evoking a world of vivid sensations which very soon fade and die – the candle flame, the oil painting, the breaking waves, the thunder, the snow, the torrents and the magnificence of natural life itself – 'Ces lyons rugissans, je les ay veus sans rage'. The last line of the poem hammers home the inescapable contradiction: 'Vivez, hommes, vivez, mais si faut-il mourir'.

De Sponde's preoccupation with a final negating of the self prompts him to play off the soul's prospects against the body's. Holding his feeble frame stiff against the wind he feels the tempest which will disperse the sands of his body and fears that his sleeping soul may share this same dissolution; so he urges it to watch, and keep itself alert to all terror – 'Garde que ce Larron ne te trouve endormie:' (*Sonnet de la Mort* x). Then what happens to the soul when the body which elements it disintegrates in the grave? De Sponde conveys the keenest apprehension of the dissolution of the body, and the nothingness of our existence:

> Et quel bien de la Mort? où la vermine ronge
> Tous ces nerfes, tous ces os; où l'ame se depart
> De ceste orde charongne, et se tient à l'escart,
> Et laisse un souvenir de nous comme d'un songe?
>
> *Sonnet de la Mort* xi

Boase justly points out that de Sponde's horror of rotting flesh is not a piece of quasi-mediaeval asceticism in the manner of a da Todi or a Villon.[12] On the contrary, the poet feels the corruption of his body as an annulment of his entire being:

> A quoy ceste Ame, helas! et ce corps desunis?
> Du commerce du monde hors du monde bannis?
> A quoy ces noeuds si beaux que le Trespas deslie?

Yet Boase crucially strains a kinship with the English metaphysical poets when he takes these lines for an assertion of the oneness of the soul and the body. De Sponde is actually urging our need to recognise the inevitability of a final separation, and anticipate it in our present lives:

> Ce n'en est pas pourtant le sentier racourcy,
> Mais quoy? nous n'avons plus ny d'Henoc, ny d'Elie.

The reference to Enoch and Elias signals that we cannot now ascend to heaven in the body, as they did, or recover our bodies there at all. Far from implying a bodily resurrection, as Boase supposes, the sestet anticipates the final separation of the soul from the body. The understanding remains the old one, however novel the tension it generates. It assumes that the body must be disjoined from the soul in death and lie as rotting trash in the grave while the soul alone goes to heaven: 'Pour vivre au Ciel il faut mourir plustost icy'. We must die to the world and the body if we wish to gain the joys of heaven. The line Boase quotes for its striking likeness to Donne's *The Ecstasy* precisely does not celebrate the oneness of body and soul, even if it refers at all to the knot which ties our being together. It ironically dismisses the vanities of the world by questioning the beautiful knots which tie us to them. What makes the poem much more than a *memento mori* is the tension between the present vitality and that consciousness of inevitable dissolution. It expresses the strongest sense of our present being as one entity which death must horribly, and finally, undo.

The claim for de Sponde only makes more conspicuous the absence of a French school of metaphysical poetry, or a Spanish or an Italian school for that matter. Boase asks himself squarely why no such French trend developed but answers in terms of competing fashions of style. He discovers an emerging mode of metaphysical wit among de Sponde's followers, and laments its early disappearance under the weight of the baroque manners brought in by du Bartas.[13]

A play of wit in a poem by D'Aubigné strikes Boase as metaphysical in a manner which would become inconceivable in France only a generation later. The passage which he settles on makes up the final stanza of D'Aubigné's *Prière du Soir*, and it follows out a prayer for a peaceful and holy night which discovers in the trappings of sleep an emblem of God's saving care of our souls in death: 'Dans l'épais des ombres funèbres . . . '. Amid the shades and images of death God must be our north star, torch of our darkness, lifting the eye of our conscience beyond the dread of our own wicked impulses, 'which are covered in lead, and twist themselves in fear on a pillow of thorns':

> A ceux qui chantent tes louanges,
> Ton visage est leur ciel, leur chevet ton giron;
> Abrités de tes mains, les rideaux d'environ
> Sont le camp de tes anges.

The double conceit of the bed plays off the grave against God's protective wardship in a way which has more in common with the Elizabethan poet George Gascoigne (*Gascoigne's good night*) than with Herbert or Vaughan. D'Aubigné's lines precisely do not work out a metaphysical relationship, much less discover a spiritual presence in the material circumstances. The poet simply claims that those whose faith is strong take their bed for a means of peaceful rest in God's care rather than a place of bad dreams and foreboding fears. The bed becomes an emblem of God's solicitude. Boase proposes a likeness to Herbert in virtue of a mode of writing, a trenchant verbal dexterity – 'This solemn and moving play of words on the trappings of a bed is wholly in the English metaphysical manner – that of George Herbert'.[14] Yet the issue between D'Aubigné and Herbert goes much beyond style. The two poets work out quite unlike expectations of reality.

The difference between an ingeniously managed emblem and the witty apprehension of a truth comes out if we put D'Aubigné's conceit alongside a singularly beautiful sonnet by 'the prodigious'[15] Lope de Vega, a poem which Gracian might have cited for the boldness of its device. Lope's poem appears at first just to work out a spiritual conceit in the manner of Ledesma, audaciously rendering Christ's suspension on the cross in the metaphor of an amorous shepherd's repose upon his crook – 'Pastor que con tus silbos amorosos . . .'. The shepherd is both lover and leader, whose amorous summons has newly aroused the errant poet to follow him devotedly, despite a misgiving lest ugly sin should frighten off even one who is dying of love:

> Espera, pues, y escucha mis cuidados . . .
> Pero ¿cómo te digo que me esperes
> si estás para esperar los pies clavados?

Wait then, and listen to my cares . . . But why do I ask you to wait for me if your feet stay nailed to make you wait?

The conceit turns out to be more than an ingenious repointing of the icon. In so movingly conflating the pastoral motive with the crucifixion, Christ as loving shepherd with Christ on the cross, Lope invites us to couple the two characters as different manifestations of a single impulse and brings out the vital link between them. Both functions work simultaneously, and interact in that Christ's character as loving shepherd is one with his character as crucified victim. The nailed feet clinch the identity, confirming the bond of love which cancels out our sins with solicitous pains. Lope's wit is neither radical nor strictly metaphysical, since the terms it relates stand in traditional proximity to one another and operate within the same order of being. Yet it does work to comprehend a truth such as only wit may articulate.

Metaphysical wit furthers a radical endeavour which is apt to shape all a poet's thinking. To find a radicalness at all like Donne's we must look to Francisco de Quevedo (1580–1645). Quevedo dislocates word-order and syntax, chops logic in conceited proofs, cultivates obscurity, startlingly materialises common figures; and he continually flouts decorum in grotesque hyperboles, discordant images, comic deflations, bizarre juxtapositions, gross effects wrung from conventional metaphors, insistently physiological images and terms, the sudden linking of seemingly unrelated and incongruous ideas. *A loose old woman, made up and painted* gives him scope for ribald invention:

> Vida fiambre, cuerpo de anascote,
> ¿cuando dirás al apetito, 'tate' . . .

Living cold meat, body of twill, when will you call halt to your appetite if you begin to look out for the arrow only when 'Have mercy on me' checkmates you?

You join the topknot to the shroud over your addled brain, between your brow and your nape; being already a living blunder you anoint your skull in sauce . . .

The seemingly grotesque transposition of toupee into shroud by way
of describing the scalp of a tarted-up old woman quite startlingly
couples erotic heat and decay. Quevedo's *bizarrie* have point. They
work a drastic coupling of contrary impulses which we can only call
metaphysical.

Quevedo's devout poems wage a spiritual drama through the senses.
They invest physical events with sacramental force, discovering a
universal consequence in the proclivities of the human body as if the
bodily constitution itself has spiritual meaning. Partaking of the
eucharistic bread and wine the poet finds Christ's birth, death and
burial enacted in his own body:

> Pues hoy pretendo ser tu monumento . . .
> Si no, retratarás tu nacimiento
> en la nieve de un ánimo obstinado,
> y en corazón pesebre, accompañado
> de brutos apetitos que en mí siento . . .

This day I seek to be a monument for you, so that you may rescue me from
sin, dress me with grace, having renewed the old man lost in blindness. If I
fail, you will retrace your birth in the snow of an obstinate soul and in a
cribbed heart, accompanied by brute appetites which I feel in myself.

Today you inter yourself in me, base slave [as I am], sepulchre to such a
guest, vile and narrow, unworthy of your sovereign body. Earth buries you
in me [who is] made of earth; conscience serves me for worm; my breast
yields the marble to cover you.

Salmo xxii

When Simon of Cyrene takes the weight of the cross he momentarily
relieves the hardpressed Christ of the whole world's burden of sin;
but he holds back from helping further lest he bring on a still worse
ordeal:

> Atlante, que en la Cruz sustentas cielo,
> Hércules que descansas sumo Atlante . . .

Atlas, who on the Cross sustains heaven, Hercules, who succours the greatest
Atlas, relieve with your strength the tender lover who humbly measures the
ground with his mouth. But do not give him help, for I fear that you hasten
his waiting death . . .

Nonetheless this humane reluctance is mistaken. Simon should bear
the cross all the more readily so as to speed Christ on his way to death,
for that death redeems us all and 'in helping Christ to lift the Cross he
helped himself':

> mas dásela Simón, que es importante
> para la Redención de todo el suelo . . .

Yet Simon gives help, for it is important for the redemption of the whole earth. But if you lighten the load with your arms you also add weight to his timber with your sin of the appletree. To take up part of the sovereign wood towards the Redemption which awaits them is to take away your sins with your hand.

Quevedo's conceits continually superimpose death upon life and life upon death, conveying a simultaneous intuition of intense present being and of not being at all. He discovers a quite extraordinary prospect in the old motif of the invisible communication of love through the eyes:

> Si mis párpados, Lisi, labios fueran,
>   besos fueran los rayos visüales
>   de mis ojos, qual al Sol miran caudales
>   águilas, y besaran más que vieran . . .

If my eyelids, Lisi, were lips, the visual rays of my eyes would be kisses which would gaze upon the sun as royal/tailed eagles and kiss more than they saw. They would hydroptically drink in your beauties and, crystals thirsty for crystals, nourishing their mortality with celestial lights and fires they would live.

Sustained by an invisible commerce, and naked of the body, my powers and feelings would enjoy your favours; my ardours would woo mutely; they would see themselves united while apart and their passions would be secret in public.

The bizarre conceit of the eyelids which become lips makes possible a powerful quickening of contemplation with sensuality, expressing a sense of present being so intense that it makes an erotic impulse of the response to divine beauty itself. The afterlife of the soul is sensuously savoured, as if to put in question the very dividing line between life and death.

This double apprehension of our state is habitual. Voluptuous ecstasy carries the warrant of its own undoing. 'En crespa tempestad del oro undoso . . . ': when Lisi lets down her sumptuous hair the lover's heart swims through gulfs of pure and burning light in the curled tempest of wavy gold, athirst for beauty. Such a consummation of sense brings instant extinction:

> Leandro en mar de fuego proceloso
>   su amor ostenta, su vivir apura; . . .

Leander in a sea of stormy fire displays his love and consumes his life; Icarus on a perilous path of gold burns his wings to die gloriously.

Yet the sumptuous self-destruction also offers him the hope of rising again from his ruin, finding new life through death; and it leaves him in the end to weigh the ambiguous benefits of a glory which so famishes the craving it arouses, the phoenix-hope whose demise he can only lament:

> Avaro y rico, y pobre en el tesoso,
> el castigo y la hambre imita a Midas,
> Tántalo en fugitiva fuente de oro.

Miserly and rich, and poor amidst the treasure, the punishment and appetite imitate Midas, or Tantalus in a fleeting fount of gold.

Sexual frustration only reinforces his yearning for the fulfilment of his entire being by way of an ecstatic oblivion.

He feels our mortality in sexual desire itself, contemplating Ash Wednesday emblems on the brow of beauty:

> Aminta, para mí cualquiera día
> es de ceniza, si merezco verte;
> que la luz de tus ojos es de suerte
> que aun encender podrá la nieve fría . . .

Aminta, it seems to me that any day whatever is of ash if I see you worthily; for the light of your eyes has power even to set fire to the frozen snow . . . Yet that which I see on your spacious brow manifests the conquests of your eyes in that whoever looks at them is ash, and they are fire.

Beauty, erotic ardour, and ashes startlingly interwork in a way that recalls Donne's coupling of vitality and dissolution, bright hair and bone. Love outbraves time only by way of its own mortality. The ashes of a lover placed in a hourglass at least sustain love's ardour, defying nature by perpetuating the stir of passion:

> ¡Oh milagro! ¡Oh portento peregrino!
> que de lo natural los estatutos
> rompes con eternar su moviemento.

> Tu miso constituyes tu destino:
> pues por días, por horas, por minutos,
> eternizas tu propio sentimiento.

O marvel! O strange portent! that you break the statutes of nature by immortalising its movement! You yourself constitute your own destiny; for you can by days, by hours, by minutes eternise your own feeling.

The experience of the moment seems to be so intensely apprehended just because it cannot be pinned down, and yet may be all we
can hope to have:

> Fue sueño ayer, mañana será tierra:
> Poco antes nada, y poco después humo . . .
>   Ya no es ayer, mañana no ha llegado,
> hoy pasa, y es, y fue, con movimiento
> que a la muerte me lleva despeñado.
>   Azadas son la hora y el momento,
> que a jornal de mi pena y mi cuidado,
> cavan en mi vivir mi monumento.

It was a dream yesterday, tomorrow it will be earth. A little before, nothing;
and a little after, smoke . . . Yesterday is already no more, and tomorrow
has not arrived; today passes, and is, and was, with a movement that carries
me headlong down to death. The hour and the moment are spades, which
at the cost of my pain and my care dig my monument out of my living
being.

'The hour and the moment are spades . . . ': the down-to-earth image
which makes a slow ossification of the process of living itself puts our
entire being in question:

> ¡Ah de la vida! . . . ¿Nadie me responde?
> ¡Aquí de los antaños que he vivido! . . .
>   Ayer se fue; mañana no ha llegado;
> hoy se está yendo sin parar un punto:
> soy un fue, y un será y un es cansado.
>   En el hoy y mañana y ayer, junto
> pañales y mortaja, y he quedado
> presentes sucesiones de difunto.

What then of life? Does no one answer me? All that remain [to me] are the
past times I have lived! Fortune has bitten out my days, my madness has
hidden the hours. For without power to know how or whither, well-being
and age have slipped away. Life fails, only the lived moments remain, and
there is no calamity that does not menace me.

Yesterday fled; tomorrow has not arrived; today continues to wander away
without stopping for a moment. I am a was, and a will be, and a worn out is.
In the today and tomorrow and yesterday I join together the nappy and the
shroud; and I have remained [no more than] present successions of a deceased
being.

The shroud displaces the nappy, and what comes between birth and
burial is no more than a continual dying. Quevedo's emblem bleakly

anticipates Rochester in its radical questioning of an existence which we can never pin down long enough to call our own.

Quevedo's poems repeatedly open such prospects in a drastic stroke of wit. 'Amor constante más allá de la muerte' well merits the attentions its strange figurative life has attracted:[16]

> Cerrar podrá mis ojos la postrera
> sombra que me llevare el blanco día;
> y podrá desatar esta alma mía
> hora a su afán ansioso lisonjera:
>   mas no de esotra parte en la ribera
> dejará la memoria, en donde ardía;
> nadar sabe mi llama la agua fría,
> y perder el respeto a ley severa.
>   Alma, a quien todo un dios prisión ha sido,
> venas, que humor a tanto fuego han dado,
> medulas, que han gloriosamente aridido,
>   su cuerpo dejará, no su cuidado;
> serán ceniza, mas tendrá sentido;
> polvo serán, mas polvo enamorado.

The ultimate shade that will take me from the white day will serve to close my eyes, and an hour flattering to its anxious zeal will have power to release this soul of mine. Yet on that other bank it will not leave behind the memory of what it burned with. My flame knows how to swim the icy water, and disregard the severe law [of death].

Soul, to which an entire god has been prison; veins, which have given fuel to so much fire; marrows, which have burned gloriously – it [the soul] will leave its body, not its care, they [veins and marrow] will be ash but will hold on to sense; they will be dust, but enamoured dust.

Sense and spirit interfuse. The flame of his ardour will destroy him and yet survive the icy water of death; the ashes of his burning veins and marrow will still feel passion; his dust itself will not cease to love. Such a *tour de force* of wit is no mere rhetorical sleight. The metaphors realise an apprehension. In so intimately confronting being with not-being the wit confirms a bodily sentience which is too intensely experienced to contemplate its own extinction, and even projects itself beyond the dissolution of the body.

7

METAPHYSICAL WIT

The double perspective of Quevedo's wit catches just the mode of self-awareness which the Jacobean dramatists stage as a drastic confrontation between vitality and corruption, or pose more intimately in the language itself in the ironic intensification of threatened sentience:

> Ay, but to die, and go we know not where;
> To lie in cold obstruction, and to rot; . . .
> *Measure for Measure*, 3.1.119–30

Quevedo's witty interchanges of heat and ashes parallel Webster's staging of death, Middleton's macabre word-juggling, Tourneur's mordant collocations of lust and bare bone. To take life for an unintelligible spasm and hold it in pawn to a momentary urge or a breath is to share Quevedo's insight:

> Are lordships sold to maintain ladyships,
> For the poor benefit of a bewildering minute?
> Why does yon fellow falsify highways,
> And put his life between the judge's lips,
> To refine such a thing . . . ?
> Tourneur, *The Revenger's Tragedy*, 3.5.73–7

Such writings convey in common a felt sense of not being. They apprehend death itself in the senses.

Shakespeare's theatrical language dramatises a more ample play of consciousness, realising in gesture and action a habit of thinking which is rooted in organic life. The fusion of feeling, act and idea in the texture of the writing peculiarly renders a condition of full sentience in which passions are apprehended with metaphysical urgency, metaphysical issues experienced in bodily impulse:

> When I have plucked thy rose
> It needs must wither. I'll smell it on the tree.
> O balmy breath, that dost almost persuade
> Justice to break her sword!
> *Othello* 5.2.13–17

Incorruptible virtue and fatal justice contend in a savoured breath. The
bodily constitution becomes the ground of spiritual engagement:

> Love's mysteries in souls do grow,
> But yet the body is his book.
>
> Donne, *The Ecstasy*

Donne's poetry dramatises an intelligent commitment to the life of
the body in a world dominated by time and change. It starts in the
stir of the senses as if all our doings in the world enact the impulses of
the animal organism itself, which quick wits can only exploit. The
physical thrust of the lines challenges the mind:

> To mew me in a ship, is to enthral
> Me in a prison, that were like to fall;
> Or in a cloister, save that there men dwell
> In a calm heaven, here in a swaggering hell.
> Long voyages are long consumptions,
> And ships are carts for executions.
> Yea they are deaths; is't not all one to fly
> Into another world, as 'tis to die?
> Here let me war; in these arms let me lie;
> Here let me parley, batter, bleed, and die.
>
> *Elegy 20*

No poetry in English confronts us more audaciously with its own
mental life, or has a greater power to compel our witness to an ever-
shifting play of wits. A few brusque lines snatch us into an action. Here
the poet-lover is harrying a woman to undress and get into bed with
him. There he is cursing a former mistress who has betrayed him. Elsewhere he turns back on the point of embarking for an expedition to
urge a last present on a mistress – 'Here take my picture'.

Donne's lines project a mind which is warily caught up in the life
of the streets, the courts, the chambers, the royal Court itself:

> 'Tis ten a-clock and past; all whom the mews,
> Balloon, tennis, diet, or the stews,
> Had all the morning held, now the second
> Time made ready, that day, in flocks, are found
> In the Presence, and I, (God pardon me).
> As fresh, and sweet their apparels be, as be
> The fields they sold to buy them; 'For a King
> Those hose are,' cry the flatterers; and bring
> Them next week to the theatre to sell;
> Wants reach all states; me seems they do as well

> At stage, as Court; all are players; . . . Now,
> The ladies come; as pirates, which do know
> That there came weak ships fraught with cochineal,
> The men board them; and praise, as they think, well
> Their beauties; they the men's wits; both are bought.
>
> *Satire 4*

The mockery is not casual. Donne's art questions the life it feeds on, provoking us with an undeceived zest for experience:

> Fond woman, which wouldst have thy husband die,
> And yet complain'st of his great jealousy; . . .
>
> *Elegy 1*

The lines catch a more complex motive than contempt for a jealous rival. This lover's cool appraisal of the advantage they will gain by the death of his mistress's husband offsets his distaste for the grossness of that self-destruction. The effrontery of the argument flouts the pieties of a bourgeois world, persuading us that wit and alert senses may be more worth admiring than bestial torpor, and that the perilous commitment to each other is a braver impulse than a blind self-love.

Donne's openness to life is more than a dramatising of his own ego. It follows out his sense of our constitutional commitment to change, flux, momentariness, a condition which he welcomes and exploits:

> Now thou hast loved me one whole day,
> Tomorrow when thou leav'st, what wilt thou say?
>
> *Woman's Constancy*

The diversity of situations and attitudes which surprises us in the love poetry reflects Donne's occasional prompting but also marks the contradictoriness of our experience, as of our natures. Donne's poetic preoccupations are of a piece. His poems work to try the poet's commitment to the competing claims upon his devotion, holding women, friends, God, in rivalry with the public world of affairs and with each other. The vitality of Donne's mind is purposeful. His poetry offers a continual commentary upon the world it evokes, as well as on the poet himself. This incessant play of a sceptical intelligence gives even his love poems the style of impassioned reasoning:

> Oh stay, three lives in one flea spare,
> Where we almost, nay more than married are.
> This flea is you and I, and this
> Our marriage bed, and marriage temple is; . . .
>
> *The Flea*

In a casual disagreement of lovers the poet finds occasion for a subtle play of argument which discovers the true end of their love.

Donne's adroit casuistries can serve to realise the dilemma of a quite un-Petrarchan lover:

> May he be scorned by one, whom all else scorn,
> Forswear to others, what to her he hath sworn,
> With fear of missing, shame of getting, torn: . . .
>   *The Curse*

Yet the searching play of mind persistently works to try a present case in a wider context of men's motives and understanding:

> Kind pity chokes my spleen; brave scorn forbids
> Those tears to issue which swell my eye-lids . . .
>   *Satire 3*

The opening lines of *Satire 3* confront us with a bizarre medley of moral questions. Should the corrupted state of religion prompt our anger, or our grief? What devotion do we owe to religion, and which religion might warrantably claim our faith? May the pagan philosophers be saved before Christian believers? What obligation of piety do children owe to their fathers in return for an upbringing in religion? Then we get a quick review of some current issues such as the participation of Englishmen in the foreign wars, colonising expeditions of discovery, the Spanish *auto da fé*, and brawls over women or honour in the London streets. The drift of Donne's argument holds all these concerns together, and brings them to bear upon the present divisions of Christendom which lead men to conclude that any worldly cause must be better worth their fealty than the pursuit of a true Christian life. The mode of reasoning is characteristic. Donne calls in a variety of circumstances in the world, weighing one area of concern against another so that we may appraise the present claim in relation to a whole range of unlike possibilities, which might even nullify one another:

> Is not this excuse for mere contraries,
> Equally strong; cannot both sides say so?

The movement of the poem amounts to a sifting of the relative claims on our devotion such as commonly distract us from our absolute obligation to seek the truth.

A love poem may make a contentious issue of the commitment to love, and move by way of a shrewd round-up of current foreign policies:

Till I have peace with thee, war other men,
And when I have peace, can I leave thee then?
All other wars are scrupulous; only thou
O fair free city, mayst thyself allow
To any one.

Elegy 20

In Flanders, France, Ireland, Spain, the indeterminate balance of
rights and wrongs, gains and losses, puts all our ventures in equal
doubt; only the skirmishes of lovers offer some hope of a stable peace.
The incessant probing of wit expresses a resolved attitude to the game
of power which so intrigues this poet. Calling in a world of external
enterprises to hold in balance with love Donne marks the contradictoriness of these public transactions and questions their claim upon
us. His lines invite us to heed the provisionalness of our assurances in
a world of conflicting imperatives.

Donne's poetry can be outrageously funny. Its comedy often comes
from the way the poet takes wantonness for granted:

Will no other vice content you?
Will it not serve your turn to do, as did your mothers?
Have you old vices spent, and now would find out others?
Or doth a fear, that men are true, torment you?
Oh we are not, be not you so,
Let me, and do you, twenty know.

The Indifferent

Yet the approach seems quite mercurial. Some poems take love for
ingenious seduction or daring adultery. Other poems argue that
sexual variety is a law of nature and the spice of life, or that being in
bed with a woman is worth more than martial glory. One self-styled
elegy offers a praise of a woman's beauty which centres on her
pudenda. Another elegy makes a comparison of women which
enlarges to the point of nauseating grotesqueness the ill-favour of some
rival's mistress:

Are not your kisses then as filthy, and more,
As a worm sucking an envenomed sore?
Doth not thy fearful hand in feeling quake,
As one which gathering flowers, still fears a snake?
Is not your last act harsh, and violent,
As when a plough a stony ground doth rent?

Elegy 8

The sheer unsavouriness of such exaggerations heightens the joke, and Donne points them with ribald zest:

> She, whose face, like clouds, turns the day to night,
> Who, mightier than the sea, makes Moors seem white,
> Who, though seven years, she in the stews had laid,
> A nunnery durst receive, and think a maid . . .
>
> *Elegy 2*

This monstrous hyperbole damns by praising, in an ironic parody of the old exercise of persuading a friend to marriage. By a *tour de force* of inventive sophistry Donne proves a woman singularly marriageable just because she is unimaginably hideous, the implication being that in our corrupting world only such a repellent creature is likely to keep her virtue.

Such comic heightenings make a commentary on the world Donne evokes and confirm his sceptical vision of it in their subversive mental life. Their exuberance licenses an intelligence which continually works to unsettle our complacent pieties in the interests of a disconcerting truth. The 'loving wretch' who praises his mistress's angelic mind, and insists that it is their minds which marry rather than their bodies, would just as soon swear that he hears the music of the spheres in 'that day's rude hoarse minstrelsy' (*Love's Alchemy*). We do well to acknowledge our real motive in love, beyond the gloss that Petrarchan lovers put upon it:

> Whoever loves, if he do not propose
> The right true end of love, he's one that goes
> To sea for nothing but to make him sick.
>
> *Elegy 18*

A continual effect of wit in these poems is an uncommitted testing of the moral currency.

So radical a play of mind enacts a complex vision of human affairs. The tensions the poet sets up between his protagonist and other people shift disconcertingly. Even Donne's formal satires deny us a secure moral vantage point:

> Away thou fondling motley humorist,
> Leave me, and in this standing wooden chest,
> Consorted with these few books, let me lie
> In prison, and here be coffined, when I die; . . .
>
> *Satire 1*

The poet writes as a solitary contemplative who is dragged from his books, partly by his own virile urge, to witness the active depravities of the streets, the courts, the Court. Yet the sages whose tomes he abandons are no more free of self-delusive folly than is public life, and have no higher claim upon him. 'Grave divines' think themselves 'God's conduits', Aristotle becomes 'Nature's secretary', 'jolly statesmen' propose a mystical union of the body politic, historians and poets display contrasting absurdities:

> Here gathering chroniclers, and by them stand
> Giddy fantastic poets of each land.

The drama Donne calls up simply stages the contradictions of our natural impulses, projecting people's animal urges into civic life. His volatile companion of the streets spies a mistress in a window and rushes after her, 'Violently ravished to his lechery'; but competing with many more for her favours he quarrels, fights, bleeds, gets kicked out of doors and returns with his lust brought down:

> Directly came to me hanging the head,
> And constantly a while must keep his bed.

Such writing vividly follows out a naturalistic expectation of the way the world goes, intimating that this world itself only mirrors the human organism in the inherent instability of its cravings and satisfactions. We find ourselves caught up in the tensions of a drama which is projected from our own cross purposes, our need to appease our self-seeking appetites and ward off the antagonisms they provoke while nonetheless sustaining the social forms which give us scope:

> Have we not kept our guards, like spy on spy?
> Had correspondence whilst the foe stood by?
> Stol'n (more to sweeten them) our many blisses
> Of meetings, conference, embracements, kisses?
> Shadowed with negligence our most respects?
> Varied our language through all dialects,
> Of becks, winks, looks, and often under-boards
> Spoke dialogues with our feet far from our words?
>
> *Elegy 12*

Donne is dexterous in dramatising his own moral detachment, which now impels an amused deflation of people's pretensions and now a disturbed diagnosis of corruption:

> The Iron Age that was, when justice was sold, now
> Injustice is sold dearer far; . . .
> Why barest thou to yon officer? Fool, hath he
> Got those goods, for which erst men bared to thee?
>
> *Satire 5*

In his rendering of the world our only guard against brute power is a shrewd self-possession which acknowledges the nothingness of all our human vanities in respect of our common end:

> All men are dust,
> How much worse are suitors, who to men's lust
> Are made preys. O worse than dust, or worm's meat,
> For they do eat you now, whose selves worms shall eat.
>
> *Satire 5*

The protagonist of the love poetry is a bolder figure. He acts the amorous hero in a world of half-men and lesser lovers who squander their manhood in the pursuit of profit, power, status:

> Take you a course, get you a place,
> Observe his Honour, or his Grace,
> Or the King's real, or his stamped face
> Contemplate; what you will, approve,
> So you will let me love.
>
> *The Canonization*

The poems set love in a world which does not favour it and must be outwitted or out-argued, as must the lovers' own natures:

> Alas, alas, who's injured by my love?
>   What merchant's ships have my sighs drowned?
> Who says my tears have overflowed his ground? . . .
> Soldiers find wars, and lawyers find out still
>   Litigious men, which quarrels move,
>   Though she and I do love.

This lover does not exempt himself from the frailties he mocks, on the contrary he is shrewdly alert to the thrust of his own ego. Donne's *Elegies* recall Jonson's comedies in their evocation of a corrupting energy which animates the world with blinkered obsessions and self-tormenting suspicions. A love affair becomes a clandestine campaign to outsmart the girl's menacing parents. Her mother sleeps all day so as to watch out for her escapades at night:

And, when she takes thy hand, and would seem kind,
Doth search what rings, and armlets she can find,
And kissing notes the colour of thy face,
And fearing lest thou art swoll'n, doth thee embrace;
To try if thou long, doth name strange meats,
And notes thy paleness, blushing, sighs, and sweats;
And politicly will to thee confess
The sins of her own youth's rank lustiness; . . .

Elegy 4

Her father bribes her little brothers – 'which like faery sprites / Oft skipped into our chamber, those sweet nights' – to spy on the two lovers, and interrogates them next day as he dandles them on his knee. One inference is that people have good reason to mistrust their own daughters when they themselves so brazenly exploit innocence and corrupt domestic affection.

The lover's involvement in the world he exposes diverts rather than disturbs him because he so keenly relishes his own part in a contest of wits, and so eagerly engages in it on its own terms. This world favours the talents of an amorous adventurer, calling for an agile mind, a freedom of resource, a grasp of all the moves:

Let me think any rival's letter mine,
     And at next nine
Keep midnight's promise; mistake by the way
The maid, and tell the Lady of that delay.

Love's Usury

His plea to love is just that he be preserved from slavery to the passion itself, or even to the pleasure of the game of love: 'Only let me love none, no, not the sport'. The manner of the address precisely hits an attitude to love as to the lady, sometimes in just a few words: 'Come, Madam, come' (*Elegy 19*). Such control of tone and wit confirms a poise which might impede a mere Don Juan and nimble wits alone could never hit.[1] This cool self-awareness is the condition of his keenest insights into love, such as discover in the act the complexity of his own ardent impulse:

O my America, my new found land,
My kingdom, safeliest when with one man manned,
My mine of precious stones, my empery,
How blessed am I in this discovering thee!

Elegy 19

The activities he rounds up so succinctly here are not obvious correlates of love or of each other, navigators' feats, imperial dominion, the vulnerableness of states, diamond mines. Yet each term makes its own point, heightening the zest of amorous discovery with the pride of unique possession while keeping us aware that such triumphs sustain themselves upon fear. This new Eden has been won out of the hazards of a dangerous world, not least the insecurities of the lovers' own natures. The lines oppose the world of profit and power to the private experience of love yet keep that world in prospect as an enhancing threat; the unease is implicit in the possession. Such writing owes more to a shrewd grasp of the complexity of people's motives than to a capacity for thinking in the midst of feeling, yet it strikingly gives us the passion and the appraisal of it together. The wit works to define and qualify even the most absolute of the heart's gestures.

Donne's self-ironic detachment in no way undersells the ardours it observes. Donne is a realist just in that he allows no essential difference between people's motives in whatever sphere they operate. The girl's father turns pale and trembles at the betraying hint of her lover's perfume, 'Like a tyrant king, that in his bed / Smelt gunpowder' (*Elegy 4*). A tyrannical king is still a man, who is reduced to ludicrous terror in bed by the mere whiff of danger. The poet's determination to remain undeceived prompts him to look to people's motives rather than their professed ends, and to follow all our pretensions back to the bodily impulses which they gloss. He challenges us to approve this naturalistic explanation of people's real promptings, implying that such an awareness of common nature is the condition of our freedom in a self-seeking world. The poetry continually invites us to see the world as it is and accept only what experience confirms.

This poet's openness to the diversity of experience respects the provisionalness as well as the complexity of our undertakings in an unstable world which we cannot even encounter in the same way two days running, if only because we ourselves are never 'just those persons, which we were' (*Woman's Constancy*). Donne flouts the convention which represents love as a singleminded devotion to an unattainable paragon of women. Love in the *Songs* and *Sonnets* and the *Elegies* is a versatile relationship which must make its own terms with the world and with human nature. To say that 'No where / Lives a woman true, and fair' (*Song*: 'Go, and catch a falling star') is to relish the corrupting commerce which permits only the ugly women to remain chaste. How may the lover satisfy his natural urge without rendering himself vulnerable or simply abject?

> Let me not know that others know
>   That she knows my pain, lest that so
> A tender shame make me mine own new woe.
>> *Love's Exchange*

Love becomes a game in which both parties manoeuvre for advantage, making bargaining counters of such principles as chastity and fidelity. Women naturally take advantage of their assumed status as objects of devotion while yielding nothing in return; they 'exact great subsidies' from heart and eyes and yet forsake the lovers who rely on them,

> And for the cause, honour, or conscience give,
> Chimeras, vain as they, or their prerogative.
>> *A Valediction: of the Book*

Men use such warrants as they may summon up, urging her obligation to reward devoted service, and threatening revenge if it is not met, in the entire expectation that her professed scruples are expedient ploys, a mere sham of virginity:

> When by thy scorn, O murderess, I am dead
> And that thou think'st thee free
> From all solicitation from me,
> Then shall my ghost come to thy bed,
> And thee, feigned vestal, in worse arms shall see; . . .
>> *The Apparition*

When the natural order itself prescribes variety the wary lover had better stay uncommitted, if only because his own amorous zeal is so brief. All the more welcome if she soon gets her fill of him, as she is apt to do since the passion itself dies with satisfaction and turns to indifference or worse. 'Changed loves are but changed sorts of meat'; and who does not fling the shell away once he has eaten the kernel (*Community*)! The lover's stylish composure keeps this ritual round from grossness. The style confirms his distance even from his own cravings:

> Our ease, our thrift, our honour, and our day,
> Shall we, for this vain bubble's shadow pay?
>> *Love's Alchemy*

Is the end of all that lofty striving no more than an empty pleasure which a servant might enjoy as much as his master, 'if he can / Endure the short scorn of a bridegroom's play'?

Tried experience remains Donne's touchstone. He scouts our

childish readiness to make a god of our unfulfilled cravings, and carries to a ribald extreme his sceptical testing of love:

> Whilst yet to prove,
> I thought there was some deity in love . . .
> *Farewell to Love*

The lover brusquely reasons his way to a flat renunciation of love, which he proposes not because he has some higher end in view but solely on the ground that his sexual urge defeats itself. Donne takes for granted a thoroughgoing naturalism which locates the source of love in our sexual organs. This iconoclastic expectation leaves no scope for idealising sentiment. It finds in our pursuit of love nothing but a degrading self-enslavement such as compels us to reiterate a performance which we know in advance cannot yield the satisfaction it promises. We recognise by repeated experience that acts of sex simply humiliate and damage us, bringing no fulfilment but only 'A kind of sorrowing dulnes to the mind'. Our sense of the contrariness of our condition just makes the urge still more perverse, impelling us to seek to reproduce ourselves so that we may lengthen our brief lives in our offspring yet mortifyingly bringing it home to us that our virility destroys itself, 'since each such act, they say, / Diminisheth the length of life a day'. So compelling is the presentiment of our brevity that we would soon kill ourselves in a frenzy of attempted self-perpetuation if nature imposed no intrinsic check upon desire. From this self-defeating cycle of thraldom to the body the only escape is renunciation, which needs no nobler exertion than the putting down of the tyrannical organ:

> If all fail,
> 'Tis but applying worm-seed to the tail.

This lover's renunciation of love also puts down the Platonisers who seek an escape from the life of the body by transcending sense altogether. It mocks such moralising lovers as Petrarch and Sidney offer us who turn from sexual passion to higher things, preferring the love of God to a secular attachment. The very movement of *Farewell to Love* works to explore rather than celebrate, simulating the play of a mind which is here and now thinking its way through a present dilemma – 'Whilst yet . . . Thus when . . . But, from late fair . . . And thence'. The continual probing of wit gives immediacy to this progression, setting up a tense unpredictableness within the ordered development to a climax. The complex formal patterning catches the interworking of the instances of men's brevity in consequence of the Fall, setting revulsion to countercheck lust,

> Because that other curse of being short,
> And only for a minute made to be
> Eager, desires to raise posterity.

The wit of this short poem is organic in that it articulates the life of the entire constitution, body and mind together.

Donne's apprehension of flux intensifies his search for stability. What human commitment may redress the shortcomings of our lives, however locally? Some of his subtlest wit goes to delineate a mutualness which depends upon more than the union of bodies, and exempts one realised condition of love from the common state. This condition is celebrated as a kind of miracle, a rare relationship which falls outside the order of nature and our normal categories of discourse, so that we may characterise the experience at all only by saying what it is not:

> If that be simply perfectest
> Which can by no way be expressed
> But negatives, my love is so.
> *Negative Love*

In *The Canonization, The Anniversary, The Good Morrow* wit works to uphold an achieved human bond in the teeth of the hazards which imperil it, whether they come from the world beyond the lovers, the lovers' own fears, or the passing of time itself:

> Busy old fool, unruly sun,
> Why dost thou thus,
> Through windows, and through curtains call on us?
> *The Sun Rising*

This love stands against time and death, as well as against the ruinous frenzy of moneymaking and power hunting. 'All other things, to their destruction draw, / Only our love hath no decay' (*The Anniversary*). The conceits confirm a mutual commitment which suffices in itself to set these two lovers apart from the self-absorbed world, and even outdoes the world's self-aggrandizing preoccupation with place, wealth, power:

> She'is all states, and all princes, I,
> Nothing else is.
> Princes do but play us, compared to this,
> All honour's mimic; all wealth alchemy.
> *The Sun Rising*

This play of witty hyperbole does more than pit their love against the claims of the world. It comprehends the public glories within the private condition, defiantly proclaiming that such lovers outgo their world in the world's own rewards. All Donne's love poems uphold our human interchanges against the obsessions which denature people. Some of the most impassioned of them oppose mutual love to whatever compulsions cramp the play of minds and affections such as the amassing of wealth, hunger for 'honours' smokes', fawning upon the great (*Elegy 6*). Love itself may be only another such bondage to our own desires. Donne's mutual lovers define their state by its freedom from such a slavery to sense. This love will not slacken with their bodily separation, however they may express it through their bodies:

> But we by a love, so much refined,
>> That our selves know not what it is,
> Inter-assured of the mind,
>> Care less, eyes, lips, and hands to miss.
>> *A Valediction: forbidding Mourning*

The nice qualification 'care less' wards off any suggestion that such a refined love does not need the senses at all. It marks the involvement of eyes, lips, hands in a union of their entire being which nonetheless does not depend on the proximity of their bodies.

Such a love cannot be the prerogative of their minds or souls alone:

> But O alas, so long, so far
> Our bodies why do we forbear?
>> *The Ecstasy*

The wit now works to prescribe the condition which assures the unchanging fidelity of such mutual lovers.[2] It intimates that their love is defined not by the body alone but by the interfusion of body and soul in our nature which makes their union possible. This oneness of the lovers' souls puts their state beyond the mutations of sense:

> For, th'atomies of which we grow,
> Are souls, whom no change can invade.

Yet their bodies are necessary to that state, for until they couple in affection the souls will remain locked in solitariness, helpless to reach each other:

> So must pure lovers' souls descend
>> T'affections, and to faculties,
> Which sense may reach and apprehend,
>> Else a great prince in prison lies.

The play of conceit submits feeling itself to intelligence, and defines the condition it celebrates:

> Where can we find two better hemispheres
> Without sharp north, without declining west?
>
> *The Good Morrow*

These lovers still need to come to terms with their own natures, acknowledging the precariousness of a mutual love whose 'first minute, after noon, is night' (*A Lecture upon the Shadow*). The chop-logic of the conceited argument points an unsentimental lesson. It prescribes for the continuance of a love which 'though 'tis got by chance, 'tis kept by art' (*Elegy 15*). Such lovers' unwavering constancy does not come by accident or by individual resolve. The lovers celebrate a rare mutual attainment which distinguishes their love from all other human attachments and opposes it to the frailty of everything else we know:

> This, no tomorrow hath, nor yesterday,
> Running it never runs from us away,
> But truly keeps his first, last, everlasting day.
>
> *The Anniversary*

When the defiant lover of *The Canonization* claims that the two of them give more wit to the riddle of the phoenix because they 'die and rise the same, and prove / Mysterious by this love' he suggests more than that their love is a singular bond which coitus confirms rather than destroys. The witty figure intimates that this is one small area of their lives in which they can defy their mortality and withstand the frailty of the entire natural creation.

The inescapable pressure of the time-bound world gives urgency to the steadfastness which resists it. Donne makes high drama of the contradiction between the momentary predicament of lovers and a condition which time cannot touch:

> Oh do not die, for I shall hate
> All women so, when thou art gone,
> That thee I shall not celebrate,
> When I remember, thou wast one.
>
> *A Fever*

A Fever is pitched just at the crisis of an illness. It dramatises the very process of change in time, catching the anxiety of a lover who confronts quite opposite possibilities which must decide his own state. Private apprehension opens into general disquiet in the vast conceited claim that the world itself depends upon the qualities of the sick lady, and may even be incinerated by the fever which destroys her:

> Oh wrangling schools, that search what fire
>   Shall burn this world, had none the wit
> Unto this knowledge to aspire,
>   That this her fever might be it?

Yet the lines oppose to the menacing drama of uncertainty the possibility of a condition of permanence. They bring out a quality of the sick lady herself which is not subject to the vicissitudes of the body and cannot suffer change and death:

> And yet she cannot waste by this,
>   Nor long bear this torturing wrong,
> For much corruption needful is
>   To fuel such a fever long.

> These burning fits but meteors be,
>   Whose matter in thee is soon spent.
> Thy beauty, and all parts, which are thee,
>   Are unchangeable firmament.

In Donne's cosmology meteors are more than bodies which quickly burn themselves out in a flash of brilliance. They possess a mixed nature like ours, in which earthly and heavenly elements interfuse:

Our nature is meteoric, we respect (because we partake so) both earth and heaven; for as our bodies glorified shall be capable of spiritual joy, so our souls demerged into those bodies are allowed to partake earthly pleasures.[3]

The lover proves his passion in the hyperbolic claim that her pure spirit gives life and soul to a world which, without her, would be no more to him than a worm-ridden carcase. Yet the lines do not limit their scope to the lover's feelings. They claim a universal consequence which may even be taken for granted. The conceit draws its force, however self-mockingly, from a myth of innocent atonement. It proclaims the power of uncorrupted virtue to revitalise a moribund world.

The poetical letters Donne wrote to a friend describing two incidents in the expedition to the Azores in 1596 divertingly reduce the heroic aspirations of such ventures to so many attempted appeasements of personal appetites or revulsions, which the enterprise itself quite nullifies anyway. Whatever private motives set them on – political disenchantment, boredom with love, the hope of gain, thirst of honour, desire of a brave death – they lose their end when they simply get becalmed in the burning heat, 'for here as well as I / A desperate may live, and a coward die' (*The Calm*). In the *Metempsychosis*, written some five years later, one of the oddest of Donne's witty devices allows him a ferocious exposure of power-politics which shows up men's lofty poses as masks for cold self-interest. The white and haughty swan which moves with state as if it disdains to look upon low things nonetheless snaps up the unwary fry as if by right:

> and yet before that one
> Could think he sought it, he had swallowed clear
> This, and much such, and unblamed devoured there
> All, but who too swift, too great, or well armed were.

To be vulnerable is to be the tool and then the prey of those with power:

> Exalted she is, but to the exalter's good,
> As are by great ones, men which lowly stood.
> It's raised, to be the raiser's instrument and food.

Donne outdoes Machiavelli in a fable which depicts the transmigration of a soul indifferently between human beings and beasts and takes our fallen creation for a predatory jungle. This satiric fiction opens a multiple perspective to his wit. It permits him to play off our present condition simultaneously against our first state, our ideal promise, and the unchanging order beyond all these contingencies. The curious device of the progress of a soul which started in the apple Eve plucked at the site of the future Calvary offers us several ways of looking at the Fall, and of mirroring ourselves in the early world:

> In this world's youth wise nature did make haste,
> Things ripened sooner, and did longer last;
> Already this hot cock in bush and tree
> In field and tent o'erflutters his next hen,
> He asks her not, who did so taste, nor when,
> Nor if his sister, or his niece she be,
> Nor doth she pule for his inconstancy
> If in her sight he change, nor doth refuse
> The next that calls; . . .

We see by ironic contrast with those early times how sadly we fall short of the true natural virility; yet the comparison with our own motives ribaldly reminds us what fallen creatures have in common:

Meat fit for men
His father steals for him, and so feeds then
One, that within a month, will beat him from his hen.

The complex movement of the poem also brings out the way in which people's inner cravings shape their outward ends and actions, especially in their lust for self-satisfaction, the drive to domination and power. The wit coolly rehearses this interaction of inward and outward life in high political transactions:

The heirs of slain kings, we see are often so
Transported with the joy of what they get,
That they, revenge and obsequies forget,
Nor will against such men the people go,
Because he's now dead, to whom they should show
Love in that act. Some kings by vice being grown
So needy of subjects' love, that of their own,
They think they lose, if love be to the dead Prince shown.

Donne invites us to recognise our own moral peril in a world which simply battens upon virtuous innocents:

If they stand armed with silly honesty,
With wishing prayers, and neat integrity,
Like Indians 'gainst Spanish hosts they be.
To Sir Henry Wotton

We feel ourselves to be so vulnerable because we know how easily we are corrupted, not least by our own cravings. We see where the moral dangers lie, 'yet our state's such, / That though than pitch they stain worse, we must touch'. The witty ironies and paradoxes rehearse the hazards of acting at all in a world in which 'Utopian youth' grows 'old Italian', and alternative courses of action may prove equally disastrous. We can never hope for more than a relatively – and temporarily – fortunate outcome of our efforts.

The *Metempsychosis* and *Farewell to Love* confirm a progressive decline in nature as well as a continual flux. Our present state can admit no absolute values. Only relative judgments of it are possible; and custom and opinion may be the best moral guides we can find:

There's nothing simply good, nor ill alone,
Of every quality comparison,
The only measure is, and judge, opinion.

The provocative parting dictum of the *Metempsychosis* bears out Montaigne's conclusion that we can have no stable grasp of a universe whose condition continually shifts. In fact we cannot know anything in nature with certainty because all our knowledge is acquired through the senses, and our sense impressions themselves are so frail.

Human nature shares the general condition of change; and human beings are moved by appetite and self-seeking will, which our wits assist and refine. Our moral professions merely colour our selfish desires. Indeed Aristotle makes it a question how far all our thinking simply elaborates the state of our appetites, which themselves reflect the condition of our bodily organs.[4] The early condition of mankind imposed no constraint upon the free satisfaction of appetite; and the only obligation people then recognised was to follow the impulsions of their own nature. The decline in the present state set in when moral laws of repression and denial were introduced:

> Men, till they took laws which made freedom less,
> Their daughters, and their sisters did ingress;
> Till now unlawful, therefore ill, 'twas not.
>
> *Metempsychosis*

Like Boccaccio and Machiavelli before him Donne portrays life in a civic jungle whose denizens are thinking creatures, and sharply self-aware. The condition puts quick wits at a premium. Sheer mental resourcefulness gives zest to life in a precarious world, even if it permits us no more than the thrill of survival. Wit enables us to understand our condition as well as master it; and it also allows us to maintain a certain distance from the values of the timebound world by keeping other possible modes of being in prospect. Donne makes his wit a means of trying the accepted values, whether by defining and weighing the world's activities relative to each other or by holding in balance quite contrary commitments to the world. Is the best life to be led in the city, the Court, or the country? Each place 'is worst equally':

> Cities are sepulchres; they who dwell there
> Are carcases, as if no such there were.
> And Courts are theatres, where some men play
> Princes, some slaves, all to one end, and of one clay.
> The country is a desert, where no good,
> Gained (as habits, not born,) is understood.
>
> *To Sir Henry Wotton*

We should mistake Donne's thinking to suppose that he played with the ideas of Sextus Empiricus and Montaigne for a time in his young manhood and then discarded them in favour of a more 'serious'

understanding of the world.[5] The evidence of all his writing is that he
never went back on his judgment of corrupted nature. His sceptical
appraisal of our natural condition persists in the poetry of his middle
years, as in his latest sermons. He simply enlarged the possibility that
nature might be amended.

The uncompromising testament of relativism which makes a
postscript to the *Metempsychosis* refuses any absolute value to the world
the poem has evoked. Yet Donne never abandons the touchstone of
final truth. He denies no more than that we are now capable of knowing true reality by means of our natural reason. Our knowledge is at
best a relative ordering of worldly affairs which can scarcely be called
truth. When we pretend to a surer grasp of our condition then we fall
into the contradictions and confusions which we see all round us in
the surmises of professed savants:

> And one soul thinks one, and another way
> Another thinks, and 'tis an even lay.
>   *The Second Anniversary*, 267–8

Far from learning more of the truth as time runs on we are actually
moving further from it, for the world itself is lapsing ever faster
towards chaos. The radical scepticism of the two great *Anniversary*
poems brings into focus all Donne's dealings with the secular world.
He poses the prospect of a double degeneration. We are perpetually
striving to order a fast-disintegrating universe by the means of our
rapidly decaying senses, so that our unaided reason can never yield us
any certainty at all. Our boldest claims to certainty are only the most
absurd, and the latest speculations are the wildest:

> And new philosophy calls all in doubt,
> The element of fire is quite put out;
> The sun is lost, and th' earth, and no man's wit
> Can well direct him where to look for it.
> And freely men confess that this world's spent,
> When in the planets and the firmament
> They seek so many new; they see that this
> Is crumbled out again to his atomies.
>   *The First Anniversary*, 205–12

Yet this is a Christian scepticism, not a recipe for despair. Donne
would agree with Charron that we have a means of absolute assurance
when we turn from the world and our present plight altogether and
anticipate the final bliss of union with Christ:[6]

                              nothing
          Is worth our travail, grief, or perishing,
          But those rich joys, which did possess her heart,
          Of which she's now partaker, and a part.
                              The First Anniversary, 431–5

Donne's radical sense of the relativeness of our understanding gives his
poetry an unremitting toughness of conceit. The wit continually
works to try our human circumstances relative to each other and to
play them off against a final order of reality, or such assurance of
permanence as we may win from an unstable world. What essential
joys may this earth afford? What permanent effect can we possibly
expect of 'transitory causes'!

                         Dost thou love
          Beauty? (and beauty worthiest is to move)
          Poor cozened cozener, that she, and that thou,
          Which did begin to love, are neither now;
          You are both fluid, changed since yesterday; . . .
                              The Second Anniversary, 389–93

Such lines from Donne's mature career do more than formally justify
the relativism which shapes all his work. They resolutely propose a
oneness in human experience which altogether annuls the decorum of
a world 'where some men play / Princes, some slaves, all to one end,
and of one clay' (*To Sir Henry Wotton*). To suppose that none of our
secular presumptions can truly be worth more than any other is to
reduce them all alike to a common condition which mocks the
dignities we conventionally observe. Donne's discomforting openness
to experience simply follows out his refusal to compartmentalise the
world in ready-made categories.

    Scepticism persists, and darkens into a foreboding which is not
abated by the recognition that some virtues still stand against corruption in the world. The apprehension of our worsening state in a
disintegrating universe portends an imminent lapse into nothingness.
This prospect of an impending dissolution haunts Donne's funeral
poems and verse letters, which discover in our physical decay the
pattern of a general decline. Such poems as *The First Anniversary* and
To the Countess of Salisbury accumulate instances of depravity so as to
bring out the distance between our possible grandeur and the squalid
actuality of our brief animal existence. They witness a manifold
deterioration, showing how far our condition now falls short of what
it might be and once was. Man, 'this world's vice-emperor', who

comprehends in himself all the faculties and graces of the natural condition, has brought about his own diminution:

> This man, whom God did woo, and loth t'attend
> Till man came up, did down to man descend,
> This man, so great, that all that is, is his,
> Oh what a trifle, and poor thing he is!
>
> *The First Anniversary*, 161–70

The celebratory hyperbole of *The First Anniversary* is wittily advanced so as to demonstrate the dependence of all the world's virtues on the personal qualities of the dead girl:

> She that was best, and first original
> Of all fair copies; and the general
> Steward to Fate; . . .
> She to whom this world must itself refer,
> As suburbs, or the microcosm of her . . .
>
> 227–9, 235–6

Donne's praise of the girl becomes his bold way of conceitedly following out the decline of our world in every one of its aspects from its state of innocence and right order. As the constitution of mankind is out of joint, so is the world's whole frame depraved by the corruption which seized the angels themselves:

> and then first of all
> The world did in her cradle take a fall,
> And turned her brains, and took a general maim
> Wronging each joint of th' universal frame.
>
> 191–8

The bizarre figure of a cot-casualty suggests that this progressive aberration of our nature from a coherence it once had takes its beginning from a specific point in time. Donne's conception of the Fall is dynamic in that it renders the worsening depravity of the world as an ever-faster decline from the true natural state. To know ourselves aright is to acknowledge our diminished standing now, at this late moment when 'mankind decays so soon, / We're scarce our fathers' shadows cast at noon' (*The First Anniversary*, 143–4). Yet we commit ourselves wholly to this world, perversely willing our own destruction when we should be striving to reverse the consequences of sin. There is a dangerous self-deception in the very attempt to fix human nature in some aggrandising formula as an ordered microcosm of creation:

> Since then our business is, to rectify
>   Nature, to what she was, we are led awry
> By them, who man to us in little show,
>   Greater than due, no form we can bestow
> On him; for man into himself can draw
>   All, all his faith can swallow, or reason chaw.
>
> *To Sir Edward Herbert, at Juliers*

In his verse letters and funeral poems Donne develops modes of wit which serve to try the value of a world of corruption and death. The paradox of what may appear to be the most extreme of his witty hyperbolising is that it too starts in a sceptical determination to see people's motives as they really are. As many who go to Rome do not esteem religion at all but merely satisfy their curiosity with the ornaments of faith, so most claimants to goodness mistake the outward trappings for the pure temple of virtue. The poet need pursue his own pilgrimage no further than his patroness herself:

> And after this survey, oppose to all
> Babblers of chapels, you th' Escurial.
>
> *To the Countess of Bedford* ('Madam, / You have refined me')

Donne's serious purpose as a panegyric poet becomes the celebration of the qualities beyond the common run of nature which may resist the general lapse towards chaos – 'Be more than man, or thou'art less than an ant' (*The First Anniversary*, 190). He makes a moral challenge of the task of praise which his patrons put upon him, countering our worldly expectations of success with virtues which are truly worth esteem. The poems pose a dynamic tension between the qualities which may be praised absolutely and substantially, and those endowments which the world rates highly for some relative and accidental profit they afford. Innocence must be one such absolute quality for its loss is both the cause and the consequence of the Fall. As an innocent person presents a pattern of our uncorrupted state so an innocent death is an ambiguous event; for in itself it is no death at all and yet in its effects it re-enacts the primal calamity. Elizabeth Drury's departure from the world left us dying but also better aware of our true state:

> This world, in that great earthquake languished;
> For in a common bath of tears it bled,
> Which drew the strongest vital spirits out:
> But succoured then with a perplexed doubt,
> Whether the world did lose, or gain in this . . .
>
> *The First Anniversary*, 11–15

With the loss of her preserving balm the world falls sick and dies, even putrefies, leaving the poet only the task of anatomising it so as to demonstrate its corruption. Donne rigorously carries this complex conceit of an innocent death right through the two anniversary poems for Elizabeth Drury, disregarding the practical disadvantage that he is thus led to attribute a great deal to a young girl he had not even met. Ben Jonson assured Drummond 'That Donne's *Anniversary* was profane and full of blasphemies', and said 'That he told Mr Donne, if it had been written of the Virgin Mary it had been something; to which he answered that he described the idea of a woman and not as she was'.[7] The disagreement between the two poets here shows up crucially divergent conceptions of wit. Donne precisely does not seek to celebrate a uniquely miraculous nature or a transcendental virtue. He shows us how an innocent young girl effectively embodied in her own human nature the qualities which alone preserve the natural creation, and why her death re-enacts the withdrawal of those qualities from the world. He pointedly declines to take the girl for an emanation of the divine spirit, another Beatrice who rose above the flesh in her life and transcends the world finally in her death. On the contrary, Elizabeth Drury is celebrated for human excellences which are spiritually refined in themselves. She was a being in whom body and spirit were at one.

Most of the people Donne praised, alive or dead, were past the age of innocence (Ben Jonson unkindly described one of them as the Court pucelle).[8] Yet the burden of the *Anniversary* poems themselves is that Elizabeth Drury's death has shown us all how to resist the corrupting force of the world, 'And that thou hast but one way, not to admit / The world's infection, to be none of it' (*The First Anniversary*, 245–6). A tried election of virtue is possible, though rarely achieved, which counters the common depravity of the Fall. Donne consoles a mourning mother with the conceit that she now incorporates her dead daughter's virtues with her own, and has thus acquired the power to preserve both their beings from corruption – 'You that are she and you, that's double she' (*To the Lady Bedford*). He claims that a woman embodies all virtue in herself and sustains the world, so that 'others' good reflect but back your light': *To the Countess of Huntingdon* ('That unripe side of earth'). He excoriates a blind world, which unknowingly owes what little vitality it still retains to the virtue of a few moral prodigies who mediate Christ's own virtue, having the quasi-alchemical power to turn 'Leaden and iron wills to good', and make 'even sinful flesh like his' (*Resurrection, imperfect*).

The terms in which Donne celebrates the people who thus in themselves resolve 'the issues of death'[9] follow out his judgment of a right order of sensible qualities:

> She, of whose soul if we may say, 'twas gold,
> Her body was th' electrum, and did hold
> Many degrees of that; we understood
> Her by her sight, her pure and eloquent blood
> Spoke in her cheeks, and so distinctly wrought,
> That one might almost say, her body thought; . . .
> *The Second Anniversary*, 241–6

The integrity Donne delineates here is not some ethereal virtue which has transcended the base flesh. He quite precisely praises the innocent girl for the rare interfusion of sense and spirit in her nature, which makes an intelligent organism of the body itself. It is central to the vision of these key poems that they appeal to an order which their subjects have effectively realised in the body. The right constitution they propose is no transcendent ideal but a historic state of the Creation in which spirit interpenetrated matter so as to sustain the organic life of the whole. The ground of Donne's praise is that this vital wholeness may be recovered now only locally, in the persons of those rare moral heroes who elect to spiritualise their senses and resist the disintegrating world. The poems plot the ways in which our arrogant self-sufficiency denies the coherence of the Creation and precipitates its own ruin:

> 'Tis all in pieces, all coherence gone;
> All just supply, and all relation:
> Prince, subject, father, son, are things forgot,
> For every man alone thinks he hath got
> To be a phoenix, and that then can be
> None of that kind, of which he is, but he.
> *The First Anniversary*, 213–18

Donne's account of the effects of the Fall assumes a universe of qualities in dispersal, a centrifugal whirl in which the general pull towards chaos is resisted only by the power of an innocent or virtuous few who are 'still / More antidote, than all the world was ill' (*The Second Anniversary*, 377–8). In this life we reaffirm a stable order of qualities when we progress from earth to glass, from brute sense to the transparent purity of the spiritualised body. The process may require our death to complete it, as it were by occult incubation in the grave:

> Parents make us earth, and souls dignify
> Us to be glass; here to grow gold we lie.
> *Epitaph on Himself*

The paradox of a virtuous dissolution must be that it is no mere dispersal into dust but a providential process which finally transmutes the once-base matter into gold.

Donne's funeral poems can seem perversely obscure and crabbed, as Ben Jonson seems to have found the *Elegy upon . . . Prince Henry*:[10]

> Look to me faith, and look to my faith, God;
> For both my centres feel this period.
> Of weight one centre, one of greatness is;
> And reason is that centre, faith is this.

Yet the lines make powerful sense when their precise articulation of the conceit points such a perilous discordance between our ways of recognising the truth, reason seeming to contradict faith. The idiom has given scandal from the first,[11] and risks ridicule anyway:

> Immortal Maid, who though thou would'st refuse
> The name of mother, be unto my Muse
> A father, since her chaste ambition is,
> Yearly to bring forth such a child as this.
> *The Second Anniversary*, 33–6

We might take indecorum for a working principle of these mourning panegyrics. Donne harps on decay and maggots, even essaying satiric asides in his contemplation of bodily corruption:

> Think thee a prince, who of themselves create
> Worms which insensibly devour their state.
> *The Second Anniversary*, 117–18

He shows by the analogy of a beheaded man how it is that our dead world still appears to have life and movement (*The Second Anniversary*, 9–18). He compares the soul in the newborn infant body with a 'stubborn sullen anchorite' who sits 'fixed to a pillar, or a grave . . . Bedded, and bathed in all his ordures' (*The Second Anniversary*, 169–71). He makes elephantine jibes at the arrogance of men who do not live long enough now to be page to Methusaleh and yet still claim to harness the heavens. He develops in nice particulars the conceit that virtuous men are clocks and that Lord Harrington was a public clock (*Obsequies to the Lord Harrington*). He continually mingles unlike orders of reference, the domestic with the metaphysical, the physical with the moral:

> Sight is the noblest sense of any one,
> Yet sight hath only colour to feed on,
> And colour is decayed: summer's robe grows
> Dusky, and like an oft dyed garment shows.
> Our blushing red, which used in cheeks to spread,
> Is inward sunk, and only our souls are red.
>
> *The First Anniversary*, 353–8

Such persistent idiosyncrasy goes beyond the will to shock. It marks the unrelenting effort to undo what we take for decorum and mistake for the true order of reality.

Donne's reluctance to take Holy Orders scarcely signals a misgiving of faith. The persuasions his ministry affirms shape all his mature verse, not least the religious poetry he wrote well before his ordination. Active innocence and virtue are instruments of grace, and grace may transform nature. Christ's becoming human perfects the union of body and soul, human nature and divine spirit, and confirms the restoration of love. The sequence of religious sonnets *La Corona* was written in a mode of ingenious meditation on the Christian senses of a crown such as Donne never essayed again:

> But do not, with a vile crown of frail bays,
> Reward my muse's white sincerity,
> But what thy thorny crown gained, that give me,
> A crown of glory, which doth flower always;
> The ends crown our works, but thou crown'st our ends . . .
>
> *La Corona* 1

This quibbling wit might have earned Gracian's approval. Yet it is no mere rhetorical flourish. Donne seeks ingenious ways of bringing out the irony of Christ's worldly degradation and the paradox of his double status, his creative presence in nature:

> Ere by the spheres time was created, thou
> Wast in his mind, who is thy son, and brother,
> Whom thou conceiv'st, conceived; yea thou art now
> Thy maker's maker, and thy father's mother.
>
> *La Corona* 2

Donne's *Divine Poems* propose that nature is transformed by the ministry of timeless virtues working in time. They posit that God's grace shapes temporal processes to eternal ends, providentially disposing events which seem to us accidental and contingent. Wit now becomes the means of apprehending final truth in our human exigencies, discovering in natural occurrences the working of a contrary condition of being. At the personal level Donne's religious wit follows out the prospect which Christ's double nature opened to us, rehearsing the paradox and the dilemma of our ambiguous state. An animal being nonetheless bears moral responsibility:

> If poisonous minerals, and if that tree,
> Whose fruit threw death on else immortal us,
> If lecherous goats, if serpents envious
> Cannot be damned; alas, why should I be?
> *Divine Meditations* 9

The struggle for grace to redeem sin may be resolved only in a drastic reformation of our entire nature such as transforms vice into penitence and guilt into shame:

> Yet grace, if thou repent, thou canst not lack;
> But who shall give thee that grace to begin?
> Oh make thyself with holy mourning black,
> And red with blushing, as thou art with sin; . . .
> *Divine Meditations* 4

The *Divine Meditations* make a universal drama of religious life, in which every moment may confront us with the final annulment of time. 'What if this present were the world's last night?' (*Divine Meditations* 13). The prospect of a present entry upon eternity also calls for a final showdown with ourselves, and with the exemplary events which bring time and the timeless together in one order:

> Mark in my heart, O soul, where thou dost dwell,
> The picture of Christ crucified, and tell
> Whether that countenance can thee affright . . .

Christ's double nature assures his power to transform events in time, as our power to outbrave death. 'Death be not proud': the declamatory rhetoric confirms the momentousness of the encounter and proclaims the possibility of a heroic triumph snatched from likely defeat:

> At the round earth's imagined corners, blow
> Your trumpets, angels, and arise, arise
> From death, you numberless infinities
> Of souls, and to your scattered bodies go . . .
> *Divine Meditations* 7

Christ's involvement in our condition lends our own moral life the grandeur of a universal struggle. God himself marshals the forces in a perpetual re-enactment of the central drama of creation. The real apprehension that final issues are imminent in our everyday lives gives the *Divine Meditations* their dramatic urgency, setting the trumpets blowing here and now to proclaim the sudden irruption of the Day of Judgment.

The sonnets play upon the ambiguous status of beings who simultaneously inhabit eternity and the world of time, opening a timeless prospect to us yet still allowing us a space in which to prepare ourselves for a final reckoning with the transgressions which might endlessly alienate us from God:

> But let them sleep, Lord, and me mourn a space,
> For, if above all these, my sins abound,
> 'Tis late to ask abundance of thy grace,
> When we are there; here on this lowly ground,
> Teach me how to repent; . . .

The present moment may define us forever. To imagine ourselves in mortal sickness or at the point of final judgment is a way of making our predicament immediate, bringing us up sharp against a reality which our daily lives obscure from us:

> I run to death, and death meets me as fast,
> And all my pleasures are like yesterday,
> I dare not move my dim eyes any way,
> Despair behind, and death before doth cast
> Such terror . . .
>
> *Divine Meditations* 1

The *Divine Meditations* make self-recognition imperative. They dramatise the spiritual dilemma of errant creatures who need God's grace in order that they may deserve it; for we must fall into sin and merit death even though our redemption is at hand, yet we cannot even begin to repent without grace:

> Yet grace, if thou repent, thou canst not lack;
> But who shall give thee that grace to begin?
>
> *Divine Meditations* 4

The poems open the sinner to God, imploring God's intervention by their forcible pledge of a will to acknowledge the need of it and submit:

> Batter my heart, three-personed God; for, you
> As yet but knock, breathe, shine, and seek to mend;
> That I may rise, and stand, o'erthrow me, and bend
> Your force, to break, blow, burn, and make me new.
>
> *Divine Meditations* 14

The sheer force of the petition marks the extremity of his struggle with himself and with God's adversary, as well as the majesty of the universal conflict which is waged in him and which God has an interest in his winning, 'Lest the world, flesh, yea Devil put thee out' (*Divine Meditations* 17). The drama brings home the enormity of the sinner's ingratitude, confronting him bodily with the irony of his obligation to Christ:

> Spit in my face ye Jews, and pierce my side,
> Buffet, and scoff, scourge, and crucify me,
> For I have sinned, and sinned, and only he,
> Who could do no iniquity, hath died: . . .
>
> *Divine Meditations* 11

Donne's pious wit can seem unaccommodatingly knotty:

> Father, part of his double interest
> Unto thy kingdom, thy Son gives to me,
> His jointure in the knotty Trinity
> He keeps, and gives me his death's conquest.
> This Lamb, whose death, with life the world hath blessed,
> Was from the world's beginning slain, and he
> Hath made two wills, which with the legacy
> Of his and thy kingdom, do thy sons invest.
>
> *Divine Meditations* 16

Yet this legal quibbling is not wanton ingenuity. It serves to follow out the intricate interrelation of divine being with human nature, timeless events with history. Donne prays for deliverance from the urge to make religion an excuse for wit, 'When we are moved to seem religious / Only to vent wit' (*A Litany*, 188–9). He is no less emphatic that wit is not just accessory to religion:

> nor must wit
> Be colleague to religion, but be it.
> *To the Countess of Bedford* ('Honour is so sublime perfection')

He proclaims a religion which is witty in itself and calls for wit to comprehend it:

> Tears in his eyes quench the amazing light,
> Blood fills his frowns, which from his pierced head fell . . .
>
> *Divine Meditations* 13

The figurative action catches the complexity of final judgment, graphically setting the evidence of Christ's love to temper God's justice yet leaving the outcome perilously within the scope of the sinner's will. The wit is the means of realising the manysidedness of religious experience, and of cutting right across the supposedly exclusive categories of Reformation theology.

Donne's devotional wit is no more self-absorbed than his secular wit. His very dramatising of his own predicament takes him outward from himself to characterise a general state and delineate the universal truth. A personal occasion, such as his own dangerous sickness, serves simply to confront him with the bleak actuality of our condition:

> Oh my black soul! now thou art summoned
> By sickness, death's herald, and champion;
> Thou art like a pilgrim, which abroad hath done
> Treason, and durst not turn to whence he is fled,
> Or like a thief, which till death's doom be read,
> Wisheth himself delivered from prison;
> But damned and haled to execution,
> Wisheth that still he might be imprisoned; . . .
>
> *Divine Meditations* 4

Far from dwelling on his own suffering the poet wittily reviews a series of situations in the world which bring home the peril to his soul such as a challenge to a combat, the quandary of a treasonous defector, the dilemma of a condemned thief. These predicaments are more than mere helps to meditation. The system implies a correspondence between the spiritual and the temporal states which annuls the supposed barriers between them.

Donne quite startlingly domesticates the universal drama of sin and redemption:

> And as a robbed man, which by search doth find
> His stol'n stuff sold, must lose or buy it again:
> The Son of glory came down, and was slain,
> Us whom he had made, and Satan stol'n, to unbind.
>
> *Divine Meditations* 15

Such wit does not work to embellish received truths. It brings the traffic of the world under the general laws which govern our fallen state. Even such a personal calamity as the death of his much-loved wife plays its providential part in the drama of God's offer for his soul against the rival enticements of his love:

> But why should I beg more love, when as thou
> Dost woo my soul for hers; offering all thine:
> And dost not only fear lest I allow
> My love to saints and angels, things divine,
> But in thy tender jealousy dost doubt
> Lest the world, flesh, yea Devil put thee out.
>
> *Divine Meditations* 17

Donne seems to have taken these feats of his wit for a way of grasping truths which would otherwise remain indefinable, realising a condition which our acceptance of the world only masks. One of their prime effects is to disturb our complacent expectations by reminding us of the shortcomings of the mind itself. This poet is always sceptically aware how little we know. Summoning the last trump from the 'round earth's *imagined* corners' he pulls us up sharp, recalling Revelation and mediaeval representations of the Last Judgment yet inviting us to ponder the gap between the speculations which we once took for knowledge and the evidence we now accept. In the act of affirmation the slight witty touch keeps us mindful of the risk of affirming anything at all.

In a fallen creation the search for truth may run counter to our unregenerate understanding. Donne's witty evocation of the life around him continually shows up the ineptitude of our secular assumptions, bringing out the ironies and paradoxes which are implicit in our dealings with a depraved world, the identities we do not suspect. As alchemists often turn to coining, so self-contempt begets self-love; as the best food provokes the worst surfeits, so humility fosters the most monstrous pride:

> therefore cross
> Your joy in crosses, else, 'tis double loss,
> And cross thy senses, else, both they, and thou
> Must perish soon, and to destruction bow.
>
> *The Cross*

To bring such human accidents within the witty order of the Christian truth he celebrates is to confirm the paradoxical nature of truth itself as we must encounter it, and point the paradox at the heart of our reality:

Or wash thee in Christ's blood, which hath this might
That being red, it dyes red souls to white.
Divine Meditations 4

Such snubs to pious propriety may shock, as readers have been
shocked by the impassioned plea for an enthralment which is freedom
and a ravishment which recovers chastity (*Divine Meditations* 14). The
paradox of a chaste abandonment to God's love becomes boldly
explicit, as does the proper object of love when he assures himself that
the casuistry he had once used to seduce women – 'all my profane
mistresses' – becomes a true praise when it is used of Christ. Beauty is
a sign of pity; only foulness signals rigour:

so I say to thee,
To wicked spirits are horrid shapes assigned,
This beauteous form assures a piteous mind.
Divine Meditations 13

The search for the true Church is resolved in a still bolder sexual
paradox. Christ is petitioned as a 'kind husband' to betray his spouse
to our view so that the poet's amorous soul may 'court thy mild dove',

Who is most true, and pleasing to thee, then
When she'is embraced and open to most men.
Divine Meditations 18

To express the principle of catholicity in a figure which makes the true
Church a whore and Christ her complaisant husband may seem
wantonly indecorous. Yet the lines startle us into a realisation, reminding us how far our presumption of exclusiveness takes us from Christ's
own ministry, and how arrogantly it denies Christ's Church.

The wit never removes the poems from common experience, on
the contrary it discovers a metaphysical presence in our daily lives. The
suddenness compels a reappraisal. 'Why are we by all creatures waited
on?' (*Divine Meditations* 12). In posing such a question to himself
Donne puts our domestic decorum in a final perspective. We could
claim no authority in a natural order which mankind itself has
deranged were it not restored to us by the supreme solicitude of the
Creator himself:

But wonder at a greater wonder, for to us
Created nature doth these things subdue,
But their Creator, whom sin, nor nature tied,
For us, his creatures, and his foes, hath died.

Such witty epiphanies work to disturb our facile acceptances and
expose the limitations of our understanding. They give calculated
offence to decorum in the service of a truth which has no truck with
our orders of decorum, confronting us with actualities which run
counter to our seeming. What makes them more than devices of
rhetoric is their warrant in occasions of scandal, paradox, irony,
incongruity, such as put no bar between natural and spiritual being.

The wit revalues the world. *Good Friday, 1613. Riding Westward*
discovers an aberration of the cosmos in a casual journey from one
friend's house to another. As the heavenly bodies lose their course
when they are subjected to 'foreign motions' so we are whirled by the
world, diverted from our true devotion by the distractions of our
everyday lives:

> Pleasure or business, so, our souls admit
> For their first mover, and are whirled by it.

Heading due west from Polesworth to Montgomery on Good Friday
1613, turning his back on Christ's cross in pursuit of pleasure, he confirms a general decay of nature which nonetheless opens him to
Christ's corrective mercy:

> Though these things, as I ride, be from mine eye,
> They are present yet unto my memory,
> For that looks towards them; and thou look'st towards me,
> O Saviour, as thou hang'st upon the tree;
> I turn my back to thee, but to receive
> Corrections, till thy mercies bid thee leave.
> O think me worth thine anger, punish me,
> Burn off my rusts, and my deformity,
> Restore thine image, so much, by thy grace,
> That thou mayst know me, and I'll turn my face.

The drastic reversal of perception discloses a providence in our very
aberrations. For this poem Christ's crucifixion consummates the
interworking of divine providence with human contingency which
is implicit in Christ's nature. A radical stroke of wit attests the co-
presence of changeless spirit with the gross bodily symptoms:

> Could I behold those hands, which span the poles,
> And turn all spheres at once, pierced with those holes?

Superimposing an image of total degradation upon an image of
absolute dominion Donne confirms the incongruity with our ordinary
understanding of an event which reorders the whole of existence. Far

from seeking novelty he finds his warrant, like Andrewes, in an icon of the early Church.[12]

Donne's wit strains to seize what he takes to be really there, to distinguish a timeless presence in the whirl of our human circumstances and apprehend the providence in which every order of existence coheres. The *Hymn to God my God, in my Sickness* turns on a still more startling device. The bizarre figure of the fevered poet as a flat map over which the physician-cosmographers anxiously pore prompts a survey of all the desirable places in the world which are reached by straits:

> Is the Pacific Sea my home? Or are
>   The eastern riches? Is Jerusalem?
> Anyan, and Magellan, and Gibraltar,
>   All straits, and none but straits, are ways to them . . .

The topographical questioning grows out of the quibble on straits, and defines a dilemma which these instances severally bring home to him. His present danger is a strait, as these are straits. Pain and sickness threaten to destroy him, yet may open an opposite prospect. He brings himself to understand that his suffering itself may be a blessing; for he shares the condition of a world in which our ultimate bliss must be won through well-endured hardship. In this *Hymn* the physical symptoms of the poet's illness become the instruments of his salvation:

> So, in his purple wrapped receive me Lord,
>   By these his thorns give me his other crown; . . .

The flushed face of a fevered man is metamorphosed into Christ's bloodied flesh, which is also the purple mantle of Christ's saving dominion; and the sufferer's spasms of pain become the thorns of Christ's crown. Intertwining Christ's agony and compassionate power with the human accidents, Donne identifies the pangs of a holy death with Christ's sufferings on the cross, which make such a death a means to glory. The wit articulates the working of a providence which shapes our human accidents in the pattern of timeless truth.

Our very language is taken to register the concurrence of the timeless with time. The puns in *A Hymn to God the Father* resolve the beautiful antiphony of petition and confession which regulates the poet's sense of sin:

> I have a sin of fear, that when I have spun
>   My last thread, I shall perish on the shore;
> But swear by thy self, that at my death thy son

> Shall shine as he shines now, and heretofore;
> And, having done that, thou hast done,
> I fear no more.

The plays on 'sun' and 'done' close the gap between the sin-burdened poet and a just God, bringing into one economy the means of temporal being and the means of abiding life. Such patterns are not arbitrarily made. They confirm the witty symmetry of a creation whose every part discovers the eternal order in the casual flux of sense.

Donne's *Devotions Upon Emergent Occasions*, pointedly so titled, grow out of a quite particular concern with a bodily condition. They discover in the symptoms of the poet's dangerous illness nothing less than an aberration of the entire cosmos, and strain to bring constitutional decay itself within the scope of God's providence. The idiosyncrasy of their manner is notorious; yet this is writing whose pattern discovers its meaning:

O eternal, and most gracious God, who having married *Man* and *Woman* together, and made them one *flesh*, wouldst have them also, to become one *soul* so, as that they might maintain a *sympathy* in their *affections*, and have a *conformity* to one another, in the *accidents* of this *world*, good or bad, so having married this soul and this body in me, I humbly beseech thee, that my soul may look, and make her use of thy merciful proceedings towards my *bodily restitution*, and go the same way to a *spiritual*. I am come by thy goodness, to the use of thine ordinary means for my *body*, to wash away those *peccant humours*, that endangered it. I have, O Lord, a *River* in my *body*, but a *Sea* in my *soul*, and a *Sea* swollen into the depth of a *Deluge*, above the *Sea*. Thou hast raised up certain *hills* in *me* heretofore, by which I might have stood safe, from these *inundations* of sin. Even our *Natural faculties* are a *hill*, and might preserve us from *some sin*. *Education, study, observation, example*, are *hills* too, and might preserve us from *some*. Thy *Church*, and thy *Word*, and thy *Sacraments*, and thine *Ordinances*, are *hills*, above these; thy *Spirit* of *remorse*, and *compunction*, and *repentance* for former *sin*, are *hills* too; and to the *top* of all these *hills*, thou hast brought me heretofore; but this *Deluge*, this *inundation*, is got above all my *Hills*; and I have sinned and sinned, and multiplied *sin* to *sin*, after all these thy assistances against *sin*, and where is there *water* enough to wash away this *Deluge*? There is a *red Sea*, greater than this *Ocean*; and there is a *little spring*, through which this *Ocean*, may pour itself into that *red Sea*. Let thy *Spirit* of true *contrition*, and *sorrow* pass all my *sins* through these *eyes*, into the *wounds* of thy *Son*, and I shall be clean, and my *soul* so much better purged than my *body*, as it is ordained for a *better*, and a *longer* life.[13]

The very occasion of such beseechments may seem bizarre. This prayer is prompted by an induced evacuation of the stomach and bowels in the latter stages of a serious illness. After some days of high fever the patient has at last begun to show signs of recovery in that he takes a little nourishment and keeps it down. So the doctors promptly seize the opportunity to purge him in an effort to expel the corrupting humours.

Donne takes this purging for a spiritual as well as a bodily process, a kind of purgatory here and now. He seeks a permanent truth in the immediate physical events, the 'accidents of this world' as he intimately experienced them in November and December 1623. These emergent occasions give the enquiry some urgency. Over those few weeks late in 1623 a protracted bout of relapsing fever – or it may have been typhus – brought him very near death.

He finds a general predicament in the progress of his illness, taking his own constitution for a little world which reproduces the economy of the world itself. His body has its natural means of conservation such as the rivers of cleansing waters which now flush out the accumulated corruptions, and the hills of his native faculties, which have only barely served to preserve him from being overwhelmed by these corruptions. Then his spiritual plight renews the Flood, as if he rehearses a universal drama in his own soul. He discovers in himself, as in the world at large, the landscape of the cosmic drama of transgression and atonement, the seas of sin, hills of our unaided spiritual endeavours, floods of pollution which ultimately inundate even those heights, and then the Red Sea of blood into which that ocean may pass by a little spring of penitent tears to be absorbed and wholly transformed.

The movement of thought may seem scarcely less wayward than the origin of these reflections. We pass quickly from purging to marriage, then to the relationship of body and soul, then to the writer's own embodiment of the universal Deluge before finally closing in on the supposed topography of the Middle East for a model of our means to grace. This curious sequence of ideas might appear arcane yet no one would think that it is random. On the contrary, the elaborately precise articulation of the syntax proposes a complex pattern of relationships such as we find in Donne's most highly wrought poems. We are offered a structure of ideas which cohere in necessary interdependence.

The passage epitomises a highly complex process of thinking in metaphor whose warrant is its ground in an actual event. If Donne did not actually compose the *Devotions* day-by-day during the stages of his illness then he wrote them up in his convalescence directly afterwards, for the work was entered in the Stationers' Register by January 1624.

It plots the progress of the fever in twenty-three formal phases or stations, each phase prompting a response in three parts, a meditation, an expostulation and a prayer. What this formula may owe to Loyola or anybody else is not the present concern.

The shaping factor is the pattern of events which the whole sequence of *Devotions* follows out, Donne's sudden disorder and progressive decline, his wavering on the very edge of death, and then his fairly swift recovery to new life, albeit under the continuing threat of a severe relapse. Yet the *Devotions* are wholly predicated upon the presumption of a close congruence of body and soul, a correspondence of the physical and spiritual states. So the fever is followed through as a spiritual trial which is enacted in the body. Its progress marks the inundation of the soul by sin, the sinner's passage through death and the grave to a purging in Christ's blood, and his joyful resurrection.

Donne's controlling supposition is that his illness actually embodies a spiritual condition and is not just a natural accident. He finds an order in its development and treatment which puts it altogether beyond mere hazard. The *Devotions* present Donne's striving to comprehend a providential design in these earthy processes, to understand the stages of his fever as the stations of a spiritual progress in which casual circumstances take on timeless consequences. Not that his body and his soul pull different ways in this extremity. On the contrary, as the King by sending his own doctor shows himself a physician to both body and soul on earth, so God will be physician to body and soul together in heaven.

This search for a design is more than just an allegorising of the sickness, such as would make it a mere sensible emblem of a moral state. His bodily sickness does not simply stand for or represent his soul's sickness but is one with it. These states are aspects of the same malaise, as he confirms in a vivid physiological conceit:

there is no *vein* in me, that is not full of the blood of thy *son*, whom I have crucified, and Crucified again, by multiplying many, and often repeating the same sins: . . . there is no *Artery* in me, that hath not the *spirit of error, the spirit of lust, the spirit of giddiness* in it; no *bone* in me that is not hardened with the custom of *sin*, and nourished, and suppled with the *marrow* of *sin*; no *sinews*, no *ligaments*, that do not tie, and chain sin and sin together.

9. *Expostulation*

Donne could scarcely bring it home to us more intimately that his physical constitution itself is moved and corrupted by sin.

At this early stage of its encroachment his sickness presents itself to him as a sudden reversal of his customary state, a dire transformation which turns his sensible pleasures to pains and portents of dissolution, his pleasurable sins to the threat of spiritual death. He immediately experiences it so in the body. The incremental consequence of Adam's sin comes home to him even more severely than it could have done to Adam, for he sweats as Adam did but earns no bread since he cannot now relish food. His slack sinews turn to iron fetters and the bedsheets to iron doors; the very feathers of a slothful bed become thorns of pain; the couch of luxury portends a tomb whose inscription is supplied by the *Devotions* themselves: 'A sick bed, is a grave; and all that the patient says there, is but a varying of his own *Epitaph*' (3. *Meditation*).

So abrupt a change points the chronic frailty of our natural state, the ironic arbitrariness of the appearance of death:

Death is in an old man's door, he appears, and tells him so, and *death* is at a young man's *back*, and says nothing; *Age* is a sickness, and *Youth* is an *ambush*; and we need so many *Physicians*, as may make up a *Watch*, and spy every inconvenience. There is scarce any thing, that hath not killed some body; a *hair*, a *feather* hath done it; Nay, that which is our best *antidote* against it hath done it; the best *Cordial* hath been *deadly* poison; Men have died of *Joy*, and almost forbidden their friends to weep for them, when they have seen them die laughing.

7. Meditation

In thus bringing home to him the general condition of man the sickness also exposes the state of the natural world. The world without grace is no more than a watch, but a watch which lacks its spring.

Man is a little world, who epitomises a world in himself and comprehends the entire cosmos in thought. Yet in our natural state even the greatest man is no more than a very little earth: 'He thinks he treads upon the *Earth*, that all is under his feet, and the *Brain* that thinks so, is but *Earth*' (11. *Meditation*). Donne marshals a telling array of metaphors to express the precarious and desperate situation of our lives in a degenerating world. We are our own executioners, tenants of a ruinous farm inherited from Adam, victims upon the faggot-pile of the world and self-martyrs to our own incendiary nature. We are patients in a hospital where the surgeon himself is sick, but to which God is the only true physician. We are as unstable as the earth in the cosmos, and as uncertain of ourselves as we are of the movement of the earth. We are the core of nature's nest of boxes, which are all concentric to ruin.

If human nature comprehends a world then the topography of the external world must itself present a map of our spiritual state. Donne elaborates this conceit in some detail. The land is man's self, the seas are our sins and miseries, the mountains are the natural faculties which rise above the seas, and also our sacred places of deliverance, God's holy hills; then again in the order of the body politic the high mountains are kings who rise beyond the rest of men as natural gods. Yet all this land to the very mountain tops may be inundated by the sea. As our physical being is entirely overwhelmed and possessed by sickness so we raise a flood of our miseries and guilt; and we augment it by our sins with a deluge of Christ's blood. In effect the human constitution precisely rehearses the condition of civil society and of the cosmos itself. It is rapidly degenerating, has already been engulfed in the Flood, and now confronts the imminent threat of a final conflagration.

Donne contemplates the prospect of his own undoing in the proximate death of an unknown man whose passing bell he hears as he lies in his bed, presumably tolling from the nearby church of St Gregory. We need scarcely remind ourselves that he makes this bell something more than a chance intimation or emblem of his own impending death. He takes it for a signal of the actual death of a part of himself. 'Any man's *death* diminisheth *me*, because I am involved in *Mankind*.' This lately dead stranger is nonetheless a partaker of Donne's own humanity whose death bell passes a piece of Donne himself out of the world, and who now serves a ghostly warning upon him:

Thou hast sent one from the dead to speak unto me. He speaks to me aloud from that *steeple*; he whispers to me at these *Curtains*, and he speaks thy words; *Blessed are the dead which die in the Lord, from henceforth.*

16. *Prayer*

That shared undoing is in one way the inescapable nadir of his fortunes, the final proof of the nothingness of our being without grace. We must encounter it, yet it need not define us. For all these evidences have an ambiguous force as they bear upon a being who stays uncertainly suspended between earth and heaven. In our natural condition what we take for the best state is quite likely to prove the worst state; so now grace may work a further transformation which will turn what seems worst to the best. The very sickness which seems to menace him with the natural outcome of his guilt may turn to a cordial instrument of regeneration, providentially working both correction and mercy.

He follows out these transformations in the physical circumstances of his illness and its treatment, often turning to advantage just the same figures which marked his decline. So vitally re-encountered, the sick bed now becomes a grave of his sins and even an altar. Its feathers are the feathers of the Dove; the very corruption which overwhelmed him brings about the descent of the Dove, whose coming he discovers in the pigeons laid to his feet to draw the bad humours forth. Sickness itself turns to cordial when his loss of taste here only sharpens his taste for the Lamb's Supper; the heats of his fever present themselves as the chafing of the wax to bear God's seal; and the very spots no longer mark the pinches of death but become constellations directing him to Christ, or even the letters of God's signature upon him which make a conveyance of him to heaven. The passing bells he hears turn their tolling to triumph as trumpets of the resurrection, signalling not death but the final transformation of nature; and death itself only translates a text whose scattered leaves will be bound up by God into one volume. What vitalises all these changes is a general transmutation of nature by love, which Donne defines in a key conceit. The deluge of Christ's redeeming blood finally counters and transforms the deluge of guilt, extinguishing the flames of our worldly lusts, swamping the sea of sins, turning death itself to lustration. God kills in order to give life. The descent of the Son requites the descent of the fallen angels and makes descent itself the necessary means to a resurrection.

Conceit may be the best term we can find for such an extraordinary *tour de force* of wit. Nonetheless the unconstrained movement between literal and metaphorical properties, as between the physical symptoms and their multifold import, is more than a literary device. It redefines such distinctions themselves, as the mode of this prose itself defines an order which remakes our conventional expectations of the world:

O eternal and most gracious *God*, who hast made *little things* to signify *great*, and conveyed the *infinite merits* of thy *Son* in the *water* of *Baptism*, and in the *Bread* and *Wine* of thy other Sacrament, unto us, receive the *sacrifice* of my humble thanks, that thou hast not only afforded me, the ability to rise out of this bed of *weariness* and *discomfort*, but has also made this *bodily rising*, by thy *grace*, an *earnest* of a *second resurrection* from *sin*, and of a *third*, to *everlasting glory* . . . Therefore I beg of thee, *my daily bread*; and as thou gavest me the *bread* of *sorrow* for many days, and since the *bread* of *hope* for some, and this day the *bread* of *possessing*, in *rising* by that strength, which thou the *God* of all strength, hast infused into me, so, O *Lord*, continue to me the *bread of life*; the *spiritual bread of life*, in a faithful assurance in *thee*; the *sacramental bread of life*, in a worthy receiving of *thee*; and the more *real bread of life*, in an everlasting *union to thee*.

21. *Prayer*

The syntax holds the pattern of this providential order, setting alternative possibilities to answer and redress one another, counter-pointing opposite conditions which turn out to be the same condition, paralleling contrary causes which have a like effect and point to one end that is always present.

We should cheapen Donne's thinking if we took him to be attempting nothing more than a virtuoso feat of *double entendre*, ingeniously playing upon opposite ways of looking at one and the same effect of the sickness. He points to a general condition of the world in which possibilities that seem opposed are nonetheless reconciled when nature is supplied by grace. The place of sickness is at once his present bedchamber and God's eternal bedchamber, the meeting place of two states of being. God's left hand lays the body in the grave as his right hand receives the soul into his kingdom. God makes one act of closing the eyes of the body here and opening the eyes of the soul there, not just because he performs these offices simultaneously but because they are the same process. Donne allows no final separation of restored nature from grace.

This relationship of nature and grace, and hence of the body's condition to the soul's, finds its warrant in God's own being and specifically in Christ's human existence. Here we must recognise that Donne is talking not just of God's mode of communicating with human beings but of the divine nature itself as it is present in our world. Our perception of that nature crucially affects the way we understand the world and our own lives in it. God is at once a literal and a metaphorical God (19. *Expostulation*). Hence his works are open to diverse and even contrary interpretations which may all have substance; and the same condition may offer quite opposite possibilities. Donne's ingrained relativism finds its final justification in the nature of God's creation, but now our response to the divergent prospects cannot be sceptical. God's creation is a creation of types and figures in which the hieroglyph and the substance are one. The Old Testament already contains what the New Testament makes manifest, not just as type to antitype but as aspects of the truth which is wholly realised in Christ.

Donne remarks that Christ's divine nature is aptly rendered in such metaphors as light, vine, bread, a gate, which imply no diminution of the direct literal fact of his human nature. Christ is at once a man and the divine being whose attributes these terms signify. He himself shows that in becoming a human being he was not separating himself from his divine nature; on the contrary, both natures then became one in him. And as the diverse multitude of mankind make up one inter-involved body so Christ's universal Church is an enlargement of his own nature and ours. In this nature body and spirit conjoin as one; in the sacraments of the Church the metaphorical and the literal come together, confirming the oneness of the sign with the thing signified, the bread with Christ's body. The bread and wine themselves are more than mere tokens or memorials of Christ; yet they do not simply change their own substance. The elements in the eucharist present both natures together. They are at once bread and wine, and the body and blood of Christ.

Donne's receiving of the bread and wine confirms a further union. He buries Christ in his body towards his own quickening and resurrection, takes the bodily and the spiritual bread so as to make himself eternally one with Christ. In effect he prays for a fourfold benefit by grace which will transform the natural bread of sorrow and of hope into substance at several levels, converting it to physical nourishment, spiritual assurance, sacramental presence, and finally to the 'more real' stuff of life in an everlasting union with God.

In the final transformation of his sickness the metaphors themselves take on a new and contrary sense. His recovery now presents itself to him in what might seem conventional terms as the discovery of land after a tempestuous voyage, or the espial of a rain cloud which gathers out of the sea itself following a deadly drought. Yet here the terms redraw the map of nature; and Donne turns their very ordinariness to account. The ocean of sin and guilt becomes redemptive, metamorphosed into the Red Sea of Christ's blood which Donne has reached through the river of Jordan. God's Ark carries us through the flood of sins; God's ship is our healing physician; the ship from which Christ preached is a type of Christ's Church. These scriptural metaphors of ships and floods confirm a recurrent predicament which Donne's case now repeats. He acknowledges that his tribulations have followed, and still follow, the universal pattern of providential care.

The pattern nonetheless admits the possibility of a dire relapse, and with it the prospect of a fatal reversal of the redemptive process after all. The metaphor accommodates this last peril of his relapsing fever as a sudden disastrous storm at sea which lifts the vessel up to heaven and then plunges it even further down to its final ruin in the depths. So his recovery may be precarious; yet this rescue from shipwreck now promises a preservation from threats to the ship thereafter, whether they present themselves as external hazards or as internal frailties. These enlargements of the controlling metaphor hold together in one order Donne's bodily sickness, his spiritual condition, and the state of the world. Their force is as much literal as metaphoric. They can work so only because Donne supposes that matter and spirit are not opposed orders but may even make up a single order when nature is transformed by grace. If we find opposite possibilities in the same course of events it is not because matter pulls us one way and spirit another but because the natural processes themselves present a double aspect to us. They follow out physical laws; yet through these laws themselves they fulfil the providential pattern of sin and redemption.

As in Christ's nature, and God's creation altogether, so in human nature. Body and soul simply are not discrete elements in us, much less opposed and conflicting elements. The interfusion of body and soul to make one nature is central to Donne's mature thinking. He takes marriage to be another mode of this sacramental making one of bodies and souls, matter and spirit, whose warrant is the eucharist itself. And from this conjunction action necessarily follows if only to prove the union; love stands revealed, so to say, in gestures, or works, or fruit. So the fusion of nature with grace declares itself in act, which in the present case is the exercise of purging whose effects are at once bodily and spiritual. We are brought back to *Devotion* 20, and the *Prayer* whose oddity prompted this enquiry.

In this *Prayer* Donne's counterbalancing syntax proposes not so much an analogy as an identity of kind between the union of man and woman in marriage and the union of body and soul in human nature. It seeks to catch nothing less than the inseparableness of physical and spiritual processes. The *Devotions* start from the assumption that the physical world presents a pattern of a spiritual state, even an embodiment of it, and that in this conjunction of the sensible and the spiritual God's creation itself simply enlarges the body and the human constitution altogether. As in the world so in our own condition; as we have such physical helps as hills to climb above the floods which swamp the valleys and plains down below so we have our natural means of evading or resisting sin, our upbringing, education, spiritual advisers, the Church itself. These benefits support the body and mind; yet they cannot be sufficient to save us in themselves. Nature, in sum, will simply go the way of nature until it can open itself to Christ's blood.

The distinctiveness of Donne's thinking, and the nub of it too, appears in his pondering of the responsibility for sin. Sin cannot be taken for the special propensity of matter or the flesh. It is the union of body and soul which constitutes human nature; neither body alone nor soul alone can make up a human being. In their present condition the two elements are wholly interdependent. As Adam was sinless without Eve, and Eve would have been sinless without Adam, so the body was sinless while it lacked soul and the soul is sinless 'before it come to the *body*'. Sin originates not when a corrupt body drags down pure soul but in the very constitution of a human being when body and soul become one; and the possibility of sin, as of glory, arises from the union itself. It is to that union of body and soul which Christ's blood specifically ministers. Hence the release from sin cannot come about by a spurning of the flesh so as to free the spirit. On the contrary, God is a God of both flesh and spirit; and 'I know that in the state of my *body*, which is more discernible than that of my soul, thou dost effigiate my *Soul* to me' (22. *Expostulation*).

Body effigiates soul; and God effigiates the state of the soul in the state of the body. No one who ponders Donne's resolved understanding of love will be startled to find him anticipating Wittgenstein – 'The human body is the best picture of the human soul'.[14] Yet the conclusion Donne draws here is that our one means to the purging of both body and soul is Christ's blood, which Christ sheds for us as a man.

In Donne's bodily recovery from his fever he discovers the final renewal brought about by the Great Physician. The resurrection of the body shows, or effigiates, the resurrection of the soul. His rising from his bed is an earnest of a double resurrection to come; it promises a second resurrection from sin and a final ascent to everlasting glory. Yet metaphor and actuality are one and this rising also portends its own fulfilment, the resurrection and restoration of the flesh itself. The natural body, left for dust and rubbish when the soul departs, will be transformed and glorified in the next world. Until that final reunion of souls with the glorified bodies the very bliss of the saints in glory cannot be complete.

We are brought back to Donne's apprehension of a timeless spiritual drama in the mundane symptoms of his sickness. He bears out his assumption that the progress of his fever repeats the universal order by showing that circumstances which seem merely accidental may nonetheless be providentially disposed and shaped. Body effigiates soul; and the pattern he draws out discloses itself precisely in the union of body and soul. There is no separation of the order of physical events in the world from the order of spiritual concerns, much less a conflict between the two orders. Body is not at deadly odds with spirit, nor are sensible appearances mere shadows of a higher reality. Body and spirit are inseparably one in human nature as in the natural creation altogether. However casual the occurrence might appear, and however ambiguous its import, it may nonetheless incarnate God's purpose; as the hieroglyphic sense is finally one with the actuality, the metaphorical sense with the literal. Donne's chance illness providentially overwhelms him in a sea of his own sins, which re-enacts the inundation of the world at the Deluge and requires the renewed shedding of Christ's blood.

Conceit seems scarcely the word. Such thinking is organic in Donne. We find it in the presumption that a young girl's death leaves the physical universe in chaos; that the straits of a dangerous illness embody simultaneously the navigational hazards of the world and the sacrificial suffering of Christ; that a casual journey west on Good Friday 1613 rehearses the progressive aberration of the entire cosmos; that Christ's outstretched arms on the cross simultaneously extend themselves to turn the universal poles.

Wit is central to the endeavour. In these *Devotions* wit is the indispensable means of holding together the physical event and the spiritual condition, the pattern of the illness and the providential consequence. This mode of wit is distinguished from other forms of wit which were current in seventeenth-century Europe in that it does not aim at figurative enlivenment. It sets itself to apprehend metaphysical issues, as it were sensibly and immediately in the contingent occurrences of the world. The wit of Donne's *Devotions* makes a providential drama of the processes of nature themselves.

George Herbert's wit works more intimately than Donne's to sustain the shock of metaphysical predicaments apprehended in the senses. *The Temple* amounts to a continual testing of the presumption that we participate in the working of two seemingly unlike orders of being whose relationship stands in question. The urgent impact of the poems challenges us with the prospect of some issue to be thought through here and now in an imperative present trial:

> Joy, I did lock thee up: but some bad man
>   Hath let thee out again:
> And now, me thinks, I am where I began
>   Seven years ago: one vogue and vein,
>   One air of thoughts usurps my brain.
> I did towards Canaan draw; but now I am
> Brought back to the Red sea, the sea of shame.
>   *The Bunch of Grapes*

Herbert's mastery of a rhetoric is wholly expressive. We feel rather than consciously register the effect of ordered spontaneity, the artful simulation of an anguished outpouring which is nonetheless tightly controlled.

This opening of *The Bunch of Grapes* arrests us with its extraordinary fusion of the personal and the general, intimate moral confession and universal history. The figures mark the nullifying of a seven-year progress, a regression from the prospect of the promised land which now leaves him vacillating unquietly between guilt and bliss, the Red Sea and Canaan, nature and grace. Yet his state is far from singular. On the contrary, he supposes that Christians re-enact the pattern of Old Testament events in the drama of their own moral lives:

> For as the Jews of old by God's command
>   Travelled, and saw no town;
> So now each Christian hath his journeys spanned:
>   Their story pens and sets us down.

Our discomforting liberty is prescribed. We are free within the scope of providential history and of God's providence itself, which is nonetheless dauntingly inclusive:

> God's works are wide, and let in future times;
> His ancient justice overflows our crimes.

In the witty manner of an Andrewes the poet discovers the signs of our oneness with the scriptural case as the correspondences strike him, the guardian fires and clouds, scripture-dew, 'sands and serpents, tents and shrouds', and not least 'our murmurings'. Yet he still lacks the realisation of God's promise:

> But where's the cluster? where's the taste
> Of mine inheritance? Lord, if I must borrow,
> Let me as well take up their joy, as sorrow.

The move from this stanza to the final one enacts a more momentous realisation:

> But can he want the grape, who hath the wine?
>   I have their fruit and more.
> Blessed be God, who prospered *Noah's* vine,
>   And made it bring forth grapes good store.

Noah's grapes yield Christ's blood. The pattern of providential history which the Old Testament exhibits is vindicated and consummated in

Christ, as the poet's own desolations must be changed to sweetness in Christ's sacrifice,

> Who of the Law's sour justice sweet wine did make,
> Even God himself being pressed for my sake.

The argument thus brings us to a prospect which the Old Testament people could not share, answering justice with Christ's Passion which transmutes law into grace in the eucharist as Christ's blood is transmuted into wine. Guilt and pain do not thereby relinquish their force, any more than the law is set aside or the grapes simply lose their nature. In the sweetness of the wine which is simultaneously Christ's blood the poet finds conclusive proof that his grief is also his joy.

The Bunch of Grapes gets its tension from the pull between opposite ways of understanding our lives in the world, which is resolved in the realisation that both ways have force since we are simultaneously subject to opposite conditions of being. The wit of Herbert's *Temple* follows out the presumption that we live two lives at once, one of them apparent to us and the other hidden and tending another way:

> One life is wrapped *In* flesh, and tends to earth:
> The other winds towards *Him*, whose happy birth
> Taught me to live here so, *That* still one eye
> Should aim and shoot at that which *Is* on high: . . .
>
> *Coloss. 3.3*

The poems intimate that we play a part in the working of two worlds, being subject to God's order in 'the grosser world' yet also sharing the mysterious life of 'thy diviner world of grace', which the Creator invokes and dissolves at will.

This dizzying prospect is opened to us by our human constitution itself. Herbert supposes that our nature uniquely commits us to a simultaneous participation in both states, a life of sense and a life of spirit or grace which we share with the angels, no less:

> Man ties them both alone,
> And makes them one,
> With th'one hand touching heaven, with th'other earth.
>
> *Man's medley*

Yet man's make-up also uniquely anguishes him, opening him to several dooms at once by way of a double winter and the fear of a double death; or his double status discomfortingly strands him between seemingly unlike conditions of being as a kind of freak:

> A wonder tortured in the space
> Betwixt this world and that of grace.
> *Affliction (iv)*

Herbert values the life of nature too highly just to oppose it to the life of grace. He needs no dire conflict of contraries to account for man's predicament. In his cosmogony earth and heaven do not pull opposite ways; on the contrary he invokes a time when their state differed little and an Adam might move indifferently between them, passing from paradise to heaven 'As from one room t'another' (*The H. Communion*). God himself then kept open house on earth by the agency of his apostles, and glorified men's condition here in this heavenly state which the stars themselves sought to share:

> The stars were coming down to know
> If they might mend their wages, and serve here.
> *Whitsunday*

Such conceits justify the reverence which Herbert continues to bring to the contemplation of natural life. He supposes that we have simply alienated ourselves from our former happy state; for God has not withdrawn his presence – 'Lord, though we change, thou art the same'. Nor has the natural creation itself lost its proper harmony and loving sympathy with its creator when herbs 'Grow green, and gay', and the stars themselves 'Simper and shine, / As having keys unto thy love, / While poor I pine' (*The Search*). Man has wilfully cut himself off from the fruitful intercourse of nature, bringing 'Neither . . . honey with the bees' nor 'flowers to make that, nor the husbandry / To water these' (*Employment i*). Herbert movingly contrasts the innocent sympathy of the very stones of the sepulchre which received Christ's body with the hardness of human hearts and wills. We show ourselves all too ready to kill Christ or arraign him falsely, while the pure rock just holds his body in silence:

> Only these stones in quiet entertain thee,
> And order.
> *Sepulchre*

Herbert's critical presumption is that the way is still open to a commerce between natural being and spiritual being, as to the ministrations of providence in the world. Christ offers us the means of recovering our access to grace, 'By this, thy heavenly blood' (*The H. Communion*). Herbert takes such a recovery for a restitution of our

former standing. Man may still assume his right state as a world in himself who is served by the entire creation:

> For us the winds do blow,
> The earth doth rest, heaven move, and fountains flow.
> Nothing we see but means our good . . .
>
> *Man*

Our correspondence with the rest of creation furthers a universal
interplay between spirit and sense which links God's love with the
vitality of stars and plants:

> The stars have us to bed;
> Night draws the curtain, which the sun withdraws;
> Music and light attend our head.
> All things unto our flesh are kind
> In their descent and being; to our mind
> In their ascent and cause.

Herbert comprehends the homely with the sublime, the solaces of
sense with the fulfilments of the mind in his stupendous vision of a
creation which has been providentially ordained to minister to man.
The ministry is to the whole being, body and spirit together:

> Each thing is full of duty:
> Waters united are our navigation;
> Distinguished, our habitation;
> Below, our drink; above, our meat;
> Both are our cleanliness. Hath one such beauty?
> Then how are all things neat!
>
> More servants wait on Man,
> Than he'll take notice of: . . .

Providence attests that the creation expresses God's love not only in
the intercourse of earth and heaven but in the provident reciprocities
of organic life itself: 'Rain, do not hurt my flowers; but gently
spend / Your honey drops'. The rain nurtures the infant flowers,
which gratefully repay it in due season by returning their ripe odours
to heaven. This poem apostrophises the rain as a fellow-participant in
a benign interchange of virtues which needs no force or strain to
accomplish its effects. The organic processes themselves express a
spiritual end. Far from pressing the flowers for some practical benefit
here and now the rain need only help them ripen and just be, when
their existence will unforcedly justify itself to heaven. The natural

creation works by the providential coupling of unlike kinds, which is justified in the natures of the creatures themselves:

> Thy creatures leap not, but express a feast,
> Where all the guests sit close, and nothing wants.
> Frogs marry fish and flesh; bats, bird and beasts;
> Sponges, non-sense and sense; mines, th'earth and plants.

The terms make a sacred ceremony of natural fruitfulness, which comes about not by individual shows of will but by the close reciprocity of unlike natures to 'express a feast'.

Herbert keeps keenly alert to our own means of resuming the commerce between earth and heaven. Such recourses need not be rare or prodigious events. Sundays may offer a recovery of Eden in their commingling of fulfilment and renewal, 'The fruit of this, the next world's bud':

> Sundays the pillars are,
>   On which heaven's palace arched lies: . . .
>   On Sunday heaven's gate stands ope;
>   Blessings are plentiful and rife,
>   More plentiful than hope,
>   *Sunday*

The images mark so many convergences of sensible and spiritual ends which Christ's own example authenticates. Christ makes Sundays his garden, in which he grows herbs to heal our wounds. Samson-like, he unhinges the day and bears away the doors between earth and heaven, albeit with nailed hands; and his blood pays the full price of the new finery which we need before we may re-enter paradise. The poems on prayer are a sustained celebration of the ways in which prayer itself expresses a feast and vitalises the interchange between heaven and earth:

> Prayer the Church's banquet, Angel's age,
>   God's breath in man returning to his birth . . .
>   *Prayer (i)*

The British Church is praiseworthy above all others because our native communion peculiarly and distinctively institutionalises the bond of heaven with earth in its middle way between Rome and Geneva, which is no mere compromise but a holding together of unlike states such as those rites have made mutually exclusive:

> But dearest Mother, what those miss,
> The mean, thy praise and glory is,
>   And long may be.
> Blessed be God, whose love it was
> To double-moat thee with his grace,
>   And none but thee.
>   *The British Church*

Some of Herbert's most extraordinary interchanges of sensible and spiritual qualities occur in his evocations of daily worship, and of the properties of the church itself:

> Mark you the floor? that square and speckled stone,
>   Which looks so firm and strong,
>   Is *Patience*: . . .
>   *The Church-floor*

The very floor of the church manifests the qualities which make up the Church itself and substantiate a holy life. The firm and strong stone embodies patience, the black stone signifies humility, the gentle rising 'to the Choir above' conducts us easily into a higher harmony; and the whole frame is tied in by love and charity. Sin stains the marble, yet nonetheless cleanses itself when it weeps; Death blows the dust around, yet actually sweeps what he thought to spoil:

> Blest be the *Architect*, whose art
> Could build so strong in a weak heart.

This is much more than a play of emblematic wit. By bringing into one order the outward material church and the inward spiritual life the poem shows how weakness may be transformed into strength, and loss itself is comprehended in God's providence as a purging and renewal.

Herbert's wit continually reminds us that our special means of grace are no more than propitious openings to a spiritual life which is there all the time. God 'hath made of two folds one' (*Antiphon* (ii)), and heaven holds a perpetual commerce with earth:

> Let th'upper springs into the low
> Descend and fall, and thou dost flow.
>   *The Size*

Seen through the purifying veil of Christ's flesh the dishes of God's balance of justice no longer loom as pits of hell but become buckets which descend and ascend interchangeably, 'Lifting to heaven from this well of tears' (*Justice* (ii)). God intertwines himself in our worldly actions, prospering them by sixfold or twentyfold when he favours them and even supplying our tears of penitence for our sins (*Praise* (*iii*)). God's providential disposition of our affairs extends to the words we use to speak of him, showing up in such special graces of the English tongue as the double sense of sun – '*The Son of Man*' (*The Son*). The poet's exchange of gifts with Hope prompts some sharp readjustments of his aspirations, returning him an anchor for a watch and an old prayer-book for an optic glass; but it brings him to a frustrating anticlimax when Hope responds to his vial of penitent tears with nothing more than 'a few green ears' of grain instead of the ring he expected (*Hope*). Where he looked to the prospect of an instant reward for his pains, such as would lift him beyond the world in an endless nuptials with God, he receives nothing more than the natural promises of renewed life.

The distance between the transcendent expectation and the seemingly down-to-earth return marks quite opposite perceptions of life in the world. Herbert points the difference when he ends the exalted search for peace at the lowly grave of a murdered man:

> He sweetly lived; yet his sweetness did not save
> His life from foes.
> But after death out of his grave
> There sprang twelve stalks of wheat
> Which many wondering at, got some of those
> To plant and set.
>
> *Peace*

Christ encountered the world not as a condescending deity but as a man; he died as a man, and renews his life and ministers in the world through his disciples, participating in an organic process which culminates in the offering of bread:

> Take of this grain, which in my garden grows,
> And grows for you;
> Make bread of it; and that repose
> And peace, which everywhere
> With so much earnestness you do pursue,
> Is only there.

The eucharist seals the work of grace in the order of nature; the universe discloses God's providence, the order of God's word in the Scriptures is mirrored in the interplay of the stars 'Seeing not only how each verse doth shine, / But all the constellations of the story' (*The H. Scriptures* (*ii*)).

Yet the stars in themselves cannot offer us the sure guidance we find in God's 'book of stars' which 'lights to eternal bliss'. Herbert crucially distinguishes a sacred engagement with the natural creation from mere secular meddling with nature. What prompts him to metaphysical wit rather than scientific enquiry is his search for God's love in the natural processes. He scouts the scrutinising of nature for mere curiosity's sake, as for its supposed prop to faith:

> Then burn thy Epicycles, foolish man;
> Break all thy spheres, and save thy head.
> Faith needs no staff of flesh, but stoutly can
> To heaven alone both go, and lead.
>
> *Divinity*

In Herbert's epistemology the impulsions of the flesh alone can be no more than seductive vanities:

> I know the ways of Learning; both the head
> And pipes that feed the press, and make it run; . . .
> All these stand open, or I have the keys:
> Yet I love thee.
>
> *The Pearl*

Learning, logic, discovery, honour, pleasure – all these worldly ends in themselves are acknowledged and savoured, yet pushed aside one by one to make way for a love which they cannot advance. They are all comprehended in the elaborate formal pattern of the rhetoric and gathered into an inclusive mastery at last: 'I know all these, and have them in my hand'. He fully acknowledges what he must relinquish for God, 'at what rate and price I have thy love'; yet the truth breaks in and vindicates his dogged devotion by pointing the self-delusion of those worldly offers:

> Yet through these labyrinths, not my grovelling wit,
> But thy silk twist let down from heaven to me,
> Did both conduct and teach me, how by it
> To climb to thee.

All the vain aspirings are heaped up on his own 'grovelling wit', whose self-entanglements are then wholly nullified by the silk twist let down from heaven which is so conclusively revealed here. 'Yet I love thee' makes way for 'To climb to thee', identifying the silk twist as God's loving response to his own persistence in love. Reciprocal love is the means by which he climbs to God; and while our grovelling wit simply indulges itself there will be no silk twists but only labyrinths.

Herbert's own mastery of formal wit precisely sustains his point. The ingenious rhetorical patterning becomes wholly expressive, and central to the life of the poem in fact; yet its end is the acknowledgment of a truth about the way wit uses the world.

The attempt to find grace at work in the world, and make a sacrament of everyday life, starts with God. Dulled as it may be for us by overfamiliarity *The Elixir* essays great boldness in extreme simplicity. In effect the poet asks his God and king to teach him how to encounter the world. To see the world aright is to see God in all things and do anything as for God; to perfect what we do by making God prepossessed of it; to apprehend heaven in and through the world, as 'A man that looks on glass' but does not 'stay his eye' on it. All existence is holy to the extent that it shares in God's love. To do something for God's sake is to touch it with a tincture which transforms it, making drudgery divine and the meanest action bright and clean. Our coaction with God's love in the world is the true philosopher's stone which turns to gold all we encounter:

> For that which God doth touch and own
> Cannot for less be told.

Herbert heightens incongruities so as to bring out the ambiguous power of a God who is also wholly human and comprehend Christ's double presence in the world. *Redemption* resolves among a lowly rabble and in humble simplicity the search for the heavenly landlord who may amend our longstanding contract with him:

> At length I heard a ragged noise and mirth
> Of thieves and murderers: there I him espied,
> Who straight, *Your suit is granted*, said, and died.

The Bag counters pain and despair with the assurance that God himself shares our condition, having loaned out the trappings of his grandeur in order to become a common traveller on earth. Cosmic properties mingle tellingly with homely effects:

> The stars his tire of light and rings obtained,
> The cloud his bow, the fire his spear,
> The sky his azure mantle gained.
> And when they asked, what he would wear;
> He smiled and said as he did go,
> He had new clothes a making here below.

Putting up at a lowly inn where he is very ill-entertained Christ endures 'many a brunt' to cancel sin, and finally gives up his life to pay our score. Set upon unarmed as he makes for home, and run through the side with a spear, he nonetheless offers us his open wound for a bag to convey messages to his father and ours:

> Unto my Father's hands and sight,
> Believe me, it shall safely come.
> That I shall mind, what you impart,
> Look, you may put it very near my heart.

The ironic ambiguity of the invitation to any friends who 'Will use me in this kind' sustains the pledge of a continuing sacrifice and atonement by which love turns to good such future offences as are truly repented:

> Sighs will convey
> Anything to me. Hark, Despair away.

The mysteries which seem so oddly posed in *Business* – 'Had he life, or had he none?', 'Did he die, or did he not?' – catch the paradox of Christ's double nature and sacrifice but also point the immediacy of Christ's death in consequence of our sins, which kill him here and now as well as there and then and are thus immediately atoned for:

> And hath any space of breath
> 'Twixt his sins and Saviour's death?

Our sins are borne as mortal sacrifice and redeemed as soon as committed. God immediately has part in our afflictions; as the poet's hard-pressed heart acknowledges for itself when it heaves and bursts out with 'O God!':

> Thy life on earth was grief, and thou art still
> Constant unto it, making it to be
> A point of honour, now to grieve in me,
> And in thy members suffer ill.
> They who lament one cross,
> Thou dying daily, praise thee to thy loss.
>
> *Affliction (iii)*

This continuing benefit of Christ's Passion is no mere historical legacy. These lines mark the harm done to Christ by 'They who lament one cross', presumably because they take the crucifixion for a single historic occurrence. Christ's sacrifice is a 'dying daily', a sharing in the burden of our sins and afflictions which is continually taken on anew.

'In Christ two natures met to be thy cure' (*An Offering*). Christ's Incarnation and Passion consummate the bringing into one order of two unlike conditions of being; God's human death as a malefactor on a cross revalues all our dealings with the world:

> Philosophers have measured mountains,
> Fathomed the depths of seas, of states, and kings,
> Walked with a staff to heaven, and traced fountains:
> But there are two vast, spacious things,
> The which to measure it doth more behove:
> Yet few there are that sound them; Sin and Love.
>
> *The Agony*

The Agony disconcerts us by its redirecting of traditional conceits to point the shocking paradox that sin and love make the only true objects of knowledge and are comprehended together in Christ's Passion. Yet its justification of this radical claim has the precise order of a proof in which the starting premise is tested term by term. The spiritual condition of sin is ironically and vividly rendered by its vicarious outcome in Christ's bodily sufferings for us, the wringing pains, the bloodied hair, skin, garments:

> Sin is that press and vice, which forceth pain
> To hunt his cruel food through every vein.

Love is likewise physically rendered as Christ's blood, which proves itself both when it is shed by him on the cross for our sins and tasted by us in the eucharist:

> Who knows not Love, let him assay
> And taste that juice, which on the cross a pike
> Did set again abroach; then let him say
> If ever he did taste the like.
> Love is that liquor sweet and most divine,
> Which my God feels as blood; but I, as wine.

Herbert wittily reworks the traditional figures of vine and winepress so that the cross becomes at once the press of torture and the press of the life-restoring juice, implement of torment and instrument of love; as the pike which pierced Christ's side is also the spile which broaches the wine. A paradoxical symmetry discloses itself which the pattern of the poem precisely catches. As Christ's agony is the immediate embodiment of the spiritual condition of sin so Christ's blood is the present witness of the spiritual disposition of love. His love responds to our sin. The decisive work of wit is to render both conditions immediately together, showing us that what Christ sheds as blood we drink as wine even as he continues to shed it. The wit discovers a double status in the events themselves, displaying them to us as at once physical and spiritual, historical and timeless, human and divine. An inglorious death is also a glorious victory, Christ's injuries there and then restore us here and now.

In the banquet of the eucharist Christ's broken body and spilled blood become the instruments of his saving power and are received as the sweetness of crushed pomanders and wood (*The Banquet*). The bread and wine seal Christ's oneness with man, paradoxically reminding us that we share a heavenly as well as an earthly nature in our very pains. God joins us on the ground when we are drowned 'In delights of earth', and drowns us in his blood to redeem us from them and draw us higher:

> Having raised me to look up,
> In a cup
> Sweetly he doth meet my taste . . .
> Wine becomes a wing at last.
>
> *The Banquet*

Bread and wine make up a feast of immortal love to which all are invited just because the dainty fare is God himself. Christ's body and blood quite literally offer themselves to us for our sustenance; yet our penitence turns his blood to wine even as we drink it.

The operation of a double nature which confirms Christ's oneness with us is providentially replicated in the natural order:

> Therefore my soul melts, and my heart's dear treasure
> Drops blood (the only beads) my words to measure: . . .
>
> *The Sacrifice*

The poet's soul melts and his heart drops blood in an immediate commerce between spirit and sense which his wit is always working to catch. Not a ritual patter but prayer wrung from suffering has the power to turn agony to joy. Physical pain is central to Herbert's understanding as the condition of a providential doubleness which Christ's own being proves. Christ lovingly transforms to spiritual succour the vinegar which they thrust upon him, mingled with gall and malice.

> yet, when they did call,
> With Manna, Angel's food, I fed them all: . . .

Eve's sin and the piercing of Christ's side are turned simultaneously to good in spite of man's ill will; the wound in the side which opened the way to sin is also the door to grace:

> Nay, after death their spite shall further go;
> For they will pierce my side, I full well know;
> That as sin came, so Sacraments might flow: . . .

Our very sins which wound Christ have their part in a universal reciprocity of love, and open us to the 'blessed streams' of grace from beyond the heavens

> whose spring and vent
> Is in my dear Redeemer's pierced side.
>
> *H. Baptism (i)*

Christ's human blood, shed in love of humankind, supplies the waters above the heavens and returns to earth again to purify nature or sustain the penitent tears we owe to God for such sins as could not be averted. The natural creation itself is coactive with spirit in this universal interchange of sympathy. Herbert's wit articulates the vision of a vast providential economy in which sin no less than affliction works the ends of love.

Herbert's vivid renderings of distress do not distinguish physical pain from spiritual anguish. Perturbations of spirit are experienced as excruciating physical sensations, the poet's bodily discomforts wholly possess his soul. Flesh blames soul for the sicknesses which cleave his bones, the agues which dwell in every vein (*Affliction (i)*); afflictions of his entire being work and wind into him more sharply than a screw or drill into timber, unrelentingly footing and clutching their prey from within like moles (*Confession*). Spiritual promptings replicate natural processes, so that the poet shares (rather than figuratively parallels) his condition with the 'young exhalation' which at first heads for heaven but then gradually sinks back to earth in a cloud of tears, glooms, lost hopes and lost friends (*The Answer*). Inward experience is so far assimilated to organic life that a spiritual crisis deranges the entire sentient organism, showing itself in distempers of feeling, sight, smell, taste. The 'shrivelled heart' which brings on his spiritual aridity is felt as an organic condition, which nonetheless promises a marvellous renewal of life:

> Who would have thought my shrivelled heart
> Could have recovered greenness? It was gone
> Quite under ground; as flowers depart
> To see their mother-root, when they have blown; . . .
>
> *The Flower*

Yet the rare elation which vivifies *The Flower* comes to the poet quite unpredictably. We support a state worse than that of the rest of the natural creation, which unreflectingly enjoys God's loving presence while we must go on seeking for it:

> Yet can I mark how herbs below
> > Grow green and gay,
> As if to meet thee they did know,
> > While I decay.

> Yet can I mark how stars above
> > Simper and shine,
> As having keys unto thy love,
> > While poor I pine.
> > > *The Search*

One function of wit in *The Temple* is to articulate a condition in which bitter storms inexplicably follow promises, frustrating the poet with seemingly arbitrary contradictions and leaving him at cross purposes with himself, or in unintelligible agonies:

> Sorrow was all my soul; I scarce believed,
> Till grief did tell me roundly, that I lived.
> > *Affliction (i)*

Affliction (i) draws him to a total impasse, and a near-rebellion before he can bring himself to acquiesce in the providence he does not understand:

> Now I am here, what thou wilt do with me
> > None of my books will show: . . .

> Yet, though thou troublest me, I must be meek;
> > In weakness must be stout.
> Well, I will change the service, and go seek
> > Some other master out.
> Ah my dear God! though I am clean forgot,
> Let me not love thee, if I love thee not.

These vividly realised stirrings of rebellion are what catch people's interest in Herbert:

> I struck the board, and cried, No more.
> I will abroad.
> > *The Collar*

Yet the force of the outburst only prepares the submission which follows his acquiescence in a universal interchange of love:

But as I raved and grew more fierce and wild
          At every word,
Me thoughts I heard one calling, *Child!*
          And I replied, *My Lord.*

The bizarre conceit of an exchange of artillery fire between God and man works out this reciprocity of love which our unqualified acceptance must complete:

Then we are shooters both, and thou dost deign
To enter combat with us, and contest
With thine own clay. But I would parley fain:
Shun not my arrows, and behold my breast.
          Yet if thou shunnest, I am thine:
          I must be so, if I am mine:
          There is no articling with thee:
I am but finite, yet thine infinitely.

                                        Artillery

The poet's struggles to accept his plight precisely turn upon the reconciliation of nature with grace.

Herbert continually finds new ways of showing how 'grace fills up uneven nature' (*Faith*), and makes good our decays. His homely conceits bring out the disparity between the two orders, as well as the singularity of their yoking. God stores up our tears in a heavenly bottle (*Praise (iii)*), stretches a crumb of dust from earth to heaven (*The Temper*), restores us with gold (*To all Angels and Saints*), makes a sceptre of the rod of correction (*Affliction (iii)*), makes man's weak arm into a sling (*Praise (i)*), raises dust to harmony (*Dooms-day*), transforms created things by their own natural virtues (*Praise (iii)*). Christ supplies our lack of tears with his blood (*Ephes.iv.30*), raises us from dust to gold, and in the tempering of his own crucified body tunes all instruments for their Easter music:

The cross taught all wood to resound his name,
          Who bore the same.
His stretched sinews taught all strings, what key
Is best to celebrate this most high day.

                                        Easter

This amendment of lapsed nature is continuous, a daily remaking and renewing which brings the 'grosser world' into consonance with 'thy diviner world of grace' (*The Temper*). Grace effects a renewal in the eucharist by interpenetrating the material elements with spirit so that they minister to body and soul alike, 'Leaping the wall that parts / Our souls and fleshy hearts' (*The H. Communion*). To reunite body and soul is also to restore the former ready commerce between earth and heaven, and close the gap between secular wit and divine wit (*Dulness; a true Hymn*), natural man and true priest (*Aaron*). Herbert works out the process by which the ministrant's will becomes one with God's will in a sustained piece of witty reasoning which significantly turns upon a complex play on hands – 'Their hands convey him, who conveys their hands' (*The Priesthood*) – and leaves him self-humbled at God's feet.

The task of reconciling our will with the divine will, 'Making two one' (*The Search*), starts in a temperate remorse for our own sinful condition. Neither harsh self-condemnation nor too easy self-acceptance will open the way to it. The wit continually holds a perilous balance between a tyranny of conscience which persuades us that we are helplessly locked in a body of sin, wholly dependent upon God's arbitrary election, and a complacent expectation of God's special favours to his followers or his elect. 'All things were more ours by being his' (*The Holdfast*); we have our part in a free return of love which opens us to the restoring power of Christ's atonement. Christ's bloody cross both physics sins and wards off conscience (*Conscience*); his resurrected hand raises us with him from our sinful state, drying our eyes and wounds with the handkerchiefs of his burial clothes (*The Dawning*).

The poet's strivings for self-reassurance against the judgment of his own conscience present themselves as bodily trials. The concurrence of God's love with man's love frees the bone which sticks in our throats, persuades God to chain up the dog of conscience at night (*The Discharge*), offers us God's hand in exchange for our eyes (*Submission*). In the critical case of Christ's loving acceptance of a deep-dyed sinner the sins of the body are pointedly made good in bodily actions:

> When blessed Mary wiped her Saviour's feet,
> (Whose precepts she had trampled on before)
> And wore them for a jewel on her head,
>   Showing his steps should be the street,
>   Wherein she thenceforth evermore
> With pensive humbleness would live and tread:
>
> She being stained her self, why did she strive
> To make him clean, who could not be defiled?
> Why kept she not her tears for her own faults,
>   And not his feet?
>
>   *Mary Magdalene*

The beautiful flow of the argument unflamboyantly takes in those strange yet telling conceits of the feet which are worn as a jewel on the head and the steps which become a street. It brings us up to a question, formally posed, which sums up the neo-Calvinist objections to her action. Our guilt exceeds the reach of our most abject penitence, the whore is utterly unworthy to kiss the feet she had previously flouted with her own:

> Though we could dive
> In tears like seas, our sins are piled
> Deeper then they, in words, and works, and thoughts.

The effective return upon the hard question thus posed is that Christ bore her sins – her filth – which she now washes away again in washing his feet:

> Dear soul, she knew who did vouchsafe and deign
> To bear her filth; and that her sins did dash
> Even God himself: wherefore she was not loth,
>   As she had brought wherewith to stain,
>   So to bring in wherewith to wash:
> And yet in washing one, she washed both.

Yet the witty counterplay of tears and feet implies the still stronger reassurance that Christ had made himself one with her in her human condition, as he makes himself one with us. It confirms the efficacy of Magdalene's loving tears. Self-oppressive guilt is redirected, turned to devotion in the bodily action itself which unites Christ with her by their oneness in love. The humble physical act seals in resolved tranquillity that momentous spiritual reunion.

Tranquil acquiescence is tested in confrontations with death and decay which school the body by bringing home to the poet the final outcome of our natural being:

> While that my soul repairs to her devotion,
> Here I intomb my flesh, that it betimes
> May take acquaintance of this heap of dust;
> To which the blast of death's incessant motion,
> Fed with the exhalation of our crimes,
> Drives all at last.

Church-monuments

The onward sweep of this syntax sustains a developing thought which is irresistibly resolved in a final mock-solicitous turn to his own flesh:

Dear flesh, while I do pray, learn here thy stem
And true descent; that when thou shalt grow fat,

And wanton in thy cravings, thou mayst know,
That flesh is but the glass, which holds the dust
That measures all our time; which also shall
Be crumbled into dust.

The close proximity of present sentience and dust is startlingly brought
home to us when we see the body as an hour-glass, which will finally
register our time by crumbling into the dust it encloses.

Herbert takes us through the very process by which his senses are
brought to savour their own extinction:

I made a posy, while the day ran by:
Here will I smell my remnant out, and tie
                    My life within this band.
But Time did beckon to the flowers, and they
By noon most cunningly did steal away,
                    And withered in my hand.

My hand was next to them, and then my heart: . . .
                                                        Life

The movement inwards from flowers to hand to heart enacts a sudden
recognition, which the phrasing of the argument points but does not
dwell on:

I took, without more thinking, in good part
                    Time's gentle admonition:
Who did so sweetly death's sad taste convey,
Making my mind to smell my fatal day;
                    Yet sugaring the suspicion.

We die, hand and heart, with the flowers we grasp; yet our oneness
with organic life also holds beyond death and decay in the transformation of the organism itself. Reconciling himself to that oneness
so serenely the poet prepares the natural consequence of it:

Farewell dear flowers, sweetly your time ye spent,
Fit, while ye lived, for smell or ornament,
                    And after death for cures.
I follow straight without complaints or grief,
Since if my scent be good, I care not if
                    It be as short as yours.

Herbert's concern with our survival of death takes in the fate of the
body. To die is to leave behind a part of ourselves 'and trust / Half that

we have / Unto an honest faithful grave' (*Death*). Nonetheless Christ's bodily resurrection justifies our trust in an ultimate reconstitution of our individual natures:

> What though my body run to dust?
> Faith cleaves unto it, counting every grain
> With an exact and most particular trust,
> Reserving all for flesh again.
>
> *Faith*

To acquiesce in our own mortality is to clear our eyes of their blinding preoccupation with dust, and open them to the true prospect of a state after death in which 'Our eyes shall see thee, which before saw dust; / Dust blown by wit, till that they both were blind' (*Love* (ii)). It is not just whimsy when Herbert evokes a doomsday drama in which our very dust will stir 'and rub the eyes' as our scattered bodies are roused back to life:

> While this member jogs the other,
> Each one whispering, *Live you brother?*
>
> *Dooms-day*

Death and the grave become the means of our restoring our lost wholeness in a transformed state of being, 'As at dooms-day' when souls themselves shall be newly arrayed in their transformed bodies, 'And all thy bones with beauty shall be clad' (*Death*). The stately house of love which grace strengthens to withstand many attacks must be rased to the ground at last by the combined assault of sin and death; yet that downfall is more than recovered:

> But *Love* and *Grace* took *Glory* by the hand,
> And built a braver Palace than before.
>
> *The World*

God's providence has care of our bodies in the grave; grace fills up uneven nature by renewing the corrupted body and reuniting it with the soul. The transformation of our being in glory comprehends the whole of our nature.

The sequence of poems which opens with *Superliminare*, the lintel over the portal to the church, closes with *Love* (iii). We start with a general invitation to join in a shared observance – 'approach, and taste / The church's mystical repast' – and conclude with the poet's final reconciliation to love and to his own unworthiness. Herbert brings us

from the entrance upon the banquet of the eucharist in the earthly
Church to the consummation of our bond with Christ in the love-
feast in Heaven:

> Love bade me welcome: yet my soul drew back,
>   Guilty of dust and sin.
> But quick-eyed Love, observing me grow slack
>   From my first entrance in,
> Drew nearer to me, sweetly questioning,
>   If I lacked any thing.

This beautiful little poem resolves the long debate with God not in
argument but in act. It takes in the concerns which have occupied the
poet from the first, the reciprocity between God's creative providence
and our free will, God's bearing the blame himself of our unkindness
and ingratitude to him, our sense of our own demerits and humble
reluctance to share what we have not deserved, Christ's testimony of
oneness with us in the eucharist. Yet all these considerations turn upon
love, which controls the relationship between God and the poet and
the poet's reception in heaven. The final reunion with Christ is
simply but vividly dramatised in the figure of an invitation to a meal,
in which Love plays the welcoming host and the poet is the humbly
reluctant guest whose self-accusing soul keeps him all too keenly
aware of his own unworthiness. Herbert's phrasing catches the
nuances of the unlooked-for encounter, the assured welcome, his
soul's sudden drawing back, the prompt considerateness of
'quick-eyed Love', the courtesy and sheer solicitude of the sweet
questioning:

> A guest, I answered, worthy to be here:
>   Love said, You shall be he.
> I the unkind, ungrateful? Ah my dear,
>   I cannot look on thee.
> Love took my hand, and smiling did reply,
>   Who made the eyes but I?

The quick exchanges beautifully characterise, by the simplest of
means, the momentous confrontation of guilt and love. The calmly
conclusive cadences of Love's reassurances meet the poet's self-vexed
perturbations all the more convincingly when they are offered to him
as questions whose responses he cannot deny. The inner drama of the
quiet contention of loving courtesies is created in the rhetoric itself
with its alternation of urgent cadences and calm sureness, its spreading
of the dialogue across the stanzas so that the very break between them

makes a pause for self-searching, its precise counterposing of key words and acts:

> Truth Lord, but I have marred them: let my shame
> Go where it doth deserve.
> And know you not, says Love, who bore the blame?
> My dear, then I will serve.
> You must sit down, says Love, and taste my meat:
> So I did sit and eat.

The subtle struggle played out in the syntax is resolved in the final line with a simple act of acquiescence, realised in the humblest words. The long wrestle with himself and with God is consummated in the modest act of sitting down and eating. His acceptance of Christ's atoning sacrifice assures his honoured place at Love's table, his sharing of Love's meat, which is 'my meat' in the intimate sense that it embodies Christ's own humanity and constitutes Christ's own body. The simple dignity of the gesture mutes the shock of an apotheosis of sense which fulfils the hunger of the spirit.

Crashaw's poetry strains to outgo simple sense. It does not work towards simplicity at all but flaunts its wit in the high conceited manner approved by Gracián and Tesauro. Its affinities lie with the verse of such heirs of Petrarchism as Marino, Góngora, Ledesma. Yet Crashaw uses Petrarchan manners for his own metaphysical ends, as when he celebrates Christ's circumcision by assuring the morning that the redness of Mary's blushes and of Christ's blood drops will outdo its natural sumptuousness:

> All the purple pride that laces
> The crimson curtains of thy bed,
> Gilds thee not with so sweet graces
> Nor sets thee in so rich a red.

> Of all the fair-cheeked flowers that fill thee
> None so fair thy bosom strows,
> As this modest maiden lily
> Our sins have shamed into a rose.

> Bid thy golden God, the Sun,
> Burnished in his best beams rise,
> Put all his red-eyed rubies on;
> These rubies shall put out their eyes.
> *An Hymn For The Circumcision Of Our Lord*[15]

The Petrarchan mode of wit becomes still more obtrusive when he
promises Christ himself that Christ's superior beauty will draw to
him all the paramours and lovers of the world, not least the sun-
worshippers of the East who can only gain by their changed allegiance:

> Thy nobler beauty shall bereave him,
>   Of all his Eastern paramours:
> His Persian lovers all shall leave him,
>   And swear faith to thy sweeter powers.
> Nor while they leave him shall they lose the sun,
>   But in thy fairest eyes find two for one.

Crashaw's wit works differently from Donne's wit or Herbert's. It
does not serve to hold together unlike orders of being, or to bring out
the working of a spiritual order in contingent events. Nor does it pose
a struggle to reconcile unlike elements in the poet's own nature.
Crashaw's poems typically present themselves in the attitude of
celebration or contemplation rather than self-debate. They tend to
offer us a devotional image which prompts a series of witty voluntaries
and heats these hyperingenuities with voluptuous ardour. The effect
of the wit in the hymn on the circumcision is to play off divine
wonders against natural splendours so as to show that Christ and Mary
outgo nature in its own sensible terms. The divine effects and the
natural effects differ in quality and substance but not in kind.

Crashaw meditates such sacred episodes in their symbolic character
as a show of iconic properties, rather than in their human circumstances. His concern with Christ's crucifixion is quite unlike George
Herbert's or Donne's. He fixes upon Christ's blood, which keeps on
flowing as the fuel of impassioned conceits:

> Jesu, no more! It is full tide.
> From thy head and from thy feet,
> From thy hands and from thy side
> All the purple rivers meet.
> *Upon The Bleeding Crucifix*

Christ's feet no longer walk about for our eternal good but now swim
in their own flood; his hands are bound yet free to offer us the supreme
gift of God himself; his 'deep digged side' pours out a 'double Nilus'
which is far more fruitful and copious than 'the Pharian tide'. All the
conceited plays, as all the separate issues of blood, draw together in the
single image of a general flood which revises the poet's mourning – 'I
counted wrong; there is but one'. The torrent of Christ's blood which
so agonisingly drains the sufferer's life 'to us is found / A deluge of

deliverance, / A deluge lest we should be drowned'. Antitype answers type, the one flood offsets the other; Christ's blood counters God's Deluge to offer us life through his vital death:

> Ne'er wast thou in a sense so sadly true,
> The well of living waters, Lord, till now.

Crashaw's poems repeatedly rehearse such mutations of the sacred attributes of suffering. The wounds sustained by Christ's martyrs become the vents of love's fires and the openings to Christ himself, 'Fair, purple doors, of love's devising; / The ruby windows which enriched the east / Of thy so oft repeated rising':

> It was the wit of love o'erflowed the bounds
> Of wrath, and made thee way through all those wounds.
> *To The Name Above Every Name*

The wit of love impels Crashaw's poetry. In this poem wit works to transpose dire injuries into sumptuous doors and windows which open the breast to Christ's dawn. The one substantial circumstance becomes the other as the literal means of a witty return of love.

This literalness is not casual, and the conceits carry it through to the point where our ordinary understanding is flouted in effects which seem bizarre or surrealistic. The answer to the fervently posed question whether Christ's wounds are mouths or eyes is that they are both, and that he thus has mouths and eyes in his feet. The wounds themselves are contemplated with Crashaw's customary fervour of lush ingenuity:

> Lo! a mouth whose full-bloomed lips
>   At too dear a rate are roses.
> Lo! a bloodshot eye! that weeps
>   And many a cruel tear discloses.
>   *On the wounds of our crucified Lord*

The erotic allure of bleeding wounds is no easier to stomach when the trappings are so insistently Petrarchan. Yet the poem effects a transposition of love which turns the wounds into a rich return of devotion. Christ's foot will now repay the kisses and tears lavished upon it by such penitent sinners as Mary Magdalene, and seal the conversion of her passions:

> This foot hath got a mouth, and lips,
>   To pay the sweet sum of thy kisses:
> To pay thy tears, an eye that weeps
>   Instead of tears such gems as this is.

His blood will answer in ruby-tears her tear-pearls of loving grief:

> The difference only this appears,
>   (Nor can the change offend)
> The debt is paid in ruby-tears,
>   Which thou in pearls did'st lend.

The bizarre mode of wit uncompromisingly follows out Crashaw's devotional reading of Christ's ministry. Crashaw emulates the witty Petrarchans who celebrate their lady by working up in a conceited play the prescribed attributes of her beauty. His poetry answers Tesauro's prescription for wit in that it draws out the cavillatious proof of a proposition which is contrary to common acceptance. Yet this wit does more than enliven a praise. It catches the assurance that Christ's reversal of his squalid death confirms the power of love, making love itself the true philosopher's stone which transmutes one essence into another, changes earthy matter to purest gold. The basis of the play of wit is the conversion of properties in like terms; loving kisses and rubies simply reshape and supplant the wounds and tears.

No doubt Crashaw sought to shock his readers into recognising that the paradoxes of Christ's human condition run counter to natural reason. His celebrated epigrams continually call for a radical revision of our ordinary understanding:

> Luke 11
> *Blessed be the paps which Thou hast sucked*
>
> Suppose he had been tabled at thy teats,
>   Thy hunger feels not what he eats:
> He'll have his teat e'er long (a bloody one)
>   The mother then must suck the Son.

Repellent as this imagery is it graphically brings out a prodigy which is not just interestingly odd, as Empson thought it,[16] but precisely comprehends the incongruous conjunction of homely sustenance, timeless sacrifice and absolute dominion. Christ's godhead supervenes so far upon the exigencies of his human state that this poem will not certainly concede even so much as motherly nurture to the infant's human needs.

Crashaw's emblematic rendering of his subjects is a function of his mode of wit. His hyper-conceited meditation upon Mary Magdalene's penitence for her sins, and devoted attachment to Christ, wholly fixes upon her tears and her undeviating pursuit of her beloved:

> Hail, sister springs!
> Parents of silver-footed rills!
> Ever bubbling things!
> Thawing crystal! snowy hills,
> Still spending, never spent!
> *Saint Mary Magdalene or The Weeper*[17]

Her eyes are 'Heavens of ever-falling stars' which even enable the earth to 'countershine' the heavens. *The Weeper* is a *tour de force* of wit, elaborating through thirty-one stanzas such lavishly conceited celebrations of Magdalene's tears. These stars only seem to fall like natural bodies but are actually too precious to deck our earth:

> Upwards thou dost weep.
> Heaven's bosom drinks the gentle stream.
> Where th'milky rivers creep,
> Thine floats above; and is the cream.
> Waters above th' heavens, what they be
> We are taught best by thy tears and thee.

> Every morn from hence
> A brisk cherub something sips
> Whose sacred influence
> Adds sweetness to his sweetest lips.
> Then to his music. And his song
> Tastes of his breakfast all day long.

The lush play of sensibility only points up the tangibleness of the terms. The procedure is Petrarchan in the way that the attributes of penitent love are worked up into a vast hyperbolic action as if they literally have cosmic effect; yet it dares us to take it for a picture of the truth. Crashaw seems to relish the bathos of a workaday change of use in this cosmic setting, as when heaven's bosom drinks the stream instead of emitting it, the tears become the cream of the Milky Way, and the cherub's song smacks of his breakfast. But then he courts absurdity in his entire conception of a woman who never lets Christ rest with her incessant weeping, and a heaven which simply transposes the bodily effects. The keeping of a mundane decorum is not his interest.

If Magdalene's tears enhance heaven's splendours then they must outdo nature altogether:

> Not in the evening's eyes
> When they red with weeping are
> For the sun that dies,

> Sits sorrow with a face so fair,
> Nowhere but here did ever meet
> Sweetness so sad, sadness so sweet . . .

> The dew no more will weep
> The primrose's pale cheek to deck,
> The dew no more will sleep
> Nuzzled in the lily's neck;
> Much rather would it be thy tear,
> And leave them both to tremble here.

Such exquisitely controlled wit simply transfers the erotic impulse from its natural object to the devout end. It effects a conceited sequence of divine transpositions of natural events. By her redirection of love Magdalene's tears wondrously revise the order of nature, paradoxically reconciling grief with joy, flood with fire, and gathering in all the waters of the world in the service of Christ:

> O wit of love! that thus could place
> Fountain and garden in one face.

Christ himself becomes the divine Cupid-gardener whose barbs inflame Magdalene with love and ward off rival lovers, or dig the wells and dress the vine that produces such fruit:

> Vain loves avaunt! bold hands forbear!
> The lamb hath dipped his white foot here.

He outgoes secular love in its own terms, as the one true object of passion who inspires pure ardour without the heat of ungentle flames such as vex the suffering rose in 'a too warm bed'; indeed Magdalene's pursuit of this lover only affords him a peripatetic means of refreshment and lustration:

> And now where'er he strays,
> Among the Galilean mountains,
> Or more unwelcome ways,
> He's followed by two faithful fountains;
> Two walking baths; two weeping motions;
> Portable and compendious oceans.

Christ's sovereignty over all temporal things appears in his power to prompt the coining of perpetual showers of silver and gold from a 'wand'ring mine' and a mint which follows him about:

> A voluntary mint, that strows
> Warm silver show'rs where'er it goes!

The turn to apostrophise the tears may look like mere feyness, Herrick fashion: 'Sweet, whither haste you then? o say / Why trip so fast away?' But it does prepare the clinching testimony of love. Magdalene's tears claim to outdo nature in their very fugitiveness, for they do not just yield themselves to earth and dust like dew or serve to refresh the flowers and fields; nor do they even seek to deck Christ's head with diadems. On the contrary,

> We go to meet
> A worthier object, *our Lord's feet.*

The simple close felicitously rounds the entire meditation by bringing the sinner's grief to its true fulfilment in that penitent self-humbling at Christ's feet.

So lavish a cascade of conceits may seem unapt to the contemplation of penitent love; and some of the conceits invite their notoriety. Crashaw's mode of wit is prone to bathos precisely because it holds sacred things and commonplace things together on like terms without regard to their practical incongruity. The divine prodigies overgo nature in nature's own effects. Crashaw distinguishes sacred being from secular being just by its power to transform the uses of nature. He needs no bridge or ladder between matter and spirit, or a means to reconcile unlike orders of being. Penitent tears transmute to gems and precious metals by the witty alchemy of love, as an impure substance changes into pure essence. Crashaw's poems rehearse a continual transmutation of natural elements into sacred properties such as outgoes all our expectations, and their necessary means is the witty conceit. The poet's ardour starts in his fierce yearning to bring about such a change in himself by wholly submitting his own life to the fire of Christ's love, a process which he seeks to further not by re-enacting Mary Magdalene's struggle to reconcile the contradictions in her own nature but by contemplating the miraculous enrichment of her tears.

Conceits which continually try the working of nature against the powers of Christ invite comparison with Vaughan's witty hieroglyphs. E. K. Chambers finds a likeness between a bold stroke in Crashaw's *A Hymn of the Nativity* and an effect in Vaughan's *The Feast.*[18] Crashaw's lines celebrate a past event:

> The babe looked up and showed his face;
> In spite of darkness, it was day
> It was Thy day, sweet! and did rise
> Not from the east, but from thine eyes.

Vaughan's lines catch a present impulse:

> Aye victory
> Which from thine eye
>   Breaks as the day doth from the east,
> When the spilt dew,
> Like tears doth shew
>   The sad world wept to be released.

Yet this divergence precisely marks the difference between the two poets. Crashaw redirects the Petrarchan hyperbole that the mistress's awakening makes a new day which dispels the darkness and forestalls the rising sun. In his version the birth of Christ marvellously displaces the order of nature. Vaughan is preparing himself to receive the sacrament here, and contemplates the effect of the bread and wine in giving our dust the victory over death, as Christ's bodily resurrection assures it. His lines catch the struggle of the world of sense to be regenerated and resurrected by the sacred virtue of Christ's sacrifice. The entire natural creation waits to be released, opened to Christ's revitalising power by his blood and grief which we experience in dew and tears. The natural order of daybreak from the east with its springing of dew is not disrupted by Christ; on the contrary it manifests his power, which sustains by just such means the life of a sacred creation. The working of nature makes a single sacred process with the ministry of Christ. Vaughan's wit does not pose a conceit but conjoins powers which work within organic life as they work through the eucharist.

Nonetheless Crashaw is not just wit-mongering or embellishing a pious praise. His device brings out the inherent paradoxicalness of the truths he contemplates, their contrariness to ordinary acceptance. This nativity hymn quite exquisitely confronts the world and the entire creation with the incongruity of Christ's lowly birth in a 'cold, and not too cleanly, manger', when the combined powers of heaven and earth would not suffice to fit a bed for so huge an event. Nature, and supernature, offer to protect and celebrate the infant Christ:

Tityrus.   I saw the curled drops, soft and slow,
                  Come hovering o'er the place's head;
        Off'ring their whitest sheets of snow
                  To furnish the fair Infant's bed:
        Forbear, said I; be not too bold.
        Your fleece is white but 'tis too cold . . .
Thyrsis.   I saw the obsequious seraphims
                  Their rosy fleece of fire bestow.

> For well they now can spare their wings
> Since Heaven itself lies here below.
> Well done, said I; but are you sure
> Your down so warm, will pass for pure?

Yet these offerings are superfluous to the sacred design, 'The Phoenix builds the Phoenix' nest, / Love's architecture is his own'. The snow, fire and light fall far short of the qualities which the holy pair already comprehend in themselves; for the child finds his chaste covering between Mary's breasts, and generates his own balmy dawn and ours:

> *Both.*   We saw thee in thy balmy nest,
>   Bright dawn of our eternal day!
>   We saw thine eyes break from their east
>   And chase the trembling shades away
>   We saw thee; and we blest the sight,
>   We saw thee, by thine own sweet light.

The conceits quite exquisitely confirm that Christ and his mother already outgo in themselves all that the creation may afford to celebrate Christ's birth. To our seeming they are living nests of paradoxes. The event reorders all existence, bringing earth and heaven into one order; and Christ's birthright marvellously enlarges human nature:

> Welcome all wonders in one sight!
>   Eternity shut in a span.
> Summer in winter. Day in night.
>   Heaven in earth, and God in man.
> Great little one! whose all-embracing birth
> Lifts earth to heaven, stoops heav'n to earth.
>
> Welcome. Though nor to gold nor silk,
>   To more than Caesar's birthright is; . . .

So bold a bathos can scarcely be flippantly meant; and we must take it that the conceits upon the Virgin's breasts and kisses advance some calculatedly down-to-earth wonders. They are clearly not gratuitously witty when they seek to bring out the miraculous temper of Christ's own human nature, in which frost and heat commingle. The fit close of a conceited observance which rehearses Christ's remaking of nature is the return to the celebrant's human state. In offering to Christ their gifts of lambs and doves these shepherds anticipate their own glorious undoing:

Till burnt at last in fire of Thy fair eyes,
   Ourselves become our own best sacrifice.

The culminating stroke of wit is the turning of a Petrarchan conceit so
as to intimate that this dissolving fire is the necessary fulfilment of love.

   The idea of a final annulment of nature in the fire of divine love
gives rise to Crashaw's distinctive commingling of wit and ardour in
his contemplation of pain. His impassioned *Descant Upon the Devout
Plainsong of Stabat Mater Doloroso* conceitedly confirms Mary's oneness
with Christ in his suffering, which the poet aspires to share:

> O costly intercourse
> Of deaths, and worse,
>   Divided loves. While son and mother
> Discourse alternate wounds to one another;
>   Quick deaths that grow
>   And gather, as they come and go;
> His nails write swords in her, which soon her heart
>   Pays back, with more than their own smart;
> Her swords, still growing with his pain,
> Turn spears, and straight come home again.

The mother feels the son's wounds as he feels her anguish; their
reciprocal griefs transpose themselves in the weapons which give them
pain, as deadly instruments of love. All that debars the poet from this
sympathetic interchange of wounds is his chill hardness of heart, which
he seeks to amend at Mary's eyes and breast so that he too might
become a 'Soft subject for the siege of love'. There is more in this siege
of love than the transposed pangs of courtly passion. It calls for the
re-experiencing of the sacred griefs and wounds:

> O teach these wounds to bleed
> In me; . . .
> Come wounds! come darts!
> Nailed hands! and pierced hearts!
> Come your whole selves, sorrow's great son and mother!
>   Nor grudge a younger brother
> Of griefs his portion . . .

   The spur of his meditation of this station of the cross discloses itself
as a yearning to dissolve his 'Days and hours' in tears and blood, so that
he may be made one with Christ in suffering as Mary is, 'till we mix
/ Wounds; and become one crucifix'. His means to this blood-union
with Christ come home to him in a drastic repointing of familiar
conceits. He craves tears to dissolve his temporal life, draughts of wine

from Christ's wounds to make him drunk to himself and oblivious to all save love − 'A lost thing to the world, as it to me'. His dedication of his entire life to Christ's death will be the final proof of his oneness with Christ in love:

> Fold up my life in love, and lay't beneath
> My dear lord's vital death.

In Crashaw's poems the fire of love becomes a radical force, revising or contradicting our natural expectations and consuming the world in its ardour. Paradoxes, seeming incongruities, violent reversals of our common assurances, must be inherent in the attempt to contemplate it. St Teresa reverses the presumption of human and womanly dependence which her picture embodies, 'As it is usually expressed with a Seraphim beside her'. The seraphim takes his ardour from her, not the other way round; the dart of love he holds truly belongs to her:

> You must transpose the picture quite,
> And spell it wrong to read it right;
> Read him for her, and her for him;
> And call the *Saint* the *Seraphim*.
>   *The Flaming Heart*

The poem justifies a general exchange of attributes between saint and seraphim, thus showing up the painter's error when he makes 'Some weak, inferior, woman saint' of the firebrand we find in St Teresa's writing:

> Give him the veil; that he may cover
> The red cheeks of a rivalled lover . . .
> Give her the dart for it is she
> (Fair youth) shoots both thy shaft and thee . . .

The rendering of devout ardour in Petrarchan terms must be taken to mark the wholesale transmutation of the effects of erotic love. What distinguishes the fire of divine love from the heat of sexual passion? The seraphim's own fire is fed by the saint's suffering, which she sustains in her oneness with Christ. Her flaming heart draws its fervour from the agony of love, the pains she shares with Christ in her devotion:

> Leave her alone *The Flaming Heart*.
> Leave her that; and thou shalt leave her

> Not one loose shaft but love's whole quiver.
> For in love's field was never found
> A nobler weapon than a wound.
> Love's passives are his activ'st part.
> The wounded is the wounding heart.

Wounds beget the power to wound; her hunger to share Christ's death gives her writings their sovereignty in the world. The prompting to martyrdom for love lifts Crashaw's verse at once, and kindles his wit:

> Live in these conquering leaves; live all the same;
> And walk through all tongues one triumphant flame
> Live here, great heart; and love and die and kill;
> And bleed and wound; and yield and conquer still.
> Let this immortal life where'er it comes
> Walk in a crowd of loves and martyrdoms.
> Let mystic deaths wait on't; and wise souls be
> The love-slain witnesses of this life of thee.

Leaves, tongues, blood, wounds and deaths: the effects boldly interchange by way of heralding her conquest of the nations of the earth, which she will bring about through the testimony of her agonised devotion as one who still walks the world in her own keen fire of love.

The astonishing peroration of the poem amounts to an impassioned plea that the saint's fire might be turned upon the poet himself, through her book, so as to take him from his own 'self and sin'. He seeks a change of state more drastic than a mere self-amendment or self-acceptance. Interweaving erotic ardour with martyrdom the wit confirms that love is consummated in a total annulment of self in the union with Christ:

> O thou undaunted daughter of desires!
> By all thy dow'r of lights and fires;
> By all the eagle in thee, all the dove;
> By all thy lives and deaths of love;
> By thy large draughts of intellectual day,
> And by thy thirsts of love more large than they;
> By all thy brim-filled bowls of fierce desire
> By the last morning's draught of liquid fire;
> By the full kingdom of that final kiss
> That seized thy parting soul, and sealed thee his;
> By all the heav'ns thou hast in him
> (Fair sister of the Seraphim!)

> Leave nothing of my self in me.
> Let me so read thy life, that I
> Unto all life of mine may die.

Crashaw's wit follows out the extraordinary transmutations wrought by a love which dies to the life of self and makes a sacrament of natural being. This wit is metaphysical to the extent that it correlates contrary states of being, converting a secular condition into a sacred order. The mutations it effects entail a change of substance and status, as when the water is turned into wine and the bread and wine become Christ's body and blood, the latter state simply overtaking the former: 'The properties of bread and wine which our senses tell us remain in this sacrament after the consecration do not have the substance of bread and wine as their subject. That substance is no longer present.'[19]

The wit is not called upon to comprehend a simultaneous presence of unlike natures or catch the interpenetration of the natural order by grace. The poems simply do not pose an issue between sense and spirit, let alone a struggle to reconcile unlike elements in the poet's own nature. They mediate some iconic paragon of a transformed life in every conceivable mutation of its defining properties. Thus a poem will take the form of a series of witty voluntaries upon the properties of an icon, each fresh stroke putting a different effect of the alteration of being. This is not the elaborative mode of Marino's wit or Góngora's. Even Ledesma proposes only a figurative reworking of stones into jewels by the potency of the martyr's blood. Crashaw strains to reproduce a metaphysical process, the effect of the wit of love in transforming quite humdrum functions into offices of grace, ingeniously redirecting to a divine end the sensible manifestations of love. Hence the calculated bathos of the treatment of sacred effects in humdrum terms. The final state is simply an extra-natural transmutation of the natural condition.

Edward Herbert of Cherbury strives to pass beyond sense in a quite different way from Crashaw. His poetry is assertively metaphysical, and flaunts Herbert's intimacy with Donne. It catches just Donne's manner of canvassing an existential conceit:

> Do we then die in him, only as we
> May in the world's harmonious body see
> An universally diffused soul
> Move in the parts which moves not in the whole?
> So though we rest with him, we do appear

To live and stir awhile, as if he were
Still quickening us? Or do (perchance) we live
And know it not?

Elegy for the Prince

This is poetry of a peculiar intellectuality, even dryness, yet quite luminous precision. Each poem starts in a specific predicament of praise or love, which need not be sensuously realised but serves to launch an abstract speculation. A lady's 'beauty and . . . lovely parts' may truly be praised as love's darts but only because they 'wound and kill, / The more depraved affections of our will', and thus become objects of contemplation rather than action:

For as you can unto that height refine
All love's delights, as while they do incline
Unto no vice, they so become divine,
We may as well attain your excellence,
As, without help of any outward sense
Would make us grow a pure intelligence.

Platonic Love

The cerebrality is no casual character. It marks an unremitting urge towards the intellectualising of ardent urges, the celebration of qualities of pure mind and spirit.

Herbert's terms of praise and admiration insist upon a refining of the affections beyond the frailties of sense. They register the lover's aspiration towards an 'exalted form . . . and sublime', which may 'transcend . . . change or time'. His argument continually carries us from sense to mind, from the sensible effect to the invisible cause. A kiss makes an infusion of souls; and her attractions work as a magnetic impulse emanating from the motions of her mind,

which was so much more refined
Than that I formerly did use,
That if one soul found joys in thee,
The other framed them new in me.

The First Meeting

His way of praising a lady's black hair and eyes is to discover in the correspondence of black with black the quintessence of a symmetry 'so well expressed / That the perfections in each part confessed / Are beauties to themselves and to the rest' (*To Mrs Diana Cecil*). He goes on to celebrate blackness itself as an image of the soul and the first cause, a revelation of infinity, a spark of the light inaccessible

'Affecting more the mind than sense' (*To Her Eyes*). Outward physical graces become an index of intellectual elevation, then an image of universal truth.

This drive from sense to idea signals Herbert's Platonic temper. Yet Herbert does not write at all like Cavalcanti or Michelangelo. There is no such personal struggle to apprehend the pure idea in the sensuous allure, or to mount a ladder of transcendence. Herbert follows out a universal process of sublimation in which particular states continually strive to rarefy themselves in higher modes of being until they become 'an essence pure, from grosser parts refined'. As our own lives die in our 'Uncessant minutes' so those minutes 'die in time, time in eternity' (*To his watch, when he could not sleep*). His most extreme detractions of the world simply repudiate the lures of the flesh which impede this refining process. He hates a lady's bodily charms, as he hates himself, just in as far as a preoccupation with the urges of sense must distract him from the veneration of her universal beauty; and a love poem becomes an attempt to answer the self-posed question, 'How hating hers, I truly her / Can celebrate?' (*Madrigal*). He apostrophises death as a 'great mistress' who far outdoes the attractions of a 'flesh mistress' in that she promises a release into universal liberty from the particular constraints of the senses:

> Hear, from my body's prison, this my call,
> Who from my mouth-grate and eye-window bawl.
> *To His Mistress For her True Picture*

Herbert categorically disjoins the fate of the body from the fate of the soul. He clinches his epitaph on a child which died in its birth with a rare stroke of metaphysical wit, a one-line paradox which plays on the ambiguity of our state:

> Nothing that ever died hath lived so long.

The *Epitaph For Himself* proclaims his indifference to his survival in the world, as one 'who was so free from either hope or fear / To have or lose this ordinary light'. He attributes this detachment from our customary apprehensions to the expectation that death will raise his purer part above the strife of the elements to which our unrefined flesh will be returned:

> So his immortal soul should find above
> With his Creator, peace, joy, faith, and love.

Yet Herbert's most uncompromising detractions of the flesh do not deny the worth of our bodily lives altogether, or envisage a total transcendence of their proclivities. His concern is always the refinement of sensible being towards a condition of harmonious purity which even vegetable life may attain. *To A Lady Who Did Sing Excellently* celebrates the coming together of sensuous elements to perfect a spiritual harmony which itself has power to restore and sublime. Voice and music breathe a refining soul into the lifeless elements of his own uncouth words and consummate their harmonious life in the beauty of her face, whose circle composes all the 'rare perfections' in 'one perfect sweet'. *Sonnet* finds just such a healing harmony of the senses in a natural scene, whose 'one even temper' of sounds, sights, sensations reconciles all our unrests in its own 'self-renewing vegetable bliss' of love. So intimate a transformation of sense marks the singularity of Herbert's poetic endeavour. His curious conceit seeks to wring a kind of permanence out of organic change itself. The bliss beyond the appetencies of sense is to be reached by the tempering of all the senses in the single exaltation of right love, a condition which works its own renewal.

What graces of our present being survive the grave? The anxiety haunts all Herbert's poetry, and is not allayed by his general presumption that our unrefined bodily constituents return to their elemental strife while the purified mind or soul enjoys its absolute bliss. *Elegy Over A Tomb* poses a Carew-like pondering of the survival of her various beauties now that her body is turned to ashes. The mode of wonderment itself supplies the only reassurance he can reach:

> Doth the sun now his light with yours renew?
> Have waves the curling of your hair?

Have her beauties sustained the stars, the sky, the flowers, and given a second birth of laws to heaven and earth? The universal conceit of Donne's *The first Anniversary* is turned to elegiac eulogy and left in the end as an unanswerable interrogation of death.

Herbert's poems vie with Donne's in their insistent questioning of the worth of our present experience in the body. What survives of our individual identity when the body dies, and of such confirmed commitments as a pure mutual love? How far does love itself depend upon the senses? Herbert draws out these issues in love poems which pointedly revise Donne's conceit of the perfecting of a present union. *I must depart* counterpoints *A Valediction: forbidding Mourning*, urging that their love is no more diminished by bodily separation and sleep than it will be by death. Far from frustrating such a love absence refines

it by removing 'Earthly effects', and it affords the lovers an image of
the unimpeded union of their souls after death:

> Thus when our souls that must immortal be,
>   For our loves cannot die, nor we (unless
> We die not both together) shall be free
>   Unto their open and eternal peace.

Their love will be perfected only when they are out of their bodies,
for 'Death unto us must be freedom and rest'.

Some poems called *Platonic Love* precisely open the prospect of a
perfecting of love beyond the instability of the passions, towards the
bliss of the lovers' souls in an eternal union of 'pure affection'
('Madam, believe't'). True love is no effect of individual appetite or
will but expresses a reconciling impulse which works to unite their
souls and gratify them equally, 'as but one voice, / Shall speak, one
thought but think the other's will'. Like the lovers of Donne's *The
Anniversary* they confirm a mutualness which will not be subject to
change, in this life or beyond the grave. But whereas Donne's lovers
know their unique bliss here and now in their embodied state,
Herbert's true lovers may realise their perfect union only when they
have left their senses far behind them in a continual refinement of pure
love which will 'Transform and fix them to one star at last'. Then their
blessedness will be perfected also, since the particular 'contents they in
each other find' will augment even the general bliss of heaven. So
slight a revision of Donne's drift poses an issue between Donne and
Edward Herbert which is far from slight.

Herbert curiously elaborates his metaphysics of love in the analogy
of a burning candle. He finds three components in the wasting candle,
each of which returns to its own 'proper principle' as the candle burns
down, a material body, the self-consuming flame, and ascending
smoke:

> Though all thy terrestrial part in ashes lies,
> Thy more sublime to higher regions flies,
>   The rest being to the middle ways exposed.

> And while thou does thy self each where disperse
> Some parts of thee make up this universe,
>   Others a kind of dignity obtain,
> Since thy pure wax, in its own flame consumed,
> Volumes of incense sends, in which perfumed
>   Thy smoke mounts where thy fire could not attain.
> *A Meditation Upon His Wax Candle Burning Out*

In the same way our own dissolution will disperse our constituent parts, our soul ascending to its place of origin while the body reverts to its own elements. Yet we live on after death even in the dispersed members of our bodies, which readily return to their natural station or sally forth in earth and air with the power to generate meteors and stars, 'Quickened again by the world's common soul'. Then 'our part divine' promises much more, having power even while we live to refine 'this dross of elements . . . into a better state', or to divest us of our earthy burdens altogether in the glorious state reserved for pure souls, 'which fills alone their infinite desire / To be of perfect happiness possessed'. This is the rarefied bliss to which the poet himself aspires, as one who lives and moves not by 'outward sense' such as impels 'inferior creatures' but only by 'faith and love', the purest impulses of the spirit: ·

> And therefore I . . .
> May unto some immortal state pretend,
> Since by these wings I thither may ascend
>   Where faithful loving souls with joys are crowned.

The endeavour which Herbert's scheme discloses counts for more than his bizarre metaphysics. He seeks a general process which will make death nothing more than a dispersal of our elements and yet assure the eternal fulfilment of a pure quintessence of our selves. The burning wax candle is so apt to his purpose because it precisely emblemises the divergence of matter and spirit which he takes to be the condition of our survival. What endures of our present being must already rise purged of its mortality.

A poem called *Idea* directly appraises the final worth of earthly virtues. This lengthy panegyric purports to have been sent from Scotland in 1639 to a lady far distant in response to the gift of her picture, and well catches the reasoning manner of Donne's complimentary verse letters. The poem proposes that all earthly beauties are at best no more than imperfect copies of heavenly beauties, while some of nature's figures crudely travesty the ideas which heaven originally prescribed. Nonetheless a truly beautiful disposition here on earth expresses the idea in which it originated, and will be transcendently beautiful in heaven when the soul perfects its nature and emerges as pure idea:

> However then you be most lovely here,
> Yet, when you from all elements are clear,
> You far more pure and glorious shall appear.

The lady's general bliss will then be heightened by the poet's heightened devotion to her:

> From whence ascending to the elect and blessed
> In your true joys you will not find it least
> That I in heaven shall know, and love you best.

Her beauty contemplated in her picture at a distance from its fleshy embodiment intimates the perfection of the idea which it expresses, and summarises the particular virtues of all other lives:

> Live all our lives then; if the picture can
> Here entertain a loving absent man,
> Much more the Idea whence you first began.

Herbert's aspiration towards pure idea overrides the imperatives of the body and prompts him to decry sexual desire. Yet he does allow personal affection, and the senses themselves, a part in the final consummation of love. His best admired and most beautiful poem essays his boldest realisation of the terms on which a present bond may survive, authenticating his curious argument in the mouths of mutual lovers whose yearning for permanence expresses their devoted constancy. These lovers lie imprisoned in each other's 'folded arms', and suffer for the joys they taste:

> Long their fixed eyes to heaven bent,
>   Unchanged they did never move,
>   As if so great and pure a love
> No glass but it could represent.
>
> When, with a sweet though troubled look,
>   She first brake silence, saying, Dear friend,
>   O that our love might take no end,
> Or never had beginning took!
>   *An Ode: Upon A Question Moved Whether Love Should Continue For Ever*

Herbert pithily reworks *The Ecstasy* so as to revise Donne's appraisal of mutual love. His lovers settle their gaze not in each other's eyes but upon heaven, whose unchanging purity mirrors their love; and the questions they pose tend a tellingly different way from the argument about the lovers' oneness. How may love escape the frailties of the flesh? Are our love and knowledge more than modes of our present being? Do we love God best in his creatures? Herbert's lovers are fixed in just the mutual raptness of Donne's ecstatic pair and look to an unchanging union; but they fear an alteration of that stasis. Their

affectionate ardour may resist change and decay but how can it
withstand the dissolution of their bodies? If love's fire is kindled
with the breath of life will it not be breathed out 'With our last
air . . . And quenched with the cold of death'? May even 'so dear a
love' resist death's power to close up the line of affections 'in our last
hour'?

The love-inspired response is that their affections and virtues will
endure because these advantages are elections of the soul. What unites
them in love are no mere 'lustful and corrupt desires' of a 'low and
dying appetite' but 'chaste desires', such as may 'hold in an eternal
bond'. Even their present state itself will be transformed rather than
changed; for in purifying their thoughts of 'All objects that may the
sense delude' they have already prepared the way for their bodies of
sense to be raised after death:

> Nor here on earth, then, or above,
>   Our good affection can impair,
>   For where God doth admit the fair
> Think you that he excludeth love?
>
> These eyes again then eyes shall see,
>   And hands again these hands enfold,
>   And all chaste pleasures can be told
> Shall with us everlasting be.
>
> For if no use of sense remain,
>   When bodies once this life forsake,
>   Or they could no delight partake,
> Why should they ever rise again?

Then their love will be perfected, and their immortality and their
union assured by their equal love:

> So when one wing can make no way
>   Two joined can themselves dilate,
>   So can two persons propagate
> When singly either would decay.
>
> So when from hence we shall be gone,
>   And be no more, nor you, nor I,
>   As one another's mystery,
> Each shall be both, yet both but one.

This lovers' colloquy ends in luminous exaltation with her face
uplifted towards the source of its beauty and her eyes looking up as if
to recover their rightful place:

> This said, in her uplifted face,
>   Her eyes, which did that beauty crown,
>   Were like two stars, that having fall'n down,
> Look up again to find their place.

Love itself is gathered into the eyes, which are wholly fixed upon their final bliss in heaven and aspire quite beyond an earthly consummation in the body. The beautiful conceit resolves in tranquil simplicity the question of love's continuance, which has provoked no heat or strain. Her misgivings serve just to measure her yearning for a changeless love and to prompt her lover's reassurance; they are countered at once, and the response begets its own mode of ecstasy in that lustrous aspiration towards a perfected union in heaven. The chaste bond of sense will be consummated in the eternal oneness of their ideal being.

Herbert's *Ode* concedes more to the body and the senses than an orthodox Neoplatonism would allow; and it affectingly seeks to perpetuate the personal bond. Their earthly love will be consummated not in the general bliss of a merger with the One but in each other. Yet his argument always tends towards the ideal, the fulfilment of our present aspirations in the spiritual contemplation of pure form. Ellrodt aptly remarked that he shows no 'metaphysical' sense of the presence of the world.[20] Certainly he imposes no tension between sense and intelligence, body and soul, contingent circumstances and final truth; and he needs no means of holding unlike elements in play together. There is no purer mode of metaphysical poetry; yet Herbert is not in essence a poet of metaphysical wit.

Vaughan's poetry uncompromisingly starts in sense. His wit articulates a universal conceit which is also a quest for salvation. Vaughan witnesses that the natural creation is alive with a providential impulse which it instinctively acknowledges and follows out:

>   Poor birds this doctrine sing,
>   And herbs which on dry hills do spring
>   Or in the howling wilderness
>   Do know thy dewy morning-hours,
>   And watch all night for mists or showers,
>   Then drink and praise thy bounteousness.
>   *Providence* (1655)[21]

God manifests himself in his creation not in ornate temples and the like but in the processes of nature themselves, which he observably sustains and vitalises:

Walk with thy fellow-creatures: note the *hush*
And *whispers* amongst them. There's not a *spring*,
Or *leaf* but hath his *morning-hymn*; Each *bush*
And *Oak* doth know *I AM*; . . .
Rules and Lessons (1650)

His presence may be best discerned in the stillness beyond the distractions of the world, as in the deep of night when Nicodemus encountered his God; and such times are especially sacred to those who are attuned to the life of the animating spirit. Vaughan renders the properties of night as manifestations of this spiritual life:

Christ's progress, and his prayer time;
The hours to which high Heaven doth chime.

God's silent, searching flight:
When my Lord's head is filled with dew, and all
His locks are wet with the clear drops of night;
His still, soft call;
His knocking time; the soul's dumb watch,
When spirits their fair kindred catch.
The Night (1655)

Natural processes themselves everywhere bear the character of their origin and providential purpose in a particular 'signature or life' (*Repentance*, 1650). They disclose their hidden mysteries to those who love God's works enough to discern his presence in them and may read them as spiritual hieroglyphs; indeed 'mighty love' designed them to be read so 'by a gracious art', foreseeing our fall from the state in which we apprehended God's presence directly:[22]

All things here show him heaven; *waters* that fall
Chide and fly up; *mists* of corruptest foam
Quit their first beds and mount; trees, herbs, flowers, all
Strive upwards still, and point him the way home . . .

Plants in the *root* with earth do most comply,
Their *leaves* with water and humidity,
The *flowers* to air draw near, and subtlety,
And *seeds* a kindred fire have with the sky.
The Tempest (1650)

'All have their *keys* and set *ascents*': Vaughan wittily applies himself to the hieroglyphic reading of commonplace events in nature, a cockerel crowing at dawn, a bird returning to a tree after a storm, the mist rising from a lake, a waterfall; and his poetic lapses often register a failure to sustain the witty endeavour. He evidently tackled this loving decipherment of natural life as a spiritual exercise upon which his eternal well-being might depend just because it fitted him to share in God's ultimate restoration of all creatures:

> Give him amongst thy works a place,
> Who in them loved and sought thy face!
> *The Book* (1655)

Vaughan took these natural hieroglyphs for more than mere emblems of innocence. In disclosing the work of providence they confirm a correspondence between the organic life around us and our own condition. Man is inescapably involved in the processes of nature, whose providential outcome is a fruitful reciprocity of all creatures,

> Where bees at night get home and hive, and flowers
> Early, as well as late,
> Rise with the sun, and set in the same bowers; . . .
> *Man* (1650)

Yet in his fallen state man alienates himself from this vital communion in barren restlessness and self-entanglement, knocking at all doors, straying and roaming aimlessly with less wit than some stones have, 'Which in the darkest nights point to their homes, / By some hid sense their Maker gave':

> Man is the shuttle, to whose winding quest
> And passage through these looms
> God ordered motion, but ordained no rest.

Or he disperses his spirit in sheer worldly distractions, making a plaything of the sacred life of nature in the interests of a newfangled pseudo-knowledge which can only engulf us:

> alas! what can
> These new discoveries do, except they drown?

Some of Vaughan's most thrilling outbursts proclaim a sudden renewal of sympathy with the vital life about him, such as Herbert had taken for his personal recovery of God's favour:

> O joys! Infinite sweetness! with what flowers,
> And shoots of glory, my soul breaks and buds!
> All the long hours
> Of night and rest
> Through the still shrouds
> Of sleep and clouds,

This dew fell on my breast;
O how it *bloods*,
And *spirits* all my earth!
The Morning-watch (1650)

This sustained outpouring of joy celebrates the renewal in the morning of a universal bond, a commerce between earth and heaven which remakes the poet's own nature, imbuing his earth with blood and spirit and rousing the entire creation in a symphony of praise:

hark! In what rings,
And *hymning circulations* the quick world
Awakes and sings;
The rising winds,
And falling springs,
Birds, beasts, all things
Adore him in their kinds.

Yet the poem is no mere overflow of feeling. It develops a complex pattern of correspondences which make organic life and spiritual vitality twin expressions of God's quickening love. The love which nourishes the organism as dew fosters spiritual life as Christ's blood. The harmonious working of the natural creation enacts a sacred order which is also the order of our own constitution; our prayers chime with nature's hymns, and the joint concord echoes the harmony of heaven:

Thus all is hurled
In sacred *hymns* and *order*, the great *chime*
And *symphony* of nature. Prayer is
The world in tune,
A spirit-voice,
And vocal joys
Whose echo is heaven's bliss.

Natural processes themselves confirm God's providential care of his creation, and our own spiritual striving:

O let me climb
When I lie down! The pious soul by night
Is like a clouded star, whose beams though said
To shed their light
Under some cloud
Yet are above,
And shine and move

> Beyond that misty shroud.
> So in my bed,
> That curtained grave, though sleep, like ashes, hide
> My lamp and life, both shall in thee abide.

The passage from darkness and sleep to light and new life rehearses the process of an incubation, such as prepares a new birth.

Ellrodt underrates Vaughan's wit when he denies Vaughan that sense of a double nature which characterises metaphysical poetry.[23] Such poems as *The Morning-watch* get their tension from the wit which brings man's spiritual vitality into one order with the organic life of nature and derives both impulses from the animating spirit of the creation. Vaughan's wit realises a universe of symmetries in which dispositions answer to one another at every level of being and make up a single design. God's providence is implicit in his primal act of creation which touches formless matter into harmonious life.

Our very coming into being out of the womb in the first place rehearses our resurrection from the earth in which we prepare to undergo a covert incubation, as the transformation of nature from chaos to fruitful order prepares the refinement of the soul from brutish slavery to a free and sacred commerce with God:

> When first thou didst even from the grave
> And womb of darkness beckon out
> My brutish soul, and to thy slave
> Becam'st thyself, both guide and scout;
>   Even from that hour
> Thou got'st my heart; and though here tossed
>   By winds, and bit with frost
>   I pine, and shrink
>   Breaking the link
> 'Twixt thee and me; and oft-times creep
> Into th'old silence and dead sleep,
>   Quitting thy way
>   All the long day,
> Yet, sure, my God! I love thee most.
>   *Alas, thy love!*
>   *Disorder and Frailty* (1650)

This poem gets its urgency from the threat to natural fruition posed by a general degeneration, which both follows out and regulates the fall and decay of mankind:

> I threaten heaven, and from my cell
> Of clay and frailty break and bud
> Touched by thy fire and breath; thy blood
> Too, is my dew, and springing well.
> > But while I grow
> And stretch to thee, aiming at all
> > Thy stars and spangled hall,
> > > Each fly doth taste,
> > > Poison, and blast
> My yielding leaves; sometimes a shower
> Beats them quite off, and in an hour
> > > Not one poor shoot
> > > But the bare root
> Hid under ground survives the fall.
> > *Alas, frail weed!*

His relapse and general frailty are built into the very ardour of his aspiration:

> Thus like some sleeping exhalation
> (Which waked by heat and beams, makes up
> Unto that comforter the sun,
> And soars and shines; but ere we sup
> > And walk two steps,
> Cooled by the damps of night, descends,
> > And, whence it sprung, there ends)
> > > Doth my weak fire
> > > Pine and retire,
> And (after all my height of flames)
> In sickly expirations tames
> > > Leaving me dead
> > > On my first bed
> Until the Sun again ascends.
> > *Poor, falling star!*

Yet the fall also prepares the recovery. Christ's revitalising blood may restore the fallen creature as the dew and sun revive the decayed organism. The wit becomes the means of confirming the oneness of man with nature, and warrants a marvellous surge of yearning:

> O, yes! but give wings to my fire,
> And hatch my soul, until it fly
> Up where thou art, amongst thy tire
> Of stars, above infinity;
> > Let not perverse
> And foolish thoughts add to my bill

> Of forward sins, and kill
> > That seed, which thou
> > In me didst sow,
> But dress and water with thy grace,
> Together with the seed, the place;
> > And for his sake
> > Who died to stake
> His life for mine, tune to thy will
> My heart, my verse.

Silex Scintillans attempts a series of raids upon infinity in the precise sense that it discovers an eternal engagement in time. The several parts, published at a five-year interval, register a sustained attempt to live in two orders of being at once. Vaughan seeks familiar opportunities to confirm the knot which ties God to man, finding them in such ordered uses as the observances of the Church. He celebrates Sundays as 'Son-days', and draws out the ways in which they regularly intermingle heaven's bliss with our own state:

> Bright shadows of true rest! some shoots of bliss,
> > Heaven once a week;
> The next world's gladness prepossessed in this;
> > A day to seek
> Eternity in time; the steps by which
> We climb above all ages; lamps that light
> Man through his heap of dark days; and the rich
> And full redemption of the whole week's flight.
> The pulleys unto headlong man; . . .
> > > > *Son-days* (1650)

Ascension Day inspires him to relive the primal state in which 'saints and angels glorify the earth', so that he moves among and with these celestial visitants 'winged with faith and love':

> I walk the fields of Bethany which shine
> All now as fresh as Eden, and as fine.
> > > *Ascension-day* (1655)

The Ascension itself spurs him to emulate those who have known how to 'Walk to the sky / Even in this life' (*Ascension Hymn*, 1655), and also to remind himself that they do not abandon their bodies when they 'Leave behind them the old Man'; for Christ will renew their dust and clay as he renewed his own earthly dress. Christ alone has the power to 'Bring to bone / And rebuild man', and to 'Make clay ascend more quick than light'. The celebration of the Virgin reaffirms the

bond of human kind which makes us one flesh with Christ himself,
'For coalescent by that band / We are his body grown' (*The Knot*,
1655). Holy Scriptures offer him the means of uniting himself with
Christ in Christ's human suffering. He longs to have the words of
Scripture cut into his hard heart so that he might

> plead in groans
> Of my Lord's penning, and by sweetest Art
> Return upon himself the *Law*, and *stones*.
>   *H. Scriptures* (1650)

His identification with Christ draws its force from this 'Return
upon himself'. The Mosaic law and tablets, enshrining strict Old
Testament justice, are to be thrown back upon Christ himself who
bears them in love. But then Christ also returns upon the Old Testament ordinances by countering them with his new order of loving
mercy. Moreover the poet himself would make a return upon Christ
by responding to Christ's groans in kind, sharing Christ's pains in his
own penitence and hence also sharing the conquest of death.

Vaughan seeks his accommodation with the infinite through
precise correspondences and identities, as a complex relationship to be
comprehended no less than an exaltation to be felt. His need is not to
transcend his present condition but to transform it by reconciling it
with its eternal state. Church services exhibit the power of harmony
and love to make us whole when they momentarily overcome our
fallen condition and focus our devotions, reuniting the crumbled and
dispersed body:

> Blest be the God of Harmony and Love!
>   The God above!
>   And holy dove!
> Whose interceding, spiritual groans
>   Make restless moans
>   For dust and stones,
>   For dust in every part,
>   But a hard, stony heart.
>
> O how in this thy choir of souls I stand
>   (Propped by thy hand)
>   A heap of sand!
> Which busy thoughts (like winds) would scatter quite
>   And put to flight,
>   But for thy might;
>   Thy hand alone doth tame
>   Those blasts, and knit my frame.

So that both stones and dust, and all of me
              Jointly agree
              To cry to thee,
And in this music by thy Martyr's blood
              Sealed and made good
              Present, O God!
          The echo of these stones
          My sighs and groans.

Church-Service (1650)

For all its manner of a spontaneous effusion of praise *Church Service* develops an elaborate conceit in a continual play of identities and contrasts. The poet takes his present concentration on the church service, which reconciles all his faculties in entire devotion and love, to be one and the same state with his wholeness in the grave and the eternal concord of his regenerated being. Yet this oneness is precariously sustained. The service brings him to it in the teeth of the impulses and evidences which deny it even there, and which likewise make up a single complex condition. His own habitual state of distractedness and hardhearted unresponsiveness is confirmed in the dust and stony monuments in the church, which witness the crumbled bodies and ossified bones in the vaults beneath. The poem gets its peculiar kick from its enactment here and now of a drama of mortality. It tremulously catches his sense of peril in a contest which he cannot win unaided. Yet he seeks his support in the Church itself, which may seal and confirm the effects of harmony and love so as to amend his mortal derangement. The integrative power of the service is reinforced by the choir of souls; the blood of Christ and the martyrs bedews the barren dust and stones into new life.

Some of Vaughan's most beautiful writing expresses a hard-won serenity. The soft counterfall of the cadences works to console the body for its temporary separation from the soul, and dispersal in dust:

Farewell! I go to sleep; but when   *Body.*
The day-star springs, I'll wake again.
Go, sleep in peace; and when thou liest.   *Soul.*
Unnumbered in thy dust, when all this frame
Is but one dram, and what thou now descriest
In several parts shall want a name,
Then may his peace be with thee, and each dust
Writ in his book, who ne'er betrayed man's trust!

The Evening-watch (1650)

Our entire nature stands to preserve or lose itself in the debate which these poems pose. Vaughan reassures himself that the resurrection of the body from the dust and its reuniting with the soul in glory are necessary to our full blessedness. The wit sustains and seeks to resolve the tension between the brutal facts of death and the forces which promise a renewal; the hope of a resurrection and reunion counters the inward impulse towards disintegration and dispersal.

Vaughan's troubled confrontation with bodily decay is nakedly rehearsed in the untitled pilcrow-poems, which struggle to come to terms with his brother's early death:

> I search, and rack my soul to see
> Those beams again,
> But nothing but the snuff to me
> Appeareth plain; . . .
> 'Silence, and stealth of days!'
> (1650)

He seeks a resolution of the unaccommodating dilemma within the terms of a witty conceit which is capable of its own beauty and has its own power to console. The death of innocence delicately engages this poet's wit:

> Blest infant bud, whose blossom-life
> Did only look about, and fall,
> Wearied out in a harmless strife
> Of tears and milk, the food of all;
>
> Sweetly didst thou expire: thy soul
> Flew home unstained by his new kin,
> For ere thou knew'st how to be foul,
> Death *weaned* thee from the world and sin.
>
> Softly rest all thy virgin-crumbs!
> *Lapped* in the sweets of thy young breath,
> Expecting till thy Saviour comes
> To *dress* them, and *unswaddle* death.
> The Burial of an Infant (1650)

The reassuring closure of the syntax reconciles the tensions of a complex response to an innocent death. Our natural fear of death and bodily corruption is turned back upon us. The simple diction sustains a play of wit which sets innocence against the corrupting world and makes this death itself the means of preservation. Bud and blossom-life, tears and milk, a harmless strife, have their fit issue in a sweet death and offset the early curtailment of a life in the world. Death and the dissolution of the body become the means of entry upon a truly adult life, weaning the infant from sin and preparing the virgin crumbs for Christ's own hand to unswaddle and renew. The wit discovers in the infant burial itself the pledge of a sweet renewal of the body which the grave must help to perfect.

Vaughan looks to Christ's human travail for the warrant of our trials in the world. He supposes that Christ's conquest of death may be shared by those who also share his Passion in a return of his love for us. Our part in this reciprocity of love becomes the measure of our oneness with Christ and the earnest of our resurgence from the grave. Vaughan's wit, like Dante's, is grounded in a metaphysics of love. His very remonstrance against the martyrdom of the British Church under Cromwell presents itself as an impassioned cry of anguish, the lament of a bereaved lover – 'O rose of the fields! O lily of the valley! How have you now become the food of wild boars!':

> Ah! he is fled!
> And while these here their *mists* and *shadows* hatch,
> My glorious head
> Doth on those hills of myrrh and incense watch.
> Haste, haste my dear,
> The soldiers here
> Cast in their lots again,
> That seamless coat
> The Jews touched not,
> These dare divide and stain.
>
> O get thee wings!
> Or if as yet (until these clouds depart,
> And the day springs)
> Thou think'st it good to tarry where thou art,
> Write in thy books
> My ravished looks,
> Slain flock, and pillaged fleeces,
> And haste thee so
> As a young roe
> Upon the mounts of spices.
> *The British Church* (1650)

Yet the feeling is implicit in the endeavour. The delicate play of wit assimilates the present sufferings of the true British Church to a pattern which comprehends Christ's Passion with the Song of Solomon, catching up the lover's anguish in the grief of the

despoiling of Christ's flesh. The British Church directly witnesses both
the perpetual re-enactment of the crucifying of Christ's human body
and the yearning of Christ's lovers for his return. To seize this double
identity of the British Church with Christ, in its afflictions and its love,
is to confirm the special standing of that ancient Church. It is also to
herald a triumphant revival.

Traherne's divergence from Vaughan becomes critical when the two
poets seem as close in their endeavour as in their provenance.
Traherne's Oxford editor memorably claimed that this obscure
Herefordshire chaplain was one of those rare adults 'to whom the
whole phenomenal world is given as his Garden of Eden', and went
on to speak of his 'living and permanent awareness of Spirit', his
'double awareness, of enjoying the phenomenal world and of belong-
ing to a spiritual life': 'No one . . . has so married the worlds of sense
and spirit, leaving the objects of sense undimmed and showing the
potencies of spirit, as "all Act"'.[24] A seventeenth-century poet who
simultaneously inhabits the world of sense and the world of spirit
might be expected to make demands upon metaphysical wit. Yet
Traherne is not notable for wit; and Ellrodt denies that he is a true
metaphysical poet at all.[25]

Traherne shares several distinctions with George Herbert and
Vaughan. He discovers a sacred presence in the processes of nature and
attends its effects in the world about him. His poems get their strength
from his readiness to argue out his intuition in lyric verse, to urge a
bold plea across the elaborate stanza pattern. Yet what lifts his writing
is the sense of an ecstatic participation in the glory of created life. He
celebrates a vital creation which perceptibly works all about us in
glory:

> How like an angel came I down!
> How bright are all things here!
> When first among his works I did appear
> O how their GLORY did me crown!
> *Wonder*

The poems repeatedly proclaim the poet's own experience of a
creation which is already glorified in its working if we could only see
it aright. Organic life is far more precious than gems and metals for a
divinity appears in God's works which his presence gives them − 'his
GODHEAD in his works doth shine' (*The Enquiry*):

> One Star
> Is better far
> Than many precious stones:
> One sun, which is above in glory seen,
> Is worth ten thousand golden thrones:
> A juicy herb, or spire of grass,
> In useful virtue, native green,
> An emerald doth surpass; . . .
>
> *The Apostasy*

Yet the divine life of the creation is concealed from us by sin, which dulls our sight or obscures its naked witness with worldly aspirations; and he ascribes to the polluted flesh this quickness to be distracted by passing vanities:

> Spew out thy filth, thy flesh abjure;
> Let not contingents thee defile.
> For transients only are impure,
> And airy things alone beguile.
>
> *The Instruction*

Flesh or clay is whatever impedes our apprehension of glory.

Traherne sets all his store by states of naked apprehension, 'an eye / That's altogether virgin' (*An Infant Eye*), which has not been clouded by the corrupting world or sin. His poems repeatedly witness our capacity to see things 'Even like unto the Deity', and recover Adam's first delight in the creation:

> When Adam first did from his dust arise
> He did not see,
> Nor could there be
> A greater joy before his eyes:
> The sun as bright for me doth shine; . . .
>
> *The World*

He confirms this innocent vision in various unhabitual states of awareness such as a prenatal condition of 'naked simple self' (*My Spirit*), or the eye of early childhood (*Wonder*), or our infant imaginings of seeing infinite space or a world beyond the moon (*News*; *The Preparative*; *The Salutation*; *On Leaping Over the Moon*); and he supposes that we may recover it momentarily in states of suddenly altered perspective upon our customary world such as we experience in dreams and in reflections in the water, both of which give us a glimpse of an unfamiliar mode of being:

> Beneath the water people drowned.
> Yet with another heaven crowned,
> In spacious regions seemed to go
> Freely moving to and fro: . . .
>   *Shadows In The Water*

Yet all that ever separates him from the people who walk those 'other worlds' in glory is a 'thin skin' of worldly being which will one day break to let him through.

Traherne insists that the glory of creation lies within ourselves as well as in the world outside us, and may be realised in our own minds:

> The moon and stars, the air and sun
>   Into my chamber come:
> The seas and rivers hither flow,
> Yea, here the trees of Eden grow . . .
>   *Hosanna*

He marvels that his soul already knows a godlike condition and a state of endless life, which it imparts to his body and senses so that he quite literally becomes 'A temple of eternity' (*An Hymn upon St Bartholomew's Day*). God is within us and a part of ourselves:

> Lord! What is man that he
> Is thus admired like a Deity.
>   *Admiration*

Traherne's poems exultantly inhabit this transfigured universe of his own vision. They assure us that no other existence can have consequence since thoughts are superior to things – 'Compared to them / I *things* as *shades* esteem' (*The Review*). Things have their full glory only as we apprehend them. The world we see in the mind is superior to the phenomenal world we commonly encounter beyond us just because 'things are dead, and in themselves are severed / From souls' (*Dreams*). To know God's creation truly is to inhabit a world of understanding which is 'nigh of kin / To those pure things we find / In his great mind / Who made the world'. Traherne is far from saying that sensible life and the senses themselves are inherently corrupt or an inescapable clog upon the soul. On the contrary, he proclaims that in its right state the body is accessory to the soul and may even share the soul's eternal joy:

> Men's bodies were not made for stripes,
>   Nor any thing but joys.
> They were not made to be alone:
>   But made to be the very throne
> Of blessedness . . .

The Estate

The body and its organs and senses were created glorious, 'Men's senses are indeed the gems' (*Admiration*). We apprehend the true splendour of human bodies when we see them in dissection:

> They best are blazoned when we see
>   The anatomy,
> Survey the skin, cut up the flesh, the veins
>   Unfold: the glory there remains.
> The muscles, fibres, arteries and bones
> Are better far than crowns and precious stones.

The Person

Discovering the glory of the creation in the symmetry of the anatomised human body we put no barrier between sense and idea. Rightly apprehended the sensible world and the intelligible world make a single order of blessedness, 'Both worlds one heaven made by love' (*Hosanna*).

Traherne is a metaphysical poet in the rare sense that he discovers a present glory in the creation. He apprehends an order of glorified being behind the patina of our habitual world or actually within ourselves. Yet he is not a poet of metaphysical wit. The poems need no wit because they set up no tension between the world we suppose we see and the world as it really is, the inert appearance and the vital reality. Nor do they struggle to reconcile unlike modes of being, since sense is assimilated to idea. The mode of the poetry is wondering affirmation. It proclaims the way the creation really shows itself to be when we can perceive it aright. The poems do not start in some intractable experience of the world, or the imperative need to reconcile seemingly contradictory claims upon our nature. They do not even stage a struggle to see contingent events in a way which is contrary to observation, for Traherne takes the glory of the creation as given and simply affirms his own participation in it. In the end whatever resists that glory must be mere illusion.

The mid-century poets who committed themselves to the profane pleasures of sense express their own yearnings for metaphysical assurance. Caroline love lyrics put love in hazard to a cosmic insecurity. They weigh opposite possibilities of being, trying present sentience against the prospect of perpetual nothingness. Their wit is inherent in a way of apprehending no less than in argument or conceit. John Hall questions the standing of love and beauty in a universe of meaningless flux which 'By chance on atoms is begot' (*An Epicurean Ode*). This lover's metaphysics contradict his present experience of love, leaving him to wonder at the transcendental aspirations of souls which are 'Immersed in matter, chained in sense'. If 'man's but pasted up of earth? / And ne'er was cradled in the skies' what substance can there be in his persuasion of her divine beauty? Habington dramatically holds love in pawn to death, playing upon the several ways in which a woman's beauty troubles our eyes, in its ruin as in her life:

> Castara, see that dust the sportive wind
> So wantons with. 'Tis haply all you'll find
> Left of some beauty: . . .
> *To Castara: Upon Beauty*

Carew's 'Ask me no more' holds a nice balance between metaphysical unease and wistful compliment. The falling cadences haunt love and beauty with the universal decline of brightness, consoling the lady with a brave conceit of survival:

> Ask me no more where Jove bestows,
> When June is past, the fading rose:
> For in your beauty's orient deep,
> These flowers as in their causes, sleep.

Cartwright sustains metaphysical sentience with Donne's metaphysical arguments in his response to a lady who objects that she is much older than her lover (*To Chloe, who wished herself young enough for me*). Love gives the lovers a second birth, in which their souls are made anew. Distinguishing our time from the timeless state the lover is able to set love against mortality to the advantage of such seemingly ill-matched lovers. Love shares with the resurrecting angel the power to abolish distinction of age or person and raise their souls in a perfected union:

> Nay, that the difference may be none,
> He makes two, not alike, but one.

All these poets show themselves quick to discover metaphysical predicaments in love. They put sense against spirit, holding bodily desire in balance with the love of souls or minds. Sides are taken, and battle is directly joined, in the spate of poems on platonic love. Cartwright shows how far this debate was conducted in Donne's terms and assumed Donne's sceptical naturalism. He scouts with robust earthiness the 'thin love' which seeks no more than a union of minds or spirits, and finds its fulfilment in thought. Experience soon teaches the aspiring lover better:

> But thinking there to move,
> Headlong I rolled from thought to soul, and then
> From soul I lighted at the sex again.
>
> *No Platonic Love*

Witty scepticism turns to cavalier hedonism in Cleveland's farcical shows of figurative ingenuity:

> For shame, thou everlasting wooer,
> Still saying grace, and never falling to her!
> Love that's in contemplation placed,
> Is Venus drawn but to the waist.
> Unless your flame confess its gender,
> And your parley cause surrender
> Y'are salamanders of a cold desire
> That live untouched amid the hottest fire.
>
> *The Antiplatonic*

What matters now is the attractive – and enslaving – power of the animal impulse:

> The soldier, that man of iron,
> Whom ribs of horror all environ; . . .
> Let a magnetic girl appear,
> Straight he turns Cupid's cuirassier . . .

The world these poets project, like the world of their theatrical heirs, is animated by sex but racked by metaphysical anxiety.

The persuasion that love is a function of our bodily appetites underlies the witty nonchalance of the Caroline poets, who seek to regulate grossness with urbanity:

> None (though Platonic their pretence)
> With reason love unless by sense.
>
> Stanley, *Changed yet Constant*

Those lovers 'who profess they spirits taste' nonetheless 'Feed yet on grosser meat'; they may boast that they convey souls to souls but still 'Howe'er they meet, the body is the way' (Cartwright, *No Platonic*

Love). The love they cultivate has no absolute value or permanence, being nothing more than a momentary quirk of taste:

> 'Tis not the meat but 'tis the appetite
> Makes eating a delight . . .
>
> Suckling, *Sonnet ii*

Beauty itself does not inhere in the lady but is bestowed upon her by her lover's desires, which claim their due return of gratitude. What marks these poems is their witty poise, the air of cool self-possession with which the audacious argument is carried off:

> Know, Celia, since thou art so proud,
> 'Twas I that gave thee thy renown: . . .
>
> Carew, *Ingrateful Beauty Threatened*

If love and beauty are no more than projections of contending appetites then the best thing a shrewd lover can do is to hold a nice balance between his conflicting interests and come to an accommodation with his mistress. Wit now becomes the elegant means of keeping opposite imperatives in play, or exploiting contrary possibilities. Whether her beauty must die or may endure, the lover needs to seek his means of outsmarting time:

> Thus, either Time his sickle brings
> In vain, or else in vain his wings.
>
> Carew, *Song. Persuasions to Enjoy*

Carew's 'Now you have given me leave to love' strikes a bargain with his relenting mistress. The poet will not only celebrate but perfect her beauty in return for her agreement to dispense with the customary disdains and get down to the real exchanges of love. If she will open her mine of pleasure then he will spend his store – 'so we each other bless'.

Poets who still seek in love an absolute beauty beyond change now feel the need to pit love's timeless graces against the forces which menace them, setting virgin purity to counter lust and death. The chaste nunnery of Castara's breasts preserves the roses which adorn it (Habington, *To Roses in the Bosom of Castara*); the drooping violet springs erect when it is 'Transplanted to those hills of snow' (Stanley, *To a Violet in her Breast*). An intricate play of ideas is refined to simple grace because it can be conducted in a well-established figurative shorthand. The issue is nonetheless urgent. These poems wistfully acknowledge the frailness of innocence and challenge innocent beauty with its own power to provoke a destructive desire. Her eyes threaten death while her apple-breasts tempt the lover to repeat Adam's fall; if Eve had been 'Half so fair / Or Adam loved but half so well' the Serpent would never have got near her to corrupt her, for the lover could not have left her allurements alone (Townshend, *Pure simple love*). Admiration is inseparable from desire, the very coolness of purity allures; opposite impulses are entertained together and find accord in a witty poise.

Life and death also enter the balance. The more perfectly soul spiritualises body the finer the division between them:

> And here the precious dust is laid;
> Whose purely-tempered clay was made
> So fine that it the guest betrayed.
>
> Else the soul grew so fast within,
> It broke the outward shell of sin,
> And so was hatched a cherubin.
>
> <div align="right">Carew, <i>Maria Wentworth</i></div>

The common mid-century intuition is that the prospect of imminent decay gives zest to present experience. Dust and nothingness set off the moment of ardour, whose intensity engenders its own ruin:

> You are a sparkling rose i' th' bud,
> Yet lost, ere that chaste flesh and blood
> Can shew where you or grew, or stood.
>
> <div align="right">Herrick, <i>A Meditation for his Mistress</i></div>

The glow-worm which Charissa takes up shows its lustre against the blackness which surrounds it and turns to ashes in the fire of her beauty, 'To shine in darkness only being made' (Stanley, *The Glow-worm*). Mortality quickens desire, the nuptial sheets portend a winding sheet, a woman's fire prepares her ashes (Cartwright, *Women*). The best that can be wished upon lovers who aspire beyond sense and the death of the body is that they will stay ardent in the grave (Stanley, *La Belle Confidente*). Love gets its fervour from its momentariness, which makes urgent our attempts to 'pinion Time' (Carew, *A Pastoral Dialogue*). All these poets seek witty ways of setting off the present moment of commitment against the certainty of change, and of bringing out the pathetic vulnerableness of love's lordship against the general onslaught upon his domain,

Where in all sorts of flow'rs are growing
Which as the early Spring puts out,
Time falls as fast a mowing.
Townshend, *A Dialogue betwixt Time and a Pilgrim*

They wonderingly question the coherence of their own impulses when a former devotion turns unaccountably to indifference (Suckling, 'Dost see how unregarded now'). The sense of a bewildering instability sharpens their urge to seize the present moment; love is 'a flame would die / Held down or up too high' (Carew, *Persuasions to Enjoy*). The preoccupation with time and change begets a presentiment of unpredictable fortunes and unsustainable fulfilment which finds its own forms of witty articulation. Lovers cannot help themselves:

(For thou and I, like clocks, are wound
Up to the height, and must move round;)
Suckling, *To His Rival* (ii)

Clocks loom large in English writing after Donne. 'Lovers have in their hearts a clock still going', which they must observe in order to find 'the critical hour', but which also marks the inevitable term of bliss (Suckling, *Love's Clock*).

Poets confirmed in the appetitive premise of Donne's *Farewell to Love* and Shakespeare's Sonnet 129 persuade themselves that sexual fruition itself destroys the bliss it seeks: 'Fruition adds no new wealth but destroys, / Even kisses lose their taste' (Suckling, *Against Fruition*). They catch the contradictoriness of our condition, discovering self-defeat in our very passion for beauty and permanence:

Cloris, it is not in our power
To say how long our love will last,
It may be we within this hour
May lose those joys we now may taste;
The blessed that immortal be
From change in love are only free.
Etherege, *To a Lady, Asking Him How Long He Would Love Her*

Desire frustrates fulfilment, our rage for perpetuity undoes itself:

But we, poor slaves to hope and fear,
Are never of our joys secure;
They lessen still as they draw near,
And none but dull delights endure.
Rochester, *The Fall*

What may possibly appease our urge to wring some permanence from the flux, and find a stay against despair? Love accompanies its assurances with disabling self-doubt, making the very prospect of heaven contingent upon our fear of eternal alienation,

> Lest once more wand'ring from that heav'n
> I fall on some base heart unblessed;
> Faithless to thee, false, unforgiven,
> And lose my everlasting rest.
>
>   Rochester, *Absent from thee*

The witty scepticism of Montaigne and Donne leads at last to the conclusion that all we can ever be sure of is the witness of the present moment:

> If I by miracle, can be
> This live-long minute true to thee,
> 'Tis all that heav'n allows.
>
>   Rochester, *Love and Life*

Marvell's best poetry is precisely contemporaneous with Vaughan's, and likewise mythologises a rural retreat from the world. Yet it continually balances one mode of being against another. Even to seek a shaping spirit in it might be to frustrate the ironic many-sidedness of the poems themselves. Nonetheless Marvell's urbane poise is far removed from the nonchalance of a Suckling or an Etherege. Marvell's wit can be dry, and it evades our attempts to pin down the poet in the poetry, yet it gives his poems a peculiar power. Marvell will scarcely strike us as a poet in travail. He is a rare kind of artist who will touch the profoundest concerns of his day in the course of an elegant compliment or graceful fiction, or a bold poetic gesture. Whether or not his wit expresses a coherent metaphysical vision we cannot account for the way it works unless we allow that for him, as for Donne and Andrewes, wit offered a means to truth.

The poetry which concerns us was written in the few years around 1650 when Marvell was in his late twenties. It coincides with the climax in Vaughan's inner life which quickens *Silex Scintillans*. Marvell's lyric poetry is exhilaratingly open to the great issues which preoccupied British minds in the middle of the seventeenth century, civic no less than spiritual. Yet it encounters these exigencies on its own terms when it transforms them into graceful wit, entertaining them speculatively and often with an amused self-irony which mocks the search for intellectual coherence or spiritual renewal. To set ourselves to see what Marvell's wit is doing, what kind of apprehension it embodies, is to trace a peculiarly subtle engagement with the predicaments of metaphysical poetry.

The poise of Marvell's lyrics is an effect of their continual counterposing of opposites. They get their life from an inner debate as attitudes set each other off, or a developing argument implicitly supposes its opposite case, or seemingly opposed qualities are brought into unexpected relation. Love reconciles unlike beauties 'in fatal harmony' to bring about the lover's downfall; so that

> while she with her Eyes my Heart does bind,
> She with her Voice might captivate my Mind.
>
> *The Fair Singer*

This is the casuistical manner which the Caroline poets picked up from Donne; but even in his modish pieces Marvell's witty sleights have a substance which is lacking in the chop-logic of a Stanley or a Cleveland. He will bring opposed forces to a tense equipoise, setting off the lover's passions, which can ignite all nature, against the beauties of his mistress which have power to repair the shortcomings of the whole world; so that their precarious coupling possesses them of the best that love and nature may offer (*The Match*). Or he will coolly leave the conflicting possibilities unresolved in the interest of a more wisely perceived equivocalness, as when he brushes aside people's ingenious explanations of Clora's tears over Strephon's body with a refusal to admit such shallow conjecture:

> How wide they dream! The *Indian* Slaves
> That sink for Pearl through Seas profound,
> Would find her Tears yet deeper Waves
> And not of one the bottom sound.
>
> *Mourning*

The curious and beautiful equation of physical exploit with intellectual enquiry, so simply done in the play on 'profound', shows how even this playing wit is open to a metaphysical question. The slight conceit keeps before us the suggestion that the unfathomableness of nature in some way projects our inability to fathom our own minds.

The poet shows us attitudes abruptly turning into their opposites as circumstances change, not in a sceptical spirit but with a humorous sense of the relativeness of our firmest assurances, the ambiguity of all our commitments. Chloe earnestly repels Daphnis just until she thinks she can prevent his departure by yielding; Daphnis is hot in his importunity just until Chloe yields, when he at once refuses the offered fruition because it would pollute the pure grief of parting and heighten the anguish of loss. Not only that but their valediction itself is a fake. In the very last stanzas of the poem the poet comes back jauntily on his own device:

> But hence Virgins all beware.
> Last night he with *Phlogis* slept;
> This night for *Dorinda* kept;
> And but rid to take the Air.

Then he manages yet another twist of the argument to finish love off:

> Yet he does himself excuse;
> Nor indeed without a Cause.
> For, according to the Laws,
> Why did *Chloe* once refuse?
> *Daphnis and Chloe*

The poem has already made it clear that the laws which condemn coyness and denial cannot themselves be received unambiguously; for Nature needs both innocence and coupling, and lays aside her own rules when the cohesion of the entire world is at stake – 'Sudden Parting closer glues'. Such measures may serve Nature well enough, but they leave us locked in our dilemma since innocence and fruition are now contradictory states.

In these neo-Caroline love lyrics Marvell elegantly entertains a possibility which he elsewhere realises with some force. He plays upon the presumption that our aspirations are hopelessly at odds with our condition. The ill success his lovers lament is brought on not by the vagaries of a cruel mistress but by the perverseness of circumstances, which set their love in hopeless opposition to fate and commit them to unending strife, as if they are 'by the malignant stars, / Forced to live in storms and wars' (*The Unfortunate Lover*). The tumult which embroils Marvell's unfortunate lover projects into the elements the condition of mature love itself in its hopeless endeavour 'To make impression upon time'. The reward of love is an eternal doom of tears, sighs, hopes, despairs, which assail the lover with an elemental force of stormy seas whose power he may defy but not resist,

> Whilst he, betwixt the flames and waves,
> Like Ajax, the mad tempest braves.

We may see what Marvell is doing here if we put this picture alongside Petrarch's bold conceit of the lover as a vessel which founders in the turbulence of its own derangement, 'Passa la nave mia'. In

Marvell's poem it is the universe not the lady which denies him a fruition of love because love as we have it now runs counter to nature's laws, which the lover can only defy:

> See how he nak'd and fierce does stand,
> Cuffing the thunder with one hand . . .

The categorical title of the poem called *The Definition of Love* points the irony of a condition in which perfect love is begotten by despair, and defined precisely by the impossibility of its fruition. To consummate such a love would be to deny or abolish altogether our present state and depose the tyrannical power of fate itself. Marvell's cool impersonal irony plays off against the assurance of Donne's *The Ecstasy*. Hard images from current sciences, iron wedges, planisphere and the like define a precisely opposite condition of right love from Donne's:

> And therefore her decrees of steel
> Us as the distant Poles have placed,
> (Though Love's whole world on us doth wheel)
> Not by themselves to be embraced.

The parenthesis so nicely takes off Donne's mode as to be all but tongue in cheek. It ironically glances at the old conceited brag of fulfilled lovers to make the point that this love is perfect and enduring just because it can have no consummation. Being enviously debarred from its natural course by Fate love must find its satisfaction in a 'conjunction of the mind, / And opposition of the stars'. These lovers stand beyond the reach of time and the world's changes not because they 'die and rise the same, and prove / Mysterious' by their love but because their passion is eternally frustrated of its end. Marvell laments the brevity of desire in his own ironic way; yet he joins with Suckling and Rochester in his disillusioned acknowledgement that our commitments must be frail when their fruition brings instant change.

The common outcry of seventeenth-century love poets is that love frustrates itself because beauty and innocence are threatened by the very passions they kindle, and passion itself is destroyed by the consummation it seeks. Poets who turn from the woman-hunt to argue against fruition have at least the logic of despair, for if passion dies with its fulfilment then the best state of love must be that in which love is not consummated, or innocence actually cools desire; as when admired beauties 'are too green / Yet for lust, but not for love' (*Young Love*). Marvell's invitation to a mutual love which might crown the lovers joint monarchs of love's empire is pointedly addressed to a

young girl not yet nubile. It wistfully sets off the yearning for changeless love against the trappings of amorous intrigue to remind us how
love destroys young innocence and itself. Deceiving her father with
their snatched sport these premature lovers might just manage to
beguile old Time also. The poet can be sure of having her to himself
only if he seizes her in infancy when he need fear no rivals. His
peremptory invitation to love is made urgent by a sense of the
momentariness of our commitments, and the uncertainty of our state
altogether:

> Now then love me: time may take
> Thee before thy time away:
> Of this need we'll virtue make,
> And learn love before we may.
>
> So we win of doubtful fate; . . .

Opposite possibilities continually confront each other in these love
poems as the poet's mind beats about for ingenious ways of outfacing
or evading the hard facts of love's case. On the one hand Arcadian
lovers turn their yearning spirits from the shortcomings of their
present state to a perfected idyll of Elysium, or the author of enduring
joys, foregoing momentary pleasures in order to antedate their future
state 'By silent thinking' (*A Dialogue between Thyrsis and Dorinda*). On
the other hand an amorous haymaker brusquely settles the question
whether women better assure love by denial or by exchanging love for
love, breaking off the nice emblematic debate with an invitation to
seize the present moment:

> Then let's both lay by our rope
> And go kiss within the hay.
> *Ametas and Thestylis Making Hay-ropes*

These Arcadian dialogues draw their poignant beauty from the way in
which they haunt love's delights with love's brevity. They offer us
pastoral lovers who feel themselves menaced from within by the frailty
of passion, the shortness of desire, some dire contradiction in their
own cravings:

> C.   I have a grassy scutcheon spied,
>   Where Flora blazons all her pride.
>   The grass I aim to feast thy sheep:
>   The flowers I for thy temples keep.
> D.   Grass withers; and the flowers too fade.
> C.   Seize the short joys then, ere they vade, . . .

> Near this, a fountain's liquid bell.
> Tinkles within the concave shell.
> D.   Might a soul bathe there and be clean,
> Or slake its drought?
>   *Clorinda and Damon*

Such a breathtaking turn from the refreshment of the body to the assuagement of a soul marks a delicate balancing of commitments. The delights of sense lie disturbingly close to the anticipated delight of spirit from which they are fatally divided.

'Had we but world enough, and time': the lover tries his mistress's coyness in a double perspective of time, measuring the urgency of present desire against an Eden-like state in which persuasion and enjoyment would be free of threatening circumstance:

> An hundred years should go to praise
> Thine eyes, and on thy forehead gaze.
> Two hundred to adore each breast:
> But thirty thousand to the rest.
>   *To His Coy Mistress*

Their need to get on with it while they may follows from our general condition now in which all our ardours stand mocked as well as heightened by the onset of a bleak eternity. Our graces get their relish from their precariousness, the threat of imminent ruin:

> Thy beauty shall no more be found;
> Nor, in thy marble vault, shall sound
> My echoing song: then worms shall try
> That long-preserved virginity:
> And your quaint honour turn to dust;
> And into ashes all my lust.
> The grave's a fine and private place,
> But none, I think, do there embrace.

Marvell's lines urbanely catch that double apprehension which makes desire so urgent, the simultaneous sense of intense present being and of blank non-existence:

> But at my back I always hear
> Time's winged chariot hurrying near:
> And yonder all before us lie
> Deserts of vast eternity.

This lover is so importunate just because he feels his mortality in the present moment of keen sensation, apprehending their ashes in his lust, the penetrative worm in his own assault upon her virginity, the frigid privacy of the grave in their present opportunity for embraces.

The lover's invitation to sport insists upon present action – 'Now . . . Now . . . And now'. It presents itself in conceits which finely catch the momentariness of sensuous zest, pointing the need to seize the instant of her new maturity:

> Now, therefore, while the youthful glue
> Sits on thy skin like morning dew,
> And while thy willing soul transpires
> At every pore with instant fires,
> Now let us sport us while we may . . .

The terms delicately hover between sense and spirit; or they call such a distinction in question when they express a vitality of her entire being which would properly fulfil itself in making love while her faculties are at their keenest. They make an ironic contrast with the images of force which prescribe the lovemaking itself:

> And now, like amorous birds of prey,
> Rather at once our time devour,
> Than languish in his slow-chapped power.
> Let us roll all our strength, and all
> Our sweetness, up into one ball:
> And tear our pleasures with rough strife,
> Thorough the iron grates of life.

In the very peremptoriness of their coupling such lovers may make a combined assault upon the iron impediments of our condition, doing as much as lies in their power to outbrave time and defy our inescapable fate even if they thus choose to bring on their own fate with a self-destructive rush:

> Thus, though we cannot make our sun
> Stand still, yet we will make him run.

In these poems the tone is all. *To His Coy Mistress* catches a complex movement of the mind in which intimations of being and not being civilly set each other off. The mind remains in control, speculatively weighing up our condition rather than raging against it or succumbing to despair, and always working to reconcile the instant claims of sense with our yearning for perpetuity. Like Donne's *The Ecstasy* Marvell's poem discovers a metaphysical predicament in the persuasion to love, holding contrary impulses of our being in one imaginative order. As Donne's love poems continually do, *To His Coy Mistress* puts love in pawn to time. Yet for Donne right love lifts the lovers uniquely beyond time and change, while Marvell allows them only the prospect of outsmarting time briefly by their brave (and witty) opportunism. The best his lovers can do is to revel in their good moment even if the consummation kills them. The finely judged wit of Marvell's poem bespeaks a mind which finds little to hold on to but its poise.

Innocence, while it lasts, might be better armed than coyness to resist the world's mortality. Marvell plays on the myth of lost innocence, striking resonances from it within the terms of a pastoral idyll or a celebratory garland. Yet innocence itself is an ambiguous state. T.C.'s sacred innocence puts her so much at one with the natural life around her that she sustains nature and amends its defects, reforming the errors of the spring, lending the tulips her sweetness, disarming the roses of their thorns, protracting the life of the violets (*The Picture of Little T.C. in a Prospect of Flowers*). Nonetheless this very involvement of innocence with the processes of organic life makes it vulnerable to the common hazards of frail creatures and the forces that work against us or corrupt us; she must spare the buds when she gathers flowers lest nature should take an apt revenge and finding such precedent for the slaughter of innocents, 'ere we see, / Nip in the blossom all our hopes and thee'.

A witty quibble upon the conceit of innocent power reminds us that innocence itself will mature into dangerous sexuality and corrupt itself in cruelty. He would 'compound, / And parley with those conquering eyes' in good time, before they have tried their force to wound him:

> Ere, with their glancing wheels, they drive
> In triumph over hearts that strive,
> And them that yield but more despise . . .

The fine praise of her innocent infancy as a beauty in shadow must be conflated with a prayer to be shielded from the deadly force of her splendours when they emerge. This lover would be laid at an admiring distance only, 'Where I may see thy glories from some shade'.

In these poems the fatal threat to retired innocence comes from the world beyond the garden, which preys upon harmless trust:

> The wanton troopers riding by
> Have shot my fawn, and it will die.
> Ungentle men! They cannot thrive
> To kill thee! Thou ne'er didst alive
> Them any harm: alas, nor could
> Thy death yet do them any good.
>
> *The Nymph Complaining for the Death of Her Fawn*

The Nymph Complaining submits an idyll of innocent ardour to the harsh actuality of betrayal and destruction. Setting the scene so discreetly between pastoral fiction and current events Marvell distances without diminishing the guilt of blood and the crime of the wanton violation of trust. We are left to conclude that innocent compassion itself may hope to survive in the world only as cold marble or alabaster, inviolable to all save its own tears. The weighed words and phrases bring out the ironic pathos of the conceit:

> First my unhappy statue shall
> Be cut in marble, and withal,
> Let it be weeping too – but there
> The engraver sure his art may spare,
> For I so truly thee bemoan,
> That I shall weep though I be stone:
> Until my tears (still dropping) wear
> My breast, themselves engraving there.

Marvell's wit continually opens fresh prospects of our dealings with nature in the present state of our desires. The amorous mower offers a complex moral perspective. In quaint yet luminous conceits the mower laments the effect of love upon his labours and upon our bond with nature's creatures, whose unforced reciprocity of use he cannot share:

> Ye living lamps, by whose dear light
> The nightingale does sit so late,
> And studying all the summer night,
> Her matchless songs does meditate; . . .
> Your courteous lights in vain you waste,
> Since Juliana here is come,
> For she my mind hath so displaced
> That I shall never find my home.
>
> *The Mower to the Glow-worms*

Sexual passion may not blast the surrounding meadows but it distracts us from our true end, whereas the mower's right labours put the life of nature in his service:

> On me the morn her dew distils
> Before her darling daffodils.
> And, if at noon my toil me heat,
> The sun himself licks off my sweat.
> While, going home, the evening sweet
> In cowslip-water bathes my feet.
>> *Damon the Mower*

Distracted by love the mower mows himself. Yet this bodily wound cannot be as severe as the wound which love itself has given him; for the natural virtues of herbs and plants will suffice to heal it whereas death alone may cure the wound of love. He reminds himself not only of his own mortality but of what it is that makes him mortal. Our unnatural and infected wounds find no such healing powers in the world as nature prescribes for its own renewal.

These mower poems turn upon the conventional paradox that their outcry against the tyranny of love makes a graceful compliment to the lady whose beauties cause such disturbance. The mower himself is a deeply ambiguous figure, being at once the accomplice of nature and a death-dealing leveller; and the larger irony of his lovelorn state is that his distraction from his task lets the meadows flourish while he himself suffers the fate he should deal out:

> But these, while I with sorrow pine,
> Grew more luxuriant still and fine,
> That not one blade of grass you spied,
> But had a flower on either side;
> When Juliana came, and she
> What I do to the grass, does to my thoughts and me.
>> *The Mower's Song*

Landscape gardening raises the whole question of our traffic with the natural world which entails so much destruction and levelling. What justifies our imposing an order upon wild nature? Or what order should we seek to impose?

> Luxurious man, to bring his vice in use,
> Did after him the world seduce,
> And from the fields the flowers and plants allure,
> Where nature was most plain and pure . . .
> With strange perfumes he did the roses taint,
> And flowers themselves were taught to paint.
> The tulip, white, did for complexion seek,
> And learned to interline its cheek: . . .
>> *The Mower against Gardens*

The mower's elaborate conceits pose a central dilemma. Should we see a garden as a necessary regulation of errant nature which brings us a step nearer the first garden? Or must we take it for a corruption of the natural state, an imposing of man's vanity and doubleness upon a creation which did not fall of itself? These slight mower poems continually invite us to feel the disparity between our present order, artificially imposed, and the wild and fragrant innocence of nature:

> 'Tis all enforced, the fountain and the grot,
>   While the sweet fields do lie forgot: . . .

Marvell makes his imagined return to Eden in the hymn of the English Protestants whose boat God's providence itself has guided to a new world altogether:

> He hangs in shades the orange bright,
> Like golden lamps in a green night,
> And does in the pom'granates close
> Jewels more rich than Ormus shows.
>   *Bermudas*

These conceits, like Milton's in the description of Eden (*Paradise Lost* IV, 224–68), simply define a right order of nature and distinguish it from our own familiar artifices. The hopeful voyagers celebrate a haven of living riches and pleasures where there is no fatal apple, the very trees recall the Holy Land, night is not black but green, the pearls are living gospels, the primal rocks make a natural temple. Yet this is no mere daydream of a place where the life of sense can be naturally at one with the sacred life of the spirit. For this unspoiled second Eden actually exists, doubtless because it stands quite apart from our blighted hemisphere; and its discovery now makes a providential recovery of a bit of the original creation which still survives in our world.

Bermudas attests that quiet and innocence are sacred plants which we now find only among the plants. Marvell makes a spiritual imperative of Walton's epigraph 'study to be quiet'. Yet his garden poetry never lets us forget the world beyond the garden or our own incapacity to sustain the state of paradise for more than a moment. *The Garden* evokes the poet's resolved quiet of mind in an authentic English garden:

> How vainly men themselves amaze
> To win the palm, the oak, or bays,
> And their uncessant labours see
> Crowned from some single herb or tree . . .

So exquisite a poise bespeaks a self-composure which the poem sustains throughout. The wit continually invites us to measure the activities of the world against these briefly enjoyed natural pleasures, humorously reminding us of the natural divinity which plants have kept and we have forfeited, or implicitly prompting us to compare our state in this garden with our fallen condition and our falls:

> Stumbling on melons, as I pass,
> Ensnared with flowers, I fall on grass.

The tone of genial rumination and the civil flow of the couplets only temper the conceited balancing of moral alternatives. Why should we value incessant public activity before inner repose, society before solitude, sexual passion before calm self-content? Or why should our lives be regulated by clockwork rather than the natural rhythms of organic life, gain rather than private wisdom? A life of innocent sense is tried against the life of mind and of soul, and then against this recovered harmony of our being in the garden:

> Meanwhile the mind, from pleasures less,
> Withdraws into its happiness: . . .

> Here at the fountain's sliding foot,
> Or at some fruit-tree's mossy root,
> Casting the body's vest aside,
> My soul into the boughs does glide:
> There like a bird it sits, and sings,
> Then whets, and combs its silver wings;
> And, till prepared for longer flight,
> Waves in its plumes the various light.

> Such was that happy garden-state,
> While man there walked without a mate: . . .

So natural a self-transcendence from sense to mind and mind to soul keeps us heedful of a state in which the life of sense was one with the life of spirit and a life of spirit inhered in the life of sense. If Eve's arrival in the Garden preluded our loss of bliss it is presumably because her coming inflamed the passions, as well as turning a solitude into a society.

Choosing known country domains for types of his natural state Marvell celebrates an achieved and not a merely wished-for retreat towards the primal felicity. Complimentary description, moral emblem and metaphysical meditation develop together by the syn-thesising power of wit as though the wit itself is no more than a means of bringing out the harmonious wholeness of its object:

> See how the arched earth does here
> Rise in a perfect hemisphere! . . .
> It seems as for a model laid,
> And that the world by it was made.
> *Upon the Hill and Grove at Bilbrough*

The terrain of the Fairfax estate at Bilbrough becomes the outward style of a moral character which was formed upon a model of celestial order; physical features express a spiritual disposition here because the estate embodies the qualities of its master:

> Here learn, ye mountains more unjust,
> Which to abrupter greatness thrust,
> That do with your hook-shouldered height
> The earth deform and heaven fright, . . .
> Learn here those humble steps to tread,
> Which to securer glory lead.

The conceits define a public eminence which is hallowed by retired meditation. They propose the rare example of a just career in the world whose glories are incidental upon a sacred calling such as the true order of nature promotes.

Upon Appleton House rehearses such a regenerative discipleship to nature. It seeks a reconciliation of sense, mind and spirit in the order of a country house. The poem is shaped by time. It progresses through the day and the year, then makes a retreat back through Old Testament times to a type of innocent virtue in the garden, before the darkening prospect itself gently returns us to our present state.

The elaborate conceit is launched in the opening laud of the dynasty of the Fairfaxes, which tells how that new sacred order replaces with a better truth the old formal regimen of the nuns who previously held the house as their convent. The nuns represent a life of retired insulation from the world which is harmless enough but enfeebling, and leaves them only superstitions and tart tongues to oppose against the onslaught of the ancestral Fairfax. This time the disruptive force from outside has justice with it and even seems irresistible, as if fate supervenes upon an old order and time-hallowed growth to make a better state. The nuns who incarcerate Fairfax's heiress-bride have no hope of preventing the union or intercepting 'the great race' of Fairfaxes which will spring from it. This better state of marriage and offspring may well be taken for the work of fate if only because it has already come about. Its consequences are there in the house.

The new sacred house thus founded, the dynasty of the Fairfaxes, embodies a sounder understanding of active life and our relation to the world than the former foundation represented. It discovers a moral order in the order of nature which its present head duly observes:

> For he did, with his utmost skill,
> Ambition weed, but conscience till –
> Conscience, that heaven-nursed plant,
> Which most our earthy gardens want.
> A prickling leaf it bears, and such
> As that which shrinks at every touch;
> But flowers eternal, and divine,
> That in the crowns of saints do shine.

Such a wise reciprocity between man and nature also helps nature, whose lapsed state may be partly restored by the harmony projected upon it. Marvell's conceits show the garden peacefully enacting the ceremonial order of the man's life as if to rectify or repel the ruin which attends such military operations beyond its bounds:

> See how the flowers, as at parade,
> Under their colours stand displayed:
> Each regiment in order grows,
> That of the tulip, pink, and rose.

These ceremonies remind us that the garden itself only imperfectly imitates the larger order which the world once observed. Yet it stands amid an alien world as a favoured place, an island of virtue which by grace and wisdom still preserves at least something of the primal state.

The poem keeps us poignantly aware of the diminution of hope which the vision of this garden represents. In the wake of the Civil Wars the elect nation dwindles to a select – and embattled – country estate. Britain has betrayed its destiny and frustrated the providence which worked to restore it to the state of Eden:

> Oh thou, that dear and happy isle
> The garden of the world ere while,
> Thou paradise of four seas,
> Which heaven planted us to please,
> But, to exclude the world, did guard
> With watery if not flaming sword;
> What luckless apple did we taste,
> To make us mortal, and thee waste?
> Unhappy! shall we never more
> That sweet militia restore,

> When gardens only had their towers,
> And all the garrisons were flowers,
> When roses only arms might bear,
> And men did rosy garlands wear?

In the early 1650s such questions give urgency to the search for an order nearer the first state.

Marvell's poem conducts this search in ingenious geniality even as it celebrates the changing life of the Fairfax estate. In the tall grass the grasshoppers become giants and mock the men who walk beneath them – 'They, in their squeaking laugh, contemn / Us as we walk more low than them'. Dew and slaughtered quails rain down together, as manna rained upon the Israelites of old. The very cattle appear in several perspectives, now scaled down as in a painting, now as spots on faces, now fleas, and at last as the heavenly constellations (stanzas 57–8). Such extraordinary conceits transact the brilliant transformation scenes by which the estate becomes a world and a cosmos in itself; and they simultaneously suggest a return through Old Testament times towards primal innocence (stanza 56). The unsettling of our worldly acceptances is a condition of the wisdom which this estate embodies. The shifting prospects dispossess humanity of its supposed pre-eminence in nature; and a metamorphosis of species and functions disturbs our expectation of a stable order. The world changes as our point of view and circumstances alter:

> Let others tell the paradox,
> How eels now bellow in the ox;
> How horses at their tails do kick,
> Turned as they hang to leeches quick;
> How boats can over bridges sail;
> And fishes do the stables scale.
> How salmons trespassing are found;
> And pikes are taken in the pound.

The instability of what we take for knowledge is caught in bizarre images of total relativeness which are the more telling because they present a world quite suddenly unfamiliar, as it is when we first see it through optical instruments.

The estate which enacts this hieroglyph of relativism also provides the purifying Flood and the saving Ark. The Ark is the green wood itself in which the poet takes refuge on equal terms with all other created life, 'And where all creatures might have shares, / Although in armies, not in pairs'. Through relativeness, chaos, and Flood we are carried back to a better state, that of the *prischi teologi* who shared the language and wisdom of the original creatures. The conceits divertingly plot the poet's progress towards that wise oneness with plants and animals which will open nature's mystic book to him:

> Thus I, easy philosopher,
> Among the birds and trees confer,
> And little now to make me wants
> Or of the fowls, or of the plants:
> Give me but wings as they, and I
> Straight floating on the air shall fly:
> Or turn me but, and you shall see
> I was but an inverted tree.

Such ironically outlandish wit half-mocks the search it furthers while nonetheless keeping us alert to the paradox that what the world takes for unnaturalness may be simple truth. The poet's better state as an animal or a plant belies mere worldly wisdom, rank, passion. The oddity of the conceit which transforms a man into a natural prelate may measure our false understanding of priesthood:

> And see how chance's better wit
> Could with a mask my studies hit!
> The oak leaves me embroider all,
> Between which caterpillars crawl:
> And ivy, with familiar trails,
> Me licks, and clasps, and curls, and hales.
> Under this antic cope I move
> Like some great prelate of the grove.

In playing off the estate against the turmoil which surrounds it the conceits never allow us to suppose that this garden presents a practical alternative to a life in the world. It is not a nirvana but a restoring refuge, which can offer its votaries an absolute point of moral reference in its version of civil life. There is no question of a daydream evasion of actuality or an exemption from the effects of sin. The poet's yearning to remain here struggles with his need to return, and may be indulged only at a price:

> Bind me, ye woodbines, in your twines,
> Curl me about, ye gadding vines,
> And, oh, so close your circles lace,
> That I may never leave this place:
> But lest your fetters prove too weak,

> Ere I your silken bondage break,
> Do you, O brambles, chain me too,
> And, courteous briars, nail me through.

The images of a ravishing bondage invite us to take this transfixion by bramble-bonds and thorn-nails for the natural penalty of sin, which must be paid even in this garden, albeit at a milder rate than that suffering which the world still imposes upon Christ.

The estate may no more isolate itself from the lapsed world than it can undo the consequences of sin. The flood which inundates it leaves a world as if born again, without malice and without deceitful distortions yet just briefly recalling the first state:

> No serpent new nor crocodile
> Remains behind our little Nile,
> Unless itself you will mistake,
> Among these meads the only snake.
>
> See in what wanton harmless folds
> It everywhere the meadow holds;
> And yet its muddy back doth lick,
> Till as a crystal mirror slick,
> Where all things gaze themselves, and doubt
> If they be in it or without.
> And for his shade which therein shines,
> Narcissus-like, the sun too pines.

Mary Fairfax's appearance in the garden only momentarily suspends the course of nature before darkness returns; and her wanderings make a far greater disturbance in nature than did Eve's ministrations in Eden. The conceits elegantly catch the admiring suspension of nature's flux which the girl's innocent beauty imposes:

> So when the shadows laid asleep
> From underneath these banks do creep, . . .
> The modest halcyon comes in sight,
> Flying betwixt the day and night;
> And such an horror calm and dumb,
> Admiring Nature does benumb.
>
> The viscous air, wheres'e'er she fly,
> Follows and sucks her azure dye;
> The jellying stream compacts below,
> If it might fix her shadow so;
> The stupid fishes hang, as plain
> As flies in crystal overta'en; . . .

The little girl's blameless virtue puts her in close communion with the garden. She converses with nature, bestows her own pure beauty upon it, learns from it how to avert love's wars and snares. Marvell's tribute to his young pupil wittily enlarges a metaphysical conceit of regeneration such as Donne and Vaughan might have approved. It brings the present state of nature back into one order with the primal state, discovering a condition of grace in an actual human being and the topography of a country seat.

Yet innocence itself cannot long hold back night or chaos. Marvell draws the poem together with a final reminder of the world's derangement, which the constitution of this garden amends:

> 'Tis not, what once it was, the world,
> But a rude heap together hurled,
> All negligently overthrown,
> Gulfs, deserts, precipices, stone.
> Your lesser world contains the same,
> But in more decent order tame; . . .

Such a microcosm of the world as it was, and might still have been, calls for more than human power to uphold. The elaborate conceit mirrors the general ruin of an order which has been recovered in this one household by particular grace. At Nun Appleton House alone the elements still hold a civil order in their fit places:

> You, heaven's centre, Nature's lap,
> And paradise's only map.

This 'You' is wittily ambiguous. The house shares with the girl the hyperbole which celebrates in this little world nothing less than that oneness of heaven with nature which makes it a unique pattern of paradise.

The notorious conceits of the final stanza follow straight on from this reminder of the disorders beyond the garden:

> But now the salmon-fishers moist
> Their leathern boats begin to hoist,
> And like Antipodes in shoes,
> Have shod their heads in their canoes.
> How tortoise-like, but not so slow,
> These rational amphibii go!

From hyperbole to burlesque. Such diverting ingenuities show the common order reasserting itself even here. There is no disorder in the garden, but no escaping from time there either as returning darkness brings back the ambiguities, reversals, topsy-turvydom of things. Light passes to the other side:

> Let's in: for the dark hemisphere
> Does now like one of them appear.

The droll analogy makes a fit close to a meditation upon the right order of nature, discovering a global parallel in the human accident and a metaphysical portent in both.

Such an emblematic oneness of thing and idea resolves for this unique case the struggle between sense and intelligence or spirit which is always going on in Marvell's lyrics. The issue is far from clear-cut. The two metaphysical dialogues do not simply pit soul against body or spiritual life against sensual indulgence, as Ellrodt supposes.[26] They show us that the relation between the several orders of our nature is more painfully complex than that. These anatomical conceits define the agony of embodied spirit, the dilemma of spiritualised sense. The soul has good claim to be the prisoner of the body. Is it not fettered in bones and limbs, deafened and blinded by the senses, hung upright as a felon condemned to torment

> in chains
> Of nerves, and arteries, and veins,
> Tortured, besides each other part,
> In a vain head, and double heart?
> *A Dialogue between the Soul and Body*

Yet the body stands at the mercy of the tyrannical soul, which racks it with moral compulsions and conflicting passions:

> O, who shall me deliver whole,
> From bonds of this tyrannic soul,
> Which, stretched upright, impales me so,
> That mine own precipice I go; . . .
>
> Whom first the cramp of hope does tear,
> And then the palsy shakes of fear;
> The pestilence of love does heat,
> Or hatred's hidden ulcer eat; . . .
> What but a soul could have the wit
> To build me up for sin so fit?

The dialogue brings out the contradiction in our nature which sets elements so interdependent to oppress and torment each other. Choice itself becomes self-denying. The gratification which the resolved soul must renounce in favour of heavenly joys is not

hedonistic self-indulgence but created pleasure, the delighted participation of sense in the natural life around it:

> Lay aside that warlike crest,
> And of Nature's banquet share:
> Where the souls of fruits and flowers
> Stand prepared to heighten yours.
> *A Dialogue, between the Resolved Soul and Created Pleasure*

These poems are not so much moral debates as attempts to define
our nature, whose complexities and self-frustrations Marvell
dramatises with hypersubtle wit. *Eyes and Tears* follows the quarrel
between sense and spirit in the functioning of a faculty which is
characterised by conflicting ends:

> How wisely Nature did decree
> With the same eyes to weep and see!
> That, having viewed the object vain,
> We might be ready to complain.

The conceit defines the peculiar anguish of a divided existence in
which sense draws us an opposite way from spirit and we know the
world at all only at the cost of our innocence. To be human is to be
pleased with the corrupted world while we nonetheless grieve at our
corruption, a dilemma which cannot be eased until sense and spirit
become one:

> Thus let your streams o'erflow your springs,
> Till eyes and tears be the same things:
> And each the other's difference bears;
> These weeping eyes, those seeing tears.

Sense and intelligence subtly interwork in the witty argument of
The Coronet, which takes flowers for emblems of poetry while still
keeping them before us as natural growths. The poem follows out
conflicting impulses which inextricably tangle, intertwining with
personal vanity even the urge to write poems of penitence to Christ:

> When for the thorns with which I long, too long,
> With many a piercing wound,
> My Saviour's head have crowned,
> I seek with garlands to redress that wrong:
> Through every garden, every mead,
> I gather flowers (my fruits are only flowers),
> Dismantling all the fragrant towers
> That once adorned my shepherdess's head.

The search for flowers becomes a moral progress, which carries the poet from sin to remorse and then from simple piety to a shrewder sense of his own involvement in the corrupted world. With the flowers which he culls and wreathes into pious art comes the disguised serpent also, the flowers interwoven with the hidden evil, the poetry folded about 'With wreaths of fame and interest'. When the very attempt to redress his sins frustrates itself then he can do nothing but submit his will to Christ. Christ alone may disentangle the loving urges from the corrupt, or simply choose to destroy the garland with the serpent:

> But Thou who only couldst the serpent tame,
> Either his slippery knots at once untie;
> And disentangle all his winding snare;
> Or shatter too with him my curious frame,
> And let these wither, so that he may die,
> Though set with skill and chosen out with care:
> That they, while Thou on both their spoils dost tread,
> May crown thy feet, that could not crown thy head.

Garlands, poems, and the poet's own corrupted nature come together as the 'curious frame' which may need to be shattered to adorn Christ, who will then be set off with the spoils of his triumph. The argument goes forward in several terms at once, coupling the blight of flowers with the poet's tainted motive for writing verses to Christ as if flowers and poetic impulse share the same malaise. The rhetoric sweeps the developing thought to its close by way of gathering the several elements into a single order, which coheres because they all confirm it. For this poet thorns and flowers at once exemplify and emblemise a spiritual condition. They share the poet's simultaneous involvement in organic life and spiritual being.

On a Drop of Dew draws out the soul's quarrel with the body in a natural emblem which is more than just a figure of speech. The morning dew in the rose poses the predicament of a pure nature in an alien element, expressing the soul's distaste for sense, and perpetual yearning towards its sacred origin:

> Yet careless of its mansion new,
> For the clear region where 'twas born
>   Round in itself incloses:
>   And in its little globe's extent,
> Frames as it can its native element.
>   How it the purple flower does slight,

> Scarce touching where it lies,
>   But gazing back upon the skies,
>   Shines with a mournful light,
>   Like its own tear,
> Because so long divided from the sphere.

Yet the rose may also claim its due, having its own sensuous beauty and its rich organic life. The issue between sense and spirit cannot be resolved while the aspiration of the soul remains unreconciled to the life of the body. Neither body nor soul alone will suffice to make us human or perpetuate our being; for the rose soon fades, while the dew simply loses itself in eternity when 'the glories of th' almighty sun' dissolve its cold white purity. The poem expresses the dilemma of creatures of a double nature who find themselves caught irresolvably between the several elements of their being, struggling to reconcile their sensible constitution with their spiritual aspirations, the life of nature with the life of grace.

An Horatian Ode stages the collision of unlike elements in the political sphere, where the contradictory aspirations of our nature best articulate themselves in a judicious balancing of moral claims. The *Ode* invests its particular public occasion with a significance which is unconfined by time and place. Marvell discovers a destiny at work in current conflicts which transforms a country gentleman into a cosmic force, and pits him against the anointed king in a clash of universal opposites:

> So restless Cromwell could not cease
> In the inglorious arts of peace,
>   But through adventurous war
>   Urged his active star.
> And, like the three-forked lightning, first
> Breaking the clouds where it was nursed,
>   Did thorough his own side
>   His fiery way divide . . .
> Then burning through the air he went,
> And palaces and temples rent;
>   And Caesar's head at last
>   Did through his laurels blast.
> 'Tis madness to resist or blame
> The force of angry heaven's flame: . . .

Divinely sanctioned power opposes ancient (and divine?) rights, necessity challenges the prescriptions of time:

> Though justice against fate complain,
> And plead the ancient rights in vain:
>   But those do hold or break
>   As men are strong or weak.
> Nature, that hateth emptiness,
> Allows of penetration less:
>   And therefore must make room
>   Where greater spirits come.

In following out his providential destiny Cromwell drastically shifts our perspective of history and our moral perspective too. He cuts right across the nice calculus of rights and wrongs which mirrors the contradictions of our own nature. Yet the human issues are too finely poised to be resolved by the constitutional outcome alone. Marvell's witty projection of the equivocalness of our state is fulfilled in the celebration of a human comportment which outbraves political mischance:

> He nothing common did or mean
> Upon that memorable scene:
>   But with his keener eye
>   The axe's edge did try:
> Nor called the gods with vulgar spite
> To vindicate his helpless right,
>   But bowed his comely head,
>   Down, as upon a bed.

An Horatian Ode gets its intellectual thrust from Marvell's bold realisation of the conceit of a providence unpredictably at work in history. The vision scarcely survived its occasion. Cromwell's death just eight years later offered scope for a metaphysical hyperbole in the manner of Donne's funeral *Anniversaries*, which Marvell had already drawn upon for his poem on the first anniversary of Cromwell's rule. Yet *A Poem upon the Death of His Late Highness the Lord Protector* attempts an eulogy of Cromwell's public and domestic virtues which needs no exercise of wit. Providence favours Cromwell just by allowing him to die unheroically of grief for his daughter's death rather than violently in battle. Nature's sorrow for his demise displays itself in a self-destructive summer storm whose violence spends itself in bombast:

> He unconcerned the dreadful passage crossed;
> But, oh, what pangs that death did Nature cost!
> First the great thunder was shot off, and sent

The signal from the starry battlement.
The winds receive it, and its force outdo,
As practising how they could thunder too; . . .
    Nature, it seemed with him would Nature vie;
He with Eliza. It with him would die . . .

Cromwell himself is celebrated as an exemplary father and leader who takes with him from this world all the qualities which give zest to our lives:

    Valour, religion, friendship, prudence died
    At once with him, and all that's good beside;
    And we death's refuse, nature's dregs, confined
    To loathsome life, alas! are left behind.

The inertness of these personifications contrasts with the witty life of the conceits in *An Horatian Ode*, or *Upon Appleton House* – not to say Donne's *Anniversaries* – which continually open a universal consequence in the natural events. The shift from metaphysical wit to a rhetorical deployment of figures of speech marks a drastic narrowing of vision. Marvell marches indefatigably on to his career as a politician and political satirist; and a half-century of metaphysical striving begins to give place to the manners of the Town.

The true legacy of Donne shows up in metaphysical endeavour rather than in the trappings of a metaphysical style, or in Cavalier attitudes. The poems in Cowley's *The Mistress*, 1647, 'became the favourite love poems of the age'.[27] They rework Donne's *Songs and Sonnets*, carrying off their borrowings with a negligent ease of manner and an elaborate elegance of complimentary conceit which quite alters their force. Cowley's lover poses just Donne's questions. How could the poet possibly love his mistress more than he loves her now, when her beauties are already unsurpassable (*The Increase*)? How may their love survive a bodily separation?

        Ask me not what my love shall do or be
            (Love which is soul to body, and soul of me)
        When I am separated from thee; . . .
                                            The Separation

The drift drolly mocks the manner. Metaphysical terms whizz around as if to make question of the steadfastness of our commitments in time, our stable identity, the relation of body to soul in love. Yet they serve just as ingenious exhortations to pleasure:

> Indeed I must confess,
> When souls mix 'tis an happiness;
> But not complete till bodies too combine,
> And closely as our minds together join;
> But half of Heaven the souls in glory taste,
> 'Till by love in Heaven at last,
> Their bodies too are placed.
>
> *Platonic Love*

Souls know beauty by 'the body's help', and simply abuse that trust if they then seek to exclude the body from love. The argument of *The Ecstasy* merges with the claim for the resurrection of the body to make a persuasion to bodily union. Spiritual love is opposed against animal coupling just to give the force of reasoning to the pleas for the satisfaction of desire:

> So angels love; so let them love for me;
> When I'am all soul, such shall my love too be:
> Who nothing here but like a spirit would do,
> In a short time (believ't) will be one too:
> But shall our love do what in beasts we see?
> Even beasts eat too, but not so well as we . . .
> Beasts do the same: 'tis true; but ancient fame
> Says, gods themselves turned beasts to do the same.
>
> *Answer to the Platonics*

Donne's mode of thinking and discourse gets turned to the ends of an amorous pursuit. This poet really does affect the metaphysical Don Juan whom Pierre Legouis thought he found in Donne's *The Ecstasy*.[28] His metaphysical knowingness sets off his all-out commitment to bodily life; the Cavalier manner puts a gloss upon his dedication to sensual pleasures. He is adept at the brisk sleight of mind which diverts the most rarefied ideas to earthy designs. A transcendental ideal gets turned to a persuasion to undress:

> Fairest thing that shines below,
> Why in this robe dost thou appear?
> Wouldst thou a white most perfect show,
> Thou must at all no garment wear: . . .
>
> *Verses Lost Upon A Wager*

The argument of *Air and Angels* suddenly issues in erotic fantasy:

If Truth it self (as other angels do
   When they descend to human view)
In a material form would deign to shine,
   'Twould imitate or borrow thine,
So dazzling bright, yet so transparent clear,
So well proportioned would the parts appear;
   Happy the eye which Truth could see
   Clothed in a shape like thee,
   But happier far the eye
Which could thy shape naked like Truth espy!

The metaphysical concerns he invokes do not shape his awareness and are never followed through, serving just to sustain a literary game. They get mummified in conceits, which are metaphysical conceits in a wholly unimportant sense:

My affection no more perish can
Than the First Matter that compounds a man.
   Hereafter if one dust of me
   Mixed with another's substance be,
'Twill leaven that whole lump with love of thee.

Let Nature if she please disperse
My atoms over all the universe,
   At the last they easily shall
   Themselves know, and together call;
For thy love, like a mark, is stamped on all.

All-over, love

The conceit of an atomised survival bears out his protestations of undying love but can scarcely have substance in itself. It wittily makes a courtesy of a current metaphysical puzzle. Comparison with Donne seems invited just to point the ingenious redirection. When this lover seeks to prove his entire dependence upon his mistress he flaunts his raid on the *Songs and Sonnets*:

Her body is my soul; laugh not at this,
   For by my life I swear it is.

The Soul

The compliment is ingeniously turned in the erotic fancy that her body is his soul because it preserves his being and breath.

Cowley pointedly domesticates the preoccupations of Cavalier poetry. His argument against fruition is the purely practical one that we spoil our appetite for sex if we get too much of it too easily. A little difficulty and danger lend sauce to desire: 'if once he lose his

sting' love 'grows a drone' (*Against Fruition*). His pondering of love
and life confronts him with the paradox that he has experienced more
than twenty years of life in a mere twelve months of love. Yet this
curious double pace does not mean that he lives two lives at once or
stands miraculously beyond the course of nature. On the contrary, it
corresponds to the natural motion of the sun which advances quickly
and slowly at the same time:

> At once with double course in the same sphere,
> He runs the day, and walks the year.
>
> *Love and Life*

So with this lover's life, which goes slowly when his soul refers itself
to his own concern alone and flies when it relates itself to her, 'and
then is love'. The paradox of the lover's double apprehension of time,
in which Donne and Rochester discover such metaphysical consequence, is here quite rationally accounted for. It is brought under a
law of nature such as the movement of the heavens confirms. The
poem gets its life from the adroitness with which the analogy is
managed, and eschews metaphysical questions.

   If *The Mistress* really did become the favourite love poems of the age
then we cannot doubt the way the age was going. Cowley openly
stakes his ground in a poem written hard upon the Restoration, some
fourteen years later than *The Mistress*. His ode *To the Royal Society*
(*c.* 1661) celebrates the advent of a true philosophy which is founded
in things rather than in words or the exploration of our own minds.
This intellectual liberation was prepared by Bacon, who urged it in the
teeth of the continuing attempts of pedagogues to divert the infant
Philosophy from its right course:

> That his own business he might quite forget,
> They amused him with the sports of wanton wit,
> With the desserts of poetry they fed him,
> Instead of solid meats t'increase his force; . . .

To turn back into our own minds from that external world would be
to go on snatching at the forbidden tree, striving to emulate God by
discovering truth and falsehood, good and evil 'Without the senses'
aid, within ourself':

> For 'tis God only who can find
> All nature in his mind.

Bacon swept aside such arrogant misconceptions and opened up the
orchard of the world to us:

> From words, which are but pictures of the thought,
> (Though we our thoughts from them perversely drew,)
> To things, the mind's right object, he it brought;
> Like foolish birds to painted grapes we flew;
> He sought and gathered for our use the True.

The right object of the mind's activity, and the touchstone of reality and truth, is the external world as we perceive it through our senses. Words must be pictures of things and not of thoughts; and to draw our thoughts from words is to fly to painted grapes instead of real ones. Such an idea of the relation of language to truth drastically limits the scope of wit, and of poetry altogether. It takes us straight out of the sphere of the metaphysical poets and into the new era of empirical science which Descartes and Locke were preparing and the Royal Society precisely inaugurated.[29] The unkindest irony is that Cowley should have become Johnson's model of the metaphysical poet.

The domestication of grace is carried to its literal limit in the poems which Edward Taylor wrote in America from the 1680s to the 1720s, seemingly as preparatory meditations upon the texts for his sermons. Taylor's witty forte is the rendering of sacramental effects in the terms of homely pursuits, a feat of correlation which he carries through in the most exotic points. Christ's human agency is presented as an alchemical process of distillation in which holy love provides the heat, Christ's body is the still, his mouth is the neck of the vessel, and grace is the liquid gold which must be dug out of its own mine to tincture the liquor of his utterances. The poet pleads that his own soul may be 'thy phial' to hold this precious essence of Christ's words:

> Grace in thy lips poured out's as liquid gold,
> Thy bottle make my soul, Lord, it to hold.
> *Meditation. Ps.45.2*

The sheer lumpishness of the writing scarcely serves a wit which seems so arbitrarily exercised. Taylor picks up his terms of correspondence from the tavern, the kitchen, the medicine chest, the common trades and professions. Souls are lost at Prisoner's Base, and sin plays nine-hole in the poet's head. His sinful heart is Satan's bowling alley 'where he shears his fleece / At Nine Pins, Nine Holes, Morrice, Fox and Geese'; or it is a gaming den in which pride and passion, atheism and blasphemy prance obscenely and Satan practises his con tricks with cards and dice, playing for souls 'At Cudgels, Kit-Cat . . . / . . . Noddy,

Ruff-and-trumped, Jing, Post-and-Pair, / Put, One-and-thirty, and such other ware' (*Meditation 1 Joh.2.2*). The poet is not sure whether he himself serves as God's money or God's purse, and asks God to be his spectacles so that he may clearly see what purpose he fulfils; his faith is a golden quill through which he sucks the vital spirits of Christ's blood; God is a judge who has Christ as his attorney, the Holy Ghost as his registrar, the angels as his sergeants, and Satan as accusing counsel; sinful men are prisoners who look to Christ for their release from the pit, and may then escape by paddling their canoes up a red sea of blood; Satan is a cook who sauces his dishes poisonously with sin.

Taylor has a strong line in culinary and alimentary wit. 'Spiritual crisping pins' regulate the assemblies of the blessed. Christ's works make a divine art of cookery in which Christ is both chef and ingredients, his deity wielding the rolling-pin upon his humanity so as to knead flesh and blood into a fine pastry, and also to press out the choicest drink:

> Here's Meat, and Drink for Souls to use: (Good Cheer,)
>   Cooked up, and Brewed by Pure Divinity
> The juice tunned up in Human Casks that ne'er
>   Were musty made by any Sluttery.
>   And tapped by Grace's hand whose table hold
> This fare in dishes far more rich than gold.
> Meditation. Joh.6.53

Christ mixes the fruits of his divine nature with his human flesh and blood to make a plum cake for the poet's soul, which gives it eternal life. Christ's Passion is the roasting of a piece of mutton in its own juices, towards which the poet offers his soul for a dripping-pan in return for a share in the sacrificial meat:

> My trencher, Lord, with thy roast mutton dress:
>   And my dry biscuit in thy dripping sap.
> And feed my soul with thy choice angel mess: . . .
> Meditation on Gal.3.16

Christ in the grave is another Jonah, whom the whale has swallowed down as a rich pill 'Of working physic full of virtue which / Doth purge death's constitution of its ill, / And womblecrops her stomach where it sticks' (*Meditation. 2 Cor.5.17*). This womble-cropping makes the whale sick, as well it might, and brings on the Resurrection:

It heaves her stomach till her hasps off fly.
And out he comes cast up, raised up thereby.
Meditation 30. Math.12.40

Witty piety could scarcely work less like metaphysical wit. For all his uncouthness Taylor does invite comparison with George Herbert in his witty sifting of grace and the eucharist. He follows Ledesma and Crashaw when he renders sacred events in homely terms. His wit has a certain rude vigour. Yet it does not embody a metaphysical apprehension.

To identify Christ's sufferings on the cross with the preparation of roast lamb for the table is not to discover a marvellous conjunction of two unlike orders of being. It is just to represent one sensible condition in terms of another so as to bring out Christ's literal offering of his body to us in the eucharist. The incongruity of the coupling does not mark the double status of a historical event which is also an eternal truth, or the working of an order of grace in and through the order of nature. It lies in the physicalising of the sacrament, the gross reduction of Christ's death to a domestic banality which the poet arbitrarily contrives for a particular rhetorical purpose.

Taylor's wit is simply a means of re-presenting the drama of sin and grace so as to accommodate its mysteries to people's daily lives. It is essentially a tool of rhetoric, which serves a doctrinal end. Yet it does follow out a conception of spiritual being. The continual rendering of the sacraments in terms of homely use assimilates grace itself to common nature. The effect of the wit in these poems is to limit the aspiration of the spirit to the perfecting of sensible life.

SACRED EARTH

When Lancelot Andrewes wittily laboured to discover in the Gun-powder Plot the trappings of an abortive birth he followed out an understanding which is central to his ministry.[1] Andrewes' own justification of his method cannot be in doubt, since it is implicit throughout his sermon. He finds in the very fortuities of the Plot not only an instance or fulfilment of the prescription in Isaiah 37 but the manifestation of a mystery. He had set out the ground of such a read-ing of occurrences in the world when he spoke of the nature of a sacrament in a Christmas Day sermon preached in the same place to a like audience some nine years earlier:

It doth manifestly represent, it doth mystically impart what it representeth. There is in it even by the very institution both a manifestation, and that visibly, to set before us this flesh; and a mystical communication to infeoffe us in it or make us partakers of it. For the elements; what can be more properly fit to represent unto us the union with our nature, than things that do unite themselves to our nature?[2]

Andrewes, in sum, simply carries through in events they had all experienced his understanding that we inhabit a creation in which 'Truth shall bud out of the earth'[3] and 'all things answer one another, first and last'.[4] Such unlikely contingencies as the thwarting of a plot to blow up the King in Parliament may discover the divine presence.

This last-second failure of the plot affords a particularly telling manifestation of God's providence. We see the providential dis-position of King James's affairs as it were by negative or contrary instance, in which God frustrates a devilish birth at the moment of its fruition. The events of that November night in 1605 simply re-enacted a timeless pattern, revealing God's peculiar design in the very narrowness of the escape. Andrewes finds an Old Testament prototype in the catastrophic frustration of Sennacherib's first assault

on Judah, and a powerful historical confirmation in the destruction of
the Armada in '88. All these instances disclose the character of God's
working in human affairs in the way they reverse our normal
estimation of success or failure. What the participants experience as
danger or disaster may actually be a proof of saving grace, the
occasion of a triumph; once that is realised then dismay on the instant
turns to joy. More than that, God's nature reveals itself in quite
unlikely circumstances which may even strike us as a bizarre embodiment of pure spirit. Indeed the very incongruity of the physical
presence with the divine attributes it incarnates marks its sacramental
status.

Andrewes pointedly controverts such refined conceits as the Neoplatonic cult of beauty, which starts in the premise that even the most
spiritualised worldly appearances only shadow a higher reality, or offer
the first steps towards it. By contrast he understands that the divine
nature conjoins itself with the earthiest material elements to work in
the world, however we mistake it at first. We discover spiritual truth
not by turning away from a world of illusions altogether, or by
leaving sense behind in our aspiration towards a higher meaning, but
by understanding physical events better in their own right, piercing
into them, as Andrewes himself tellingly describes the process of
coming to comprehend Christ's Passion.[5]

'The Passion is a piece of perspective':[6] to grasp the true nature of
happenings in the world we must take a double perspective of them,
or even a triple perspective if we consider our own condition and
posture in the face of inevitable death and judgment. When he
meditates on Christ's Passion Andrewes shows why we may need to
see the same event in quite opposite ways:

Two pieces therefore He maketh choice of, and but two, and presenteth Him
to our eye in two forms only: 1. As hanging on the cross; 2. as sitting on the
throne. 1. His Passion, and 2. His Session; these two. And these two, with
very good and perfect correspondence to the two former. By the cross He is
Author; by the throne He is Finisher of our faith. As Man on the cross,
Author; as God on the Throne, Finisher.[7]

Then he goes on to contrast the corresponding properties of the two
conditions, a regal crown and a crown of thorns, an imperial robe and
a body covered in blood, and so on. S. L. Bethell pointed out the
liturgical warrant for such a double vision of the cross in the Good
Friday hymn *Vexilla regis* of the sixth-century Bishop Venantius
Fortunatus:[8]

Arbor decora et fulgida,
Ornata regis purpura,
Electa digno stipite
Tam sancta membra tangere.

Beata, cujus brachiis
Pretium perpendit saeculi,
Statera facta corporis,
Tulitque praedam tartari.[9]

Donne as well as Andrewes seems to have pointedly looked back to this celebrated Good Friday conceit. Yet it would be piffling to speculate whether Andrewes was picking up Donne's Good Friday *tour de force* of some three and a half years earlier. We must acknowledge the bond of a shared understanding, a common vision which is inherently witty because it requires us to discover quite precise points of correspondence between conditions which seem radically unlike each other, and even represent quite opposite orders of being.

In the 1616 Gunpowder Treason sermon Andrewes shows how God's providence may bring good ends out of bad human intentions when he points to the contrary issue of the failed birth in a new and triumphant birth of prayers, thanksgiving, praises, understanding. This new birth must be properly human, manifesting itself in flesh and blood no less than in the spirit, good works as well as spiritual renewal. The implicit yet proving antitype of a right birth – the countertype of the failed diabolic birth – is the nativity of Christ in a cattle trough, the event which definitively conjoins human nature with divine being. This conjunction presents the absolute manifestation of God's involvement in the life of nature, and authenticates our expectation that the most unlikely looking human contingencies may embody divine presence and purpose, which will manifest themselves in the physical character of the events themselves. George Herbert struggles to realise this insight.

Verbum caro factum est. The Vulgate version of the proclamation in St John shapes Andrewes's ontology. For him the key to history is the continual conjoining and reconciling in complete union of two diverse natures, and two opposite roles. Quite dissimilar states of being are made one, unlike elements interfused without changing their own essential nature, as the material bread and wine become the body and blood of Christ while nonetheless remaining bread and wine.

Andrewes' understanding of what happens in the eucharist, his insistence that a sacrament actually re-enacts a sacrifice, takes him right to the storm centre of Renaissance theology. Cranmer had argued for a double perspective in the eucharist without accepting the idea of a consubstantiation. The elements remain substantially bread and wine while they spiritually present Christ's body and blood.[10] Cranmer's English successors are more concerned to follow out the distinctive idea that the consubstantial union of manhood and divinity in Christ authenticates an interfusion of sense and spirit in human nature, as in the natural creation altogether. This is not Neoplatonic, or Augustinian, or Calvinist, though there is an English antecedent for it in the writings of Sir Thomas More.[11] More's descendant John Donne expresses this conviction forcibly and repeatedly as a defining article of his own Anglican persuasion;[12] the English metaphysical poets all follow out its consequences in their own ways.

The presumption was that God's entry into full humanity manifests the divine presence in history in a quite particular sense. It offers absolute warrant that human contingencies may not only shadow but actually incarnate timeless truths, even sacramentally re-enact Christ's life and sacrifice. Marvell's poetry gains as much by its playing off the sensible here-and-now against the prospect of an eternal disposition of our affairs as by its interchanges of body and spirit.

Yet human history itself is just part of a larger order. The commingling of spirit with sense, heaven with earth, is taken for a peculiarly intimate assurance of the sacred life of the natural creation itself. Truth lies incubating as a seed underground and then springs forth from the earth, as Andrewes preaches:[13] 'His work to this day [is] to continue and uphold in their being all that He hath made to be'.[14] Henry Vaughan has this high sanction to seek the vitalising presence of the divine spirit in the very conduct of natural life. Vaughan's *Silex Scintillans* is largely the record of an attempt to discover God in natural processes, which the poet simply takes for hieroglyphic manifestations of sacred being.

Other poets feel in their senses their involvement in the working of fallen nature yet must will their acceptance of the consequences. Herbert's poems powerfully remind us that true metaphysical wit is not theology or rhetoric but a way of experiencing, of which Andrewes's sermons offer a doctrinal substantiation rather than a cause. The wit realises the vision because it articulates an ambiguous apprehension of our natural being in the world, continually trying the present experience against a larger prospect of time or questioning what our senses affirm. Wit is the means of putting at issue our own involvement in a natural order which always fails our desires yet intimates a providence in its working. Caroline love poetry is peculiarly poignant in the way it simultaneously realises opposed motives, balancing the intense momentary delight against a yearning for an order beyond change. Indeed the sense of present awareness seems so acute just because the divided impulse itself puts it immediately in question. To set this order of courtly wit alongside the conceited wit of a Serafino or a Marino, or the rhetorical wit which Gracián and Tesauro prescribe for, is to bring out the distinctive unease of the English poets. It is also to see why Crashaw finds such a different use for wit from Donne or Herbert, and why Herbert of Cherbury and Traherne do not need wit at all.

The collocation of vivid life and mortality – bright hair about the bone and the like – is simply one of the more dramatic expressions of a double awareness which haunts all these poets with the ephemeralness of their own ardours. Sceptical self-mockery, an ironic poise, offers another way of holding in balance quite opposite possibilities of our being. Some poets tried to resolve their quarrel with their own disposition by pursuing the sacred processes of uncorrupted nature into rural seclusion. But then by the middle of the seventeenth century other accounts of human nature and of natural processes too were drifting in from France and Italy; and it may be that such modes of experience as the metaphysical poets enact express themselves most intensely when they are already coming in question. What seems certain is that these modes could not survive the quite particular metaphysical understanding which engendered them. Metaphysical poetry follows out in various ways that local expectation of the vital presence of the divine creator in the natural order and in human nature. The revival of interest in it from the time of the Oxford Movement helps us to locate our own disquiets.

Galileo's atomic physics implicitly denied the Aristotelean distinction between substance and accidents from which followed the doctrine of transubstantiation confirmed at the Council of Trent.[15] Yet it was Descartes rather than Galileo or Newton who framed the mechanistic model of the universe which came to dominate European thinking from the middle of the seventeenth century on. Descartes's disjoining of mind from body, spirit from sense, is also a separation of God from the creation if not a dispensing with God in effect, as Pascal thought it.[16] The Cartesian account of human nature led straight to Locke's separation of ideas from things. For Locke ideas are archetypes of the mind's own making which conform only to themselves, so that disagreements about moral ideas are simply differences about the proper use of the words by which we choose to name them, and may be resolved by a dictionary.[17] The basic unit of meaning is the word; and the yoking together of heterogeneous ideas is a wholly arbitrary procedure which becomes possible only when words are used corruptly. Cowley's praise of Bacon for drawing our thoughts from words to things, painted grapes to true grapes, marks a rejection of the double perspective of nature which engendered metaphysical wit. Cowley favours a brusque way with nature:

> And when on heaps the chosen Bunches lay,
> He pressed them wisely the Mechanic way,
> Till all their juice did in one Vessel join,
> Ferment into a Nourishment Divine . . .
>
> *To the Royal Society*

The dualism of Descartes, and Locke's exploitation of it, denied a way of thinking which started in the presumption that mind and body, spirit and sense, are wholly interdependent in our nature. For the English metaphysical writers human nature epitomises a universe which works as a living organism and manifests sacred purpose in all its processes. Their conception of a natural order in which spiritual and material natures continually interwork led them to assume that effective ideas are not discrete mental objects but complex inter-relationships between seemingly (if not actually) unlike orders of being. Such ideas cannot be developed in mere successions of words but are to be comprehended in the whole sentence or poem. Descartes and Locke now fathered a conception of nature which negated these assumptions at every point; and it is a matter of record that metaphysical poetry could not be properly grasped again while it held sole sway. Coleridge is no mere chance rediscoverer of Donne.

The idea of nature which shaped metaphysical poetry did not survive the 1650s, save as aberration and whimsy. We might set the topography of Donne's *Devotions* against the cosmology projected in a notorious controversy of the 1680s and after, in which Newton and John Ray joined among others. This debate centred precisely on the geological evidence of God's operations in the Creation and the Deluge.

A real index to what was happening in English intellectual life in the late seventeenth century is the quiet assimilation of Christian doctrine to the laws of natural science. This process accompanied the assumption that God's providence works through natural laws: '*that* Doctrine which takes away the certainty of Sense does in so doing overthrow the certainty of Christian Religion' is Tillotson's short rebuttal of the idea of a mysterious mutation of bread and wine into the body and blood of Christ.[18] It brought among other consequences the avowed abandonment of a sacramental ministry in favour of a homiletic mission whose incumbents took their charge to be the prescribing of general principles of conduct, 'To recommend Religion to men from the great and manifold advantages which it brings both to public Society and to particular persons'.[19]

The tendency is blatant in a curious work published in two parts in 1681 and 1689 with the suggestive title of Telluris Theoria Sacra, englished by the author as The Sacred Theory of the Earth. This essay by the Cambridge divine Thomas Burnet, who became Master of the Charterhouse in 1685, provoked a bustle of contention in its day which embroiled some leading scientists.[20] It comes before us now as at once a dinosaur and a portent. We might take it for the very last attempt to explain the earth's present state as a stage in an apocalyptic process; but it is also one of the earliest endeavours to make the Mosaic account of creation conform to natural laws.

Burnet offers us a startlingly unorthodox way of handling the myth of the Creation and Fall. He sets out to prove by scientific evidence that the world was created perfect but is now ruined, reduced to chaotic disorder through sin. His chief evidence for this assumption is the present state of the earth. The irregularity and confusion of the physical world as we now find it extends even beyond external appearance to the areas within the earth's surface, and to the regions under the seas.

Burnet essays a geological account of the state of paradisal perfection. He supposes that as the earth settled down after its formation from chaos it produced a thick crust over its entire surface, a mixture of earth and oily liquid which was perfectly smooth and regular. This flawless regularity constituted the condition of paradise, and paradise extended over the whole earth. Burnet argues that while the earth was in this state it enjoyed perpetual equinox because it was in a 'right posture' to the sun. Moreover it remained properly watered, despite the absence of mountains and seas, by the condensation at the poles of vapours which arose through the earth's crust and their subsequent precipitation towards the equator. All in all, Burnet claims that this world of perfect geometrical symmetry constituted a true golden age in which men lived long lives in peace and innocence.

The cataclysm which ruined this Eden, and produced the present disorderly state of the world, was the Flood. Burnet is quite categorical that a general Flood occurred; but he finds the Mosaic account of it scientifically inadequate, having no more worth than a popular exposition. For one thing, he claims, forty days and forty nights of rain simply would not have produced enough water to drown the entire earth.

Hence a more scientific explanation of the Flood is needed. Burnet posits a gradual drying and shrinking of the earth's crust throughout the patriarchal period, and the opening up of cracks in the surface. Then by weight of accumulated sin, as he supposes, parts of the crust collapsed and fell inwards upon the waters below, forcing them out over the earth: 'the fountains of the great deep were opened'. The abatement of the force of the convulsion, and the subsidence of the waters, left the world as we now see it with the collapsed portions constituting the ocean beds and the heaped-up bits the hills and mountains. It goes without saying that all symmetry and order are now quite lost; and they will not be recovered until a new apocalypse restores them.

In the second part of the *Sacred Theory*, 1689, Burnet shows how the world is to be destroyed by fire, which will likewise have natural causes. This general conflagration will be precipitated by an eruption of all volcanoes at once, augmented by fiery meteors from above. Fire will break out first at Rome, as the seat of Antichrist, but it may be expected to rage with particular heat in England just because there is so much coal in the ground there. After the fire there must follow a new precipitation of elements which will reproduce the condition of the paradisal earth. This will bring in the thousand-year reign of Christ and his Saints, and the final overthrow of Satan; then the earth itself will become a fixed star.

The striking thing about Burnet's thinking is his implicit assumption that these divine events must operate by the scientific laws of matter and display God's providence in their working. Thus the world was ruined by the agency of natural causes; yet these causes were themselves set in motion by the loss of innocence and the weight of sin. God's providence itself works by natural means through the ordinary course of nature, 'the regular effects' of 'second causes'. Indeed our best evidence of God's wisdom is that he works through his own regular ordinances. Divine providence shows its highest art in the way it brings spiritual and moral determinations into consonance with the order of natural events:

it is no detraction from Divine Providence, that the course of Nature is exact and regular, and that even in its greatest changes and revolutions it should still conspire and be prepared to answer the ends and purposes of the Divine Will in reference to the *Moral* World. This seems to me to be the great Art of Divine Providence, so to adjust the two Worlds, Human and Natural, Material and Intellectual, as seeing through the possibilities and futuritions of each, according to the first state and circumstances he puts them under, they should all along correspond and fit one another, and especially in their great Crises and Periods.[21]

In fact Burnet does also notionally allow for the extra-ordinary working of God's providence in the 'greater Scenes' and 'greater revolutions of Nature'. But in practice he continually offers scientific explanations of difficulties raised by the Mosaic account, and by his own account also, when it fails to answer the 'strict and physical nature of things'. Thus he already has his solution to those hoary old geological puzzles, the marine fossils found on mountain tops and the stratified evidence of the earth's antiquity. All such present phenomena are simply signs of ruin, the arbitrary residue of the Deluge. He also poses himself some practical questions. How did Noah's progeny spread after the Flood? How was America peopled? Have other planets been subject to the same processes as ours? He replies that perhaps each continent had its Noah's Ark, and Moses told us only of the particular ark which concerns our own part of the world. Moreover other planets may well have had their own floods, brought on by their own original sins.

Yet Burnet's most revealing answer was made in his later reviews of the controversy, to critics who found his theory at odds with the Mosaic account of the Creation.[22] He avers that Moses did not 'Philosophise or Astronomise in that description' but offered 'a narration suited to the capacity of the people, and not to the strict and physical nature of things'. Moses 'must be so interpreted', in sum, 'as not to . . . be repugnant to clear and uncontested Science'.[23] As he explains in the Preface to the *Sacred Theory* itself:

'Tis a dangerous thing to engage the authority of Scripture in disputes about the Natural World, in opposition to Reason; lest Time, which brings all things to light, should discover that to be evidently false which we had made Scripture to assert: . . .

And he adds at once, 'We are not to suppose that any truth concerning the Natural World can be an Enemy to Religion'.[24] Presumably the test of all truths concerning the natural world would be that they conform to reason.

Some of Burnet's commentators and critics accused him of a blasphemously inappropriate application of scientific criteria to revealed truth; others dismissed him as far more fanciful than scientific.[25] Argument chiefly centred on his account of the Deluge. This account was generally denied, and various other geophysical hypotheses were offered instead. Whiston, for example, notoriously ascribed the Flood to the influence of a comet which then came too near the earth.[26] Such rival speculations scarcely signify in themselves. What matters is that so many of these commentators fully accepted the need for scientific explanations of Christian cosmology and simply differed in the causes they ascribed.

Scepticism itself had changed its ground. Donne's scepticism assumed the accelerating degeneration of nature and of our faculties in consequence of the Fall. Joseph Glanvill takes up Bacon's succinct subversion of that view of history – *Antiquitas seculi est juventus mundi*.[27] The vanity of dogmatising is that we essay it without the hard evidence which alone would justify our views. We cannot know the universe with certainty through our senses because science has not yet developed sufficiently to yield us sure knowledge by experimental means.[28]

Almost all Burnet's critics deny that the earth was created perfectly smooth. Most of them agree that the present variety of landscapes is itself both necessary to life and extremely pleasing; and some of them evidently assume that the earth was created more or less as we find it, requiring only our regulation to bring it back to a state akin to Eden. They are moving towards a tacit abandonment of the idea of a primitive cataclysm in favour of an acceptance of what we have, as the outcome of a long evolution of civilised order. 'Whatever is, is right', or can be made right at least:

> See Pan with flocks, with fruits Pomona crowned,
> Here blushing Flora paints th'enamelled ground,
> Here Ceres' gifts in waving prospect stand,
> And nodding tempt the joyful reaper's hand,
> Rich Industry sits smiling on the plains,
> And peace and plenty tell, a STUART reigns.
> Pope, *Windsor Forest*, 37–42 (first part, 1704)

Pope's lines precisely mirror a creation which is ordered by regular physical laws and harmoniously manageable by mind. A mere fifty years separates them from Vaughan's *Silex Scintillans*. But then we may feel the want of metaphysical sentience much more intimately in eighteenth-century renderings of metaphysical poems. Here is a version of Herbert's 'Life', written about 1737:

> I plucked this morn these beauteous flowers
>   Emblem of my fleeting hours;
> 'Tis thus, said I, my life-time flies,
>   So it blooms, and so it dies.
> And, lo! how soon they steal away
>   Withered e'er the noon of day.
> Adieu! well pleased, my end I see,
>   Gently taught philosophy:
> Fragrance and ornament alive,
>   Physic after death they give,
> Let me throughout my little stay
>   Be as useful, and as gay:
> My close as early let me meet,
>   So my odour be as sweet!

The author was John Wesley, who cherished Herbert's poetry and undoubtedly meant to help it out here. It is no surprise to find that another eighteenth-century scholar-poet, Thomas Warton, devoted many pages of commentary to the poetry of Joseph Hall yet dismissed Hall's contemporary Donne in a few sentences. For all his antiquarian receptiveness and reclamatory zeal Warton seems indifferent to the metaphysical bearing of writers from Donne on. Andrewes, George Herbert, Vaughan, Marvell are not as much as noticed in his work; and there is nothing to suggest that the unwritten fourth volume of the *History of English Poetry* would have acknowledged them. The sea-change from Andrewes to Tillotson, Donne to Burnet and Warton, Vaughan's wit to Pope's wit, registers more than an adjustment of sensibility. It confirms a decisive shift of faith.

NOTES

1. DRASTIC DEVICES

1 L. Andrewes, in *Ninety-Six Sermons*, Oxford, 1841, IV, pp. 341–60.

2 *A Discourse Concerning the Original and Progress of Satire*, 1693, in *The Poems of John Dryden*, ed. J. Kinsley, Oxford, 1958, II, pp. 603–4.

3 *Life of Cowley*, in *Lives of the English Poets* (1779–81), ed. G. Birkbeck Hill, Oxford, 1905, I, pp. 18–35.

4 Marginal annotations in J. Chalmers, *The Works of the English Poets*, 1829, given in *Literary Remains*, ed. H. N. Coleridge, 1836–8, I, pp. 148–50; and Notebook No. 43, March–May 1830.

5 For example A. D'Ancona, 'Del Secentismo nella Poesia Cortigiana del Secolo XV', in *Studi sulla Letteratura Italiana de' Primi Secoli*, Ancona, 1884, pp. 151–237.

6 *Secentismo e Marinismo in Inghilterra*, Florence, 1925, pp. 135–7; *John Donne*, Turin, 1958, pp. 13–17.

7 *John Donne, Petrarchist*, Detroit, 1966.

8 'Eliot and the Metaphysicals', in *Accent* 1, pp. 148–56. Reprinted in *The New Criticism*, Norfolk, Conn., 1941, pp. 175–92.

9 *Elizabethan and Metaphysical Imagery*, Chicago, 1947.

10 'The Metaphysical Poets', *TLS* 20, October 1921, pp. 669–70. Reprinted in *Homage to John Dryden*, 1924, and *Selected Essays*, 1932.

11 'Note sur Mallarmé et Poe', *Nouvelle Revue française* 27, 1926, pp. 524–6.

12 'Deux Attitudes mystiques: Dante et Donne' in *Le Roseau d'or, Oeuvres et chroniques* 14 (3), 1927, pp. 149–73.

13 'On Metaphysical Poetry', *Scrutiny* 2, 3, December 1933, pp. 222–39. Given in *Shakespearean and Other Essays*, ed. E. M. Wilson, Cambridge, 1974, pp. 262–78.

14 'Wit and Mystery: A Revaluation in Mediaeval Latin Hymnody', *Speculum* 22, 3, July 1947, pp. 310–41.

15 'A Seventeenth-Century Theory of Metaphysical Poetry', *Romanic Review* 42, 1951, pp. 245–55; 'Metaphysical Poetry and the Poetic of Correspondence', *JHI* 14, 1953, pp. 221–34. Both essays are reprinted in J. A. Mazzeo, *Renaissance and Seventeenth Century Studies*, 1964, pp. 29–59.

16 'Gracian, Tesauro, and the Nature of Metaphysical Wit', *The Northern Miscellany* 1, pp. 19–40. Given as 'The Nature of Metaphysical Wit' in *Discussions of John Donne*, ed. F. Kermode, Boston, 1962, pp. 136–49.

17 *Les Poètes métaphysiques anglais*, Paris, 1960 and 1973.

2. MIRROR OF CREATION

1 Aristotle, *Metaphysics Z*, VII, VIII, in *The Works of Aristotle*, transl. J. A. Smith and W. D. Ross, Oxford, 1908, VIII, 1033^{a-b}.

2 *The Rule of Reason*, 1551, Bi^r–Pv^r.

3 Dvii^r.

4 Lviii^r.

5 Nvii^v–Oi^v.

6 Oi^v.

7 Cicero, *De Inventione* 11, 12, IV, transl. H. M. Hubbell, (1949), 1976, pp. 176–7.

8 *De Poeta*, Venice, 1559; *L'Arte Poetica*, Venice, 1563, especially Books 1 and 4.

9 *Modo di Comporre una Predica*, Venice, 1603.

10 *La Fabrica del Mondo*, Venice, 1546–8.

11 *L'Idea del Theatro*, in *L'Opere*, Venice, 1584, p. 60.

12 Aquinas, *Summa Theologiae*, 1a 22, 4; in the Blackfriars translation, 1964, 5, p. 103. Dante, *Divina Commedia, Purg.* XVIII, 40–54, and *Par.* XXXIII, 88–93.

13 See Notes 15 and 16.

14 See Chapter 4.

15 M. Ficino, *Epistolarum Liber II. Quaestiones quinque: de mente* (1495), in *Opera omnia*, Basle, 1576, I, ii, p. 677.

16 Pico della Mirandola, *De hominis dignitate* (1495–6), ed. E. Garin, Florence, 1942, I, pp. 106–7.

17 M. Ficino, *Opera omnia*, I, ii, p. 681.

18 S. Bargagli, *Dell'Imprese*, Venice, 1589, p. 330. See Chapter 4, p. 43.

19 *Genealogia Deorum Gentilium*, Venice, 1473, 8^r. See A. J. Smith, 'Theory and Practice in Renaissance Poetry: Two Kinds of Imitation', *Bulletin of the John Rylands Library* 47, 1, September 1964, p. 230 fn. 2.

20 A. Segni, *Rettorica et Poetica d'Aristotele*, Florence, 1549, p. 336.

21 B. Partenio, *Della Imitatione Poetica*, Venice, 1560, pp. 2–3.

22 A. Lionardi, *Dialoghi . . . della Inventione Poetica*, Venice, 1554, p. 68.

23 T. Campanella, *Poetica 2*, in *Tutte le Opere*, ed. L. Firpo, Milan, 1954, p. 963.

24 T. Wilson, *The Rule of Reason*, 1551, Uv^v.

25 For a developed account of sixteenth-century uses of the word wit see A. J. Smith, 'Wit in the Poetry of John Donne', unpublished dissertation for the University of Wales, 1954.

26 Sir P. Sidney, *An Apology for Poetry*, 1595, F3ʳ, ed. G. Shepherd, 1965, p. 121.

27 T. Nash, *The Anatomy of Absurdity*, 1589, in *The Works of Thomas Nash*, ed. R. B. McKerrow, 1910, I, pp. 25–6.

28 *Genealogia di gli Dei*, Venice, 1581, p. 232.

29 *Saturnalia* v, i, 18–20.

30 *Problemi di Estetica* (1909), Bari, 1923, pp. 311–12.

31 See Pico's debate with Ermalao Barbaro, 1485/6, and Poliziano's debate with Paolo Cortese, *c.* 1490. The letters are given in *Prosatori Latini del Quattrocento*, ed. E. Garin, Milan–Naples, 1952, pp. 504–23 and 902–11.

32 See R. Tuve, *Elizabethan and Metaphysical Imagery*, Chicago, 1946, ch. 12; and W. J. Ong, *Ramus Method, and the Decay of Dialogue*, Cambridge, Mass., 1958, especially chs. 11 and 12. For an extended scrutiny of the bearing of Ramism on metaphysical wit see A. J. Smith, 'An Examination of some Claims for Ramism', *RES* n.s. 7, 28, October 1956, pp. 348–59.

33 Abraham Fraunce, *The Arcadian Rhetoric*, 1588, ed. Ethel Seaton, Oxford, 1950, p. 26.

34 *Saturnalia*, IV, i–vi, and v, xi.

35 Giulio Camillo, *Due Trattati*, Venice, 1544, 38ʳ⁻ᵛ, 23ʳ.

36 B. Partenio, *Della Imitatione Poetica*, Venice, 1560, p. 42.

37 *Discorso . . . Intorno al Comporre dei Romanzi* (1549), Milan, 1864, pp. 89–90.

38 G. Giraldi Cintio, *Discorso*, p. 178.

39 Camillo, *Due Trattati*, 23ʳ.

40 32ᵛ.

41 *Discorsi del Poema Eroico*, in *Prose*, ed. F. Flora, Milan–Rome, 1935, p. 156.

42 Camillo, *Due Trattati*, 37ᵛ and 40ᵛ.

43 *Comparatione di Homero, Virgilio e Torquato*, Padua, 1607, p. 40.

44 *Discorsi del Poema Eroico*, p. 356.

45 *La Deffence et illustration de la langue francayse*, ed. H. Chamard, Paris, 1948, p. 42.

46 B. Partenio, *Della Imitatione Poetica*, Venice, 1560, pp. 26 and 31.

47 L. Castelvetro, *Poetica d'Aristotele Volgarizzata et Sposta*, Basle, 1576, p. 28.

48 *La Cavalletta Ovvero della Poesia Toscana*, in *Dialoghi Scelti*, ed. A. Mortara, Milan, 1878, p. 180.

49 Camillo, *Due Trattati*, 7ʳ.

50 T. Tasso, *La Cavalletta*, p. 175.

51 *La Cavalletta*, p. 176.

52 B. Tomitano, *Ragionamenti della Lingua Toscana*, Venice, 1545, 86ʳ.

53 T. Tasso, *Discorsi del Poema Eroico*, p. 462.

54 William Alabaster, *Penitential Sonnets* No. 17 (*c.* 1598).

55 B. Tomitano, *Ragionamenti*, 116ʳ.

56 *Il Petrarcha con l'Espositione di Messer G. A. Gesualdo*, Venice, 1581, 380ʳ⁻ᵛ.

57 N. Franco, *Le pistole vulgari*, Venice, 1538, 191ʳ.

58 *To My Worthy Good Cousin Master W.S.*, in *Saint Peter's Complaint*, (1595), 1616, A2ᵛ. Given in *The Poems of Robert Southwell S.J.*, ed. J. H. McDonald and N. P. Brown, Oxford, 1967, p. 1.

59 *The Epistle Dedicatory to S. Mary Magdalen's Funeral Tears*, 1616, p. 46.

60 Henry Constable, *Spiritual Sonnets* (*c.* 1591), *To St Mary Magdalen*.

61 G. Ruscelli, *Del Modo di Comporre in Versi*, Venice, 1582, p. 18.

62 G. Fracastoro, *Naugerius, Sive de Poetica Dialogus* (1555), ed. M. W.Bundy, Illinois, 1924, p. 69.

63 T. Tasso, *Discorsi del Poema Eroico*, p. 528.

64 *Discorsi del Poema Eroico*, p. 528.

65 Tasso, *Discorsi del Poema Eroico*, pp. 457–8.

66 E. Bulgarini, *Alcune Considerazioni*, Siena, 1583, p. 90.

67 J. Mazzoni, *Difesa di Dante*, Cesena, 1573, 41ʳ.

68 L. Castelvetro, *Poetica d'Aristotele Volgarizzata et Sposta*, Basle, 1576, p. 450.

69 T. Tasso, *Le Considerazioni sopra Tre Canzoni di G. B. Pigna*, in *Le Prose Diverse di Torquato Tasso*, ed. C. Guasti, Florence, 1875, II, p. 122.

3. COURTLY CONCEITS

1 A. D'Ancona, 'Del Secentismo nella Poesia Cortigiana del Secolo xv' in *Studi sulla Letteratura Italiana de' Primi Secoli*, Ancona, 1884, pp. 151–237.

2 See Chapter 2, pp. 15–17.

3 See F. R. Leavis, *Revaluation* (1936), 1962, pp. 10–41.

4 See Chapter 5, pp. 47–8, 67.

5 For Serafino see *Le Rime di Serafino de' Ciminelli dall' Aquila*, ed. M. Menghini, Bologna, 1894. For Tebaldeo see G. A. Barotti, *Memorie Istoriche di Letterati Ferraresi*, Ferrara, 1792, I, pp. 187–203; L. Coddè, *Notizie Biografiche di Antonio Tebaldeo*, Rovigo, 1845; U. Renda, *Rime volgari di Antonio Tebaldeo*, Modena, 1909, and *Nuove rime volgari di Antonio Tebaldeo*, Teramo, 1910. For Cariteo see E. Ciavarelli, *Il Cariteo e le sue opere volgari*, Bologna, 1887, and *Le Rime di Benedetto Gareth Detto il Chariteo*, ed. E. Percopo, Naples, 1892. I quote Cariteo's poems here from the edition by Percopo. Menghini's incomplete edition of *Le Rime di Serafino* does not include the *strambotti*. The edition of the *Opere* by B. di Giunta, Florence, 1516, gives more than five hundred *strambotti*, and this is the text I use here. Tebaldeo's poems are quoted from *L'Opere d'Amore*, Venice, 1534.

6 D. L. Guss, *John Donne, Petrarchist*, Detroit, 1966.

7 *Poeti e Scrittori del Pieno e del Tardo Rinascimento*, Bari, 1945, I, pp. 52–3.

8 For Serafino's court career and reputation see J. Dennistoun, *Memoirs of the Dukes of Urbino*, 1851, II, p. 140; P. Ferrato, *Serafino Aquilano: Rappresentazione allegorica data in Mantova nel 1495*, Naples 1877 (the

Rappresentazione itself is given in M. Menghini's edition of the *Rime*, pp. 267–75); A. Luzio and R. Renier, *Mantova e Urbino: Isabella d'Este e Elisabetta Gonzaga nelle Relazioni Famigliari e nelle Vicende Politiche*, Turin–Rome, 1893, pp. 89–96; J. Cartwright, *Isabella d'Este*, 1903, I, p. 170. For Cariteo's court career see the edition of Cariteo's *Rime* by E. Percopo, Part I, especially pp. xliii–xlix. For Tebaldeo's court career see G. Bertoni, *Poeti e Poesie del Medio Evo e del Rinascimento*, Modena, 1922, pp. 245–54.

9 Ducal competition for Serafino's services is documented in A. Luzio and R. Renier, *Mantova e Urbino*, Turin–Rome, 1893; J. Cartwright, *Isabella D'Este*, 1903; *Le Rime di Serafino*, ed. M. Menghini, Bologna, 1894.

10 *Collettanee Grece Latine e Vulgari per diversi Auctori Moderni nella Morte del'ardente Serafino Aquilano*, ed. C. Bazaleri, Bologna, 1504.

11 The following accounts are notable: F. Flavio in *Opere del facondissimo Seraphino Aquilano*, Rome, 1502 and Venice, 1502; C. Bazaleri in *Opere*, Milan, 1503; A. Colocci, *Apologia . . . nell'Opere De Seraphino*, in *Opere*, Rome, 1503 and Venice, 1505; V. Calmeta, *Vita del Facondo Poeta Vulgare Seraphino Aquilano*, in the *Collettanee . . . nella Morte del'ardente Seraphino Aquilano*, Venice, 1505. Extracts from these memorials are given in Menghini's edition of the *Rime*.

Some twenty editions of Serafino's poems appeared between 1502 and 1516, and at least eleven more followed up to 1550. Six editions of Tebaldeo's poems were published between 1498 and 1500, and six more followed by 1550.

12 F. Flavio in *Opere*, Rome, 1502 and Venice, 1502, given in *Le Rime di Serafino de' Ciminelli dall'Aquila*, ed. M. Menghini, Bologna, 1894, I, p. cxiii.

13 A. Colocci, *Apologia . . . nell'Opere De Seraphino*, Rome, 1503, given in M. Menghini, *Le Rime*, Bologna, 1894, I, p. 28.

14 Colocci, *Apologia*, in Menghini, *Le Rime*, I, p. 26.

15 V. Calmeta, *Vita del Facondo Poeta Vulgare Seraphino Aquilano*, in the *Collettanee*, ed. C. Bazaleri, Bologna, 1504, p. 9. Calmeta's *Vita* was also published together with Colocci's *Apologia* in the Venetian edition of Serafino's *Opere*, 1505.

16 In Menghini, *Le Rime*, pp. 28–31.

17 *John Donne, Petrarchist*, Detroit, 1966.

18 *Nuova Antologia*, 1898, p. 138.

4. INTELLIGIBLE IMAGES

1 'I Trattatisti Italiani del Concettismo e Baltasar Gracian', in *Problemi di Estetica e Contributi alla Storia dell'Estetica Italiana*, (1909), Bari, 1923, pp. 311–48. Croce also discussed this theorising in *Estetica come scienza dell'espressione e linguistica generale*, Bari, (1902), 1950, 2.iii and 2.xix,

pp. 206–23 and 471–534; in *Saggi di letteratura italiana nel seicento*, Bari, (1911), 1962, pp. 172–4; and in *Storia della Età Barocca in Italia*, Bari, 1929, pp. 161–210.

2 *Secentismo e marinismo in Inghilterra*, Florence, 1925, pp. 135–7; *Studies in Seventeenth Century Imagery*, (1939), Rome, 1964, pp. 14–25; *Studi sul Concettismo*, Florence, 1946, pp. 209ff.; *John Donne*, Turin, 1958, pp. 16–17; *The Flaming Heart*, New York, 1958, pp. 206–7.

3 J. A. Mazzeo, 'A Seventeenth Century Theory of Metaphysical Poetry', in *Romanic Review* 42, 1951, pp. 245–55; and 'Metaphysical Poetry and the Poetic of Correspondence' in *JHI* 14, 1953, pp. 221–34. Both essays were reprinted in Mazzeo's *Renaissance and Seventeenth Century Studies*, 1964, pp. 29–59. S. L. Bethell, 'Gracian, Tesauro, and the Nature of Metaphysical Wit', in *The Northern Miscellany* 1, Autumn 1953, pp. 19–40.

4 *The Hieroglyophics of Horapollo Nilous*, transl. A. T. Cory, 1839, pp. 40 and 46–7.

5 *Ori Apollinis Niliaci, De Sacris Ægyptiorum notis, Ægyptiace expressis*, Paris, 1574, introductory address to the reader, ★ii^r.

6 B. Arnigio, *Rime di gli Academici Occulti con le loro Imprese et Discorsi*, Brescia, 1568, 'Discorso Intorno al Sileno', unpaginated.

7 A. Farra, *Tre Discorsi*, Pavia, 1564, Aiiii^r.

8 P. Aresi, *Delle Imprese Sacre*, Verona, 1616, p. 163.

9 For Tesauro see Chapter 5. D. F. Picinelli, *Mondo Simbolico Formato d'Imprese*, Venice, 1670. C.-F. Menestrier, *La Philosophie des images*, Paris, 1682; *La Science et l'art des devises*, Paris, 1686.

10 *La Philosophie des images*, Paris, 1682, p. 12.

11 D. F. Picinelli, *Mondo Simbolico*, Venice, 1670, subtitle.

12 G. P. Valeriano, *Hieroglyphica sive de sacris Aegyptiorum aliarumque gentium literis, commentarii*, Basle, 1556, ★3^r–★4^r, esp. ★3^v. The title of the Italian translation, Venice, 1602, described the work as a 'Commentary on the Occult Significations of the Egyptians and Other Nations'.

13 *Ragionamento . . . sopra VIIII Inventioni e loro Origine, Impropriamente Chiamate Imprese*, Pavia, 1574, 31^r, 38^r.

14 *I Discorsi . . . sopra l'Imprese*, Bologna, 1575, pp. 5–6.

15 L. Contile, *Ragionamento*, 3^r, 27^v, 38^r.

16 C. Ripa, *Iconologia*, Siena, 1613, Proemio, unpaginated.

17 St Eucherius's *Commentaria in Genesim et in libros Regum* was published in Rome in 1564.

18 See A. J. Smith, *The Metaphysics of Love*, Cambridge, 1985, pp. 64–6, 102–14, 260.

19 A. Farra, *Tre Discorsi*, Pavia, 1564, Aiiii^r–Bvi^r.

20 V. Cartari, *Le Imagini. Con la spositione de i dei de Gliantichi*, Venice, 1556, *passim*. G. P. Valeriano, *Hieroglyphica*, Basle, 1556, title page; *Ieroglifici*, Venice, 1602, A3–4 and pp. 580–5. N. Conti, *Mythologiae*, (1568), Venice,

1612, p. 213 and *passim*. L. Contile, *Ragionamento*, Pavia, 1574, 121ᵛ–2ʳ. G. A. Palazzi, *I Discorsi . . . sopra l'Imprese*, Bologna, 1575, pp. 5–6.

21 L. Contile, *Ragionamento*, Pavia, 1574, 27ʳ.

22 A. Farra, *Tre Discorsi*, Pavia, 1564, Aiiiiʳ.

23 *Ieroglifici*, Venice, 1602, additional books p. 912.

24 C. Ripa, *Iconologia* (1593), Siena, 1613, Proemio, unpaginated. G. Whitney, *A Choice of Emblems*, Leyden, 1586, ★4. Valeriano, *Hieroglyphica*, Basle, 1556, Epistole Nuncupatoria ★3–★4; *Ieroglifici*, Venice, 1602, pp. 87 and 685.

25 *A Choice of Emblemes*, Leyden, 1585, Dedicatory Epistle ★4.

26 *Ragionamento*, Pavia, 1584, 2ᵛ.

27 S. Bargagli, *Dell'Imprese*, Venice, 1589, p. 79.

28 L. Contile, *Ragionamento*, Pavia, 1574, 1ʳ⁻ᵛ.

29 Contile, *Ragionamento*, 1574, 27ᵛ.

30 *Tre Discorsi*, Pavia, 1564, Biiiiᵛ.

31 *Tre Discorsi*, Bviʳ.

32 *Hieroglyphica*, Basle, 1556, p. 94.

33 *Ieroglifici*, Venice, 1602, p. 93.

34 L. Contile, *Ragionamento*, Pavia, 1574, 27ʳ. B. Arnigio, *Rime*, Brescia, 1568, 'Discorso Intorno al Sileno', unpaginated.

35 L. Contile, *Ragionamento*, Pavia, 1574, 1ᵛ–2ʳ.

36 Contile, *Ragionamento*, 3ʳ and 29ᵛ.

37 H. C. Agrippa, *De Occulta Philosophia*, 1529, transl. J.F. as *Three Books of Occult Philosophy*, 1651, p. 567.

38 B. Arnigio, *Rime*, Brescia, 1568, 'Discorso Intorno al Sileno', unpaginated.

39 Arnigio, *Rime*, 87ʳ.

40 C. Ripa, *Iconologia*, Siena, 1613, Proemio, unpaginated.

41 S. Pallavicino, *Del Bene*, Rome, 1644, p. 470.

42 G. B. della Porta, *Magiae Naturalis*, Naples, 1558, pp. 13–15 and 201. Agrippa, *Occult Philosophy*, pp. 26–32.

43 This figure of the naked baby, or *putto*, first appears in *Emblematum libellus*, Paris, 1534. It replaces the figure in the crude edition of 1531, that of a robed man who is similarly winged and weighted but lacks the counterpull of earth and heaven. Later editions of Alciati tend to bear out the banal motto rather than the Humanistic image which is at odds with it; they turn the figure into a decrepit old man who is plainly borne down by poverty.

44 J. Sambuco, *Emblemata*, Antwerp, 1564, pp. 74–5.

45 C. Labia, *Dell'Imprese Pastorali*, Venice, 1685, i, pp. 12–22. I am indebted to Professor Aldo Celli of the University of Florence for help in tracking down this reference.

46 *Le Sententiose Imprese*, Lyons, 1650, p. 4.

47 P. Giovio, *Dialogo dell'Imprese Militari et Amorose*, Rome, 1555.

G. Ruscelli, *Le Imprese Illustre*, Venice, 1566. A. Fraunce, *Insignium, Armorum, Hieroglyphicorum, et Symbolorum*, London, 1588. T. Tasso, *Il Conte, ovvero dell'Imprese*, Naples, 1594.

48 S. Ammirato, *Orazioni . . . con un Dialogo delle Imprese*, Florence, 1598, p. 10.

49 G. Tiraboschi lists some 171 academies in Italy alone, in his *Storia della letteratura italiana* (1772–93), Florence, 1812, VIII, i, pp. 45–64.

50 *Tre Discorsi*, Biiii^v–v^r.

51 See Chapter 5, pp. 41–3, 61–2, 66. Paolo Giovio gave this *impresa* its fame when he reproduced and commended it in his *Dialogo dell'Imprese Militari et Amoroso* [*sic*], Lyons, 1574, p. 26.

52 *Rime de gli Academici Occulti con le loro Imprese e Discorsi*, Brescia, 1568, 'Discorso Intorno al Sileno', unpaginated.

53 *Rime*, 86^v–89^v.

54 S. Bargagli, *Dell'Imprese*, Venice, 1589, p. 330.

55 P. Aresi, *Delle Imprese Sacre*, Verona, 1616, p. 163. C. Paradin, *Devises heroiques*, Lyons, 1557, transl. P.S. as *The Heroicall Devises*, 1591, pp. 70–1.

56 *Rime*, 1568, 86^v–89^v.

57 *Dell'Imprese*, Venice, 1589, p. 48.

58 Bargagli, *Dell'Imprese*, p. 330.

59 C. Ripa, *Iconologia*, Siena, 1613, Proemio, unpaginated.

60 G. A. Palazzi, *I Discorsi . . . sopra l'Imprese*, Bologna, 1575, pp. 200–1. S. Bargagli, *Dell'Imprese*, Venice, 1589, p. 24.

61 S. Ammirato, *Orazioni . . . con un Dialogo delle Imprese*, Florence, 1596, p. 6. B. Arnigio, *Rime*, Brescia, 1568, 'Discorso Intorno al Sileno', unpaginated.

62 *Iconologia*, Siena, 1613, Proemio, unpaginated.

63 G. A. Palazzi, *I Discorsi . . . sopra l'Imprese*, Bologna, 1575, p. 202.

64 B. Taegio, *Il Liceo*, Milan, 1571, 10^r.

65 S. Bargagli, *Dell'Imprese*, Venice, 1589, *passim*. T. Tasso, *Il Conte*, 1594, *passim*.

66 L. Contile, *Ragionamento*, Pavia, 1574, 30^v.

67 *Ragionamento*, 31^v–35^v.

68 See Chapter 5.

5. ARTS OF INGENUITY

1 See Chapter 4, Note 1.

2 This work follows up Minozzi's *Delle Libidini dell'Ingegno*, Venice, 1636, which Croce does not mention.

3 An earlier version of the *Trattato* had been published in Rome in 1646 as *Considerazioni sopra l'Arte dello Stile e del Dialogo*.

4 *John Donne*, Turin, 1958, pp. 13–17.

5 See Chapter 4, Note 3.

6 *Elizabethan and Metaphysical Imagery*, Chicago, 1947, *passim*.
7 *The Works of Garcilaso de la Vega*, 1823, p. 81.
8 *Historia de las Ideas Esteticas en España*, Madrid, 1884, ii, ii, pp. 536–40.
9 *Problemi*, Bari, 1923, p. 313.
10 Tesauro, *Il Canocchiale*, 1682, p. 150 and *passim*. The augmented edition of 1682 is referred to throughout, save where an earlier edition is specifically indicated.
11 *Gli Sfogamenti d'Ingegno*, Venice, 1641, p. 257.
12 *Il Canocchiale*, p. 302.
13 *Agudeza*, Discourse xxv.
14 *Agudeza*, Discourse ii.
15 *Del Bene*, Rome, 1644, p. 470.
16 *Il Canocchiale*, pp. 38–49.
17 *Il Canocchiale*, p. 291.
18 pp. 5, 66, 185–6.
19 pp. 170–2.
20 Discourses iv–xvii and *passim*.
21 Discourses iv, viii and *passim*.
22 Discourses ii and iv.
23 Discourses x–xiv.
24 Discourse xv.
25 Discourse xiv.
26 Discourse liv.
27 Discourse li.
28 Discourse liii.
29 Discourse li.
30 See Chapter 6, p. 81.
31 Discourse iv.
32 Discourse xxxvi.
33 Discourse x.
34 Discourse viii.
35 Discourse viii.
36 Discourse v.
37 Discourse xiii.
38 Discourses vi and xvi.
39 Discourse xvi.
40 Discourse v.
41 Discourse xvi.
42 Discourse v.
43 Discourse lii.
44 Discourse v.
45 See Chapter 6, p. 79.
46 Discourse vii.
47 Discourse xxxi.

48 Discourse xvii.
49 Discourse xvii.
50 Discourse v.
51 *Il Canocchiale*, pp. 164–289 and *passim*.
52 *Delle Acutezze*, Genoa, 1639, pp. 33–47.
53 *Delle Acutezze*, pp. 39 and 118.
54 H. C. Agrippa, *De occulta philosophia*, Lyons, 1529, *passim*; *Three Books of Occult Philosophy*, transl. J.F., 1651, p. 568.
55 *Il Canocchiale*, pp. 184–5 and Chs. vii and viii *passim*.
56 *Delle Acutezze*, p. 141.
57 *Del Bene*, pp. 452–79.
58 *Trattato dello Stile*, Rome, 1662, pp. 152–61.
59 *Il Canocchiale*, pp. 165–8.
60 *Il Canocchiale*, pp. 293–301.
61 Chapter vii, *passim*.
62 *Il Canocchiale*, p. 183.
63 *Problemi*, 1923, p. 318.
64 *Il Canocchiale*, pp. 330–50.
65 Discourse x.
66 *Trattato*, pp. 119–45.
67 Discourse iii.
68 Discourse vii.
69 Discourse viii.
70 Discourse viii.
71 Discourse xxi.
72 Discourse xxvi.
73 Discourse xxv.
74 Discourse xxxvi.
75 *Delle Acutezze*, p. 118, 131, 179.
76 *Trattato*, pp. 111–18, 148–78.
77 *Il Canocchiale*, pp. 293–301.
78 *Indice* to p. 300.
79 *Il Canocchiale*, p. 297.
80 *Il Canocchiale*, pp. 325–7.
81 *Il Canocchiale*, pp. 302–25.
82 *Delle Acutezze*, pp. 212–13.
83 Pellegrini, *Delle Acutezze*, pp. 212–13; Minozzi, *Gli Sfogamenti*, pp. 250–74.
84 'A Seventeenth Century Theory of Metaphysical Poetry', and 'Metaphysical Poetry and the Poetic of Correspondence', in *Renaissance and Seventeenth Century Studies*, 1964, pp. 34–40, 48–9.
85 *Il Canocchiale*, p. 302.
86 *Il Canocchiale*, pp. 330–50.
87 *Il Canocchiale*, p. 352.

88 *Il Canocchiale*, p. 390.
89 See Chapter 4, pp. 40–5.
90 Tesauro, *Il Canocchiale*, p. 297.
91 *Il Canocchiale*, pp. 325–6.

6. METAPHORICAL WIT

1 *The Life of Michelangelo Buonarroti*, 1893, II, pp. 153–4.
2 See O. De Mourgues, *Metaphysical Baroque and Précieux Poetry*, Oxford, 1953, pp. 7–25.
3 *Dicerie Sacre*, Turin, 1614, 10ʳ.
4 *Lettere*, ed. M. Guglielminetti, Turin, 1966, p. 600.
5 F. De Sanctis, *Storia della Letteratura Italiana* (1870–1), Milan, 1955, III, pp. 34–7. See *Marino e i Marinisti*, ed. G. G. Ferrero, 1954, p. 68.
6 I am indebted to my colleague Professor Henry Ettinghausen for help with readings of Spanish poets.
7 Letter to an unknown recipient, 1613 or 1614. In *Obras Completas*, ed. J. M. Y. Giminez and I. M. Y. Giminez, Madrid, 1961, p. 897.
8 *Poems of Góngora*, Cambridge, 1966, p. 12.
9 See O. De Mourgues, *Metaphysical Baroque and Précieux Poetry*, Oxford, 1953, pp. 47–56.
10 See A. Boase, *The Poetry of France*, 1964, I, pp. c–ci, 181–2, 245–6.
11 A. Boase, *The Poetry of France*, 1964, I, pp. lxxxiv–xc.
12 A. Boase, *Sponde: Poésies*, Geneva, 1949, p. 124; *The Poetry of France*, I, p. xcvii.
13 *Sponde: Poésies*, pp. 142–3; *The Poetry of France*, I, p. xcvii.
14 *Sponde: Poésies*, p. 143.
15 Gracián, *Agudeza*, Discourse iv.
16 See A. Terry, 'Quevedo and the Metaphysical Conceit', *Bulletin of Hispanic Studies* 35, 4, October 1958, pp. 211–22.

7. METAPHYSICAL WIT

1 See P. Legouis, *Donne the Craftsman* (1928), New York, 1962, p. 70.
2 See A. J. Smith, *The Metaphysics of Love*, Cambridge, 1985, pp. 188–95.
3 Letter 'To all my friends: Sir H. Goodyer', *c.* 1612, in E. Gosse, *Life and Letters*, 1899, II, p. 7.
4 *De Anima*, III, x.
5 See L. I. Bredvold, 'The Naturalism of Donne in Relation to some Renaissance Traditions', *JEGP* 22, 1923, pp. 471–502.
6 P. Charron, *De la Sagesse*, Bordeaux, 1601, 2, v, pp. 351–72.
7 *Conversations With William Drummond of Hawthornden*, 3, in *Ben Jonson*, ed. I. Donaldson, Oxford, 1985, p. 596.
8 *Conversations with Drummond*, 5, pp. 596–7.

9 Sermon: *Death's Duel*, 1630, text and *passim*.

10 *Conversations with Drummond*, 7, p. 597.

11 See Donne's letter to George Gerrard from Paris, 14 April 1612, Gosse I, pp. 301–4.

12 See Chapter 8, pp. 243–4 and Note 9.

13 20. *Prayer*. In *John Donne: Devotions Upon Emergent Occasions*, ed. A. Raspa, Montreal and London, 1975, p. 10 (spelling modernised).

14 *Philosophical Investigations* II, iv, p. 178e.

15 This is the version of the poem given in the 1646 edition of Crashaw's poems with the title as here. In the editions of 1648 and 1652 the poem is given as *New Year's Day*, with some minor amendments of phrasing and the omission of the final couplet.

16 *Seven Types of Ambiguity* (1930), 1961, pp. 221–2.

17 This is the version of the poem given in the editions of 1648 and 1652.

18 *Henry Vaughan: Poems*, I, p. 316.

19 Aquinas, *Summa Theologiae*, vol. 57, 77.1, transl. T. McDermott, 1989, p. 578.

20 *Les Poètes métaphysiques anglais*, I, ii, p. 48.

21 The date which follows each title indicates the part of *Silex Scintillans* in which the poem first appeared, that part published in 1650 or that published in 1655.

22 See A. J. Smith, *The Metaphysics of Love*, Cambridge, 1985, pp. 255–322.

23 *Les Poètes métaphysiques anglais*, I, ii, pp. 173–260.

24 *Centuries, Poems and Thanksgivings*, ed. H. M. Margoliouth, Oxford, 1958, II, p. xii.

25 *Les Poètes métaphysiques anglais*, I, ii, pp. 391–2.

26 *Les Poètes métaphysiques anglais*, I, ii, pp. 138–44 and 159–65.

27 Leslie Stephen, *DNB*, Cowley.

28 *Donne the Craftsman* (1928), New York, 1962, p. 70.

29 See Chapter 8, pp. 246–7, and A. J. Smith, 'Sacred Earth. Metaphysical Poetry and the Advance of Science', *Proceedings of the British Academy* 71, 1985, pp. 260–1.

8. SACRED EARTH

1 See Chapter 1, pp. 1–2.

2 *Ninety-Six Sermons*, Oxford, 1841, I, p. 43. Andrewes' sermons are quoted throughout from this edition save where its text is less clear than that of the edition of 1629.

3 *Ninety-Six Sermons*, I, p. 175.

4 Mark Frank, *Sermons* (1672), Oxford, 1849, II, p. 131.

5 *Ninety-Six Sermons*, II, p. 178.

6 *Ninety-Six Sermons*, II, p. 178.

7 *Ninety-Six Sermons*, II, p. 163.

8 'Gracian, Tesauro, and the Nature of Metaphysical Wit', *The Northern Miscellany* 1, Autumn 1953, p. 36.

9 Roman Missal, Order for Good Friday. Fortunatus's hymn is sung at Vespers in Holy Week, towards the end of the Adoration of the Cross, during the procession to bring back the Blessed Sacrament from the place where it was deposited the previous day.

10 *A Defence of the True and Catholic Doctrine of the Sacrament of the Body and Blood of Our Saviour Christ*, ed. H. J. Todd, 1825, especially pp. 63, 65, 77.

11 *A Treatise Upon the Passion* (1534), in *The Complete Works of Sir Thomas More* XIII, ed. G. E. Haupt, New Haven, 1976, pp. 105–52 and *passim*.

12 See A. J. Smith, 'No Man is a Contradiction', *John Donne Journal* 1, 1982, pp. 21–38; and Chapter 3 of *The Metaphysics of Love*, Cambridge, 1985, pp. 187–220.

13 *Ninety-Six Sermons*, 1, p. 186.

14 *Ninety-Six Sermons*, 1, p. 110.

15 See P. Redondi, *Galileo: Heretic* (1983), 1988, pp. 163–4.

16 *Pensées*, 11.77.

17 I am indebted to my colleague Professor Antony Palmer for helpful discussion of Locke's arguments, and of the bearing on them of Wittgenstein's engagement with language in the *Philosophical Investigations*.

18 J. Tillotson, *The Rule of Faith* (1665), in *The Works*, 1696, p. 760.

19 Tillotson, Preface to *The Works*, 1696, A2^r.

20 I am indebted to my colleague Professor Frank Hodson for his generous help with this curious episode. Page references are given to the facsimile of the 1690/1 edition of the *Sacred Theory*, 1965, introduced by Basil Willey.

21 *Sacred Theory*, p. 89.

22 *A Review of the Theory of the Earth*, 1690, in *Sacred Theory*, 1965, pp. 381–412; *Archaeologiae Philosophicae*, 1692, Chapters 8 and 9, pp. 297–329 and *passim*; *De Statu*, 1720, last part, *passim*; *A Re-Survey of the Mosaic System of Creation*, 1728, *passim*.

23 *Sacred Theory*, pp. 407–8.

24 *Sacred Theory*, p. 16.

25 The commentators whose views are summarised here are Isaac Newton, c. 1680, Bishop Herbert Croft, 1685, Erasmus Warren, 1690, John Ray, 1691–2, John Beaumont, 1693, John Woodward, 1695, William Whiston, 1696 and 1698, John Keill, 1698. Keill stood out against the impulse to seek natural causes of Old Testament events, dismissing Burnet's theory as unnecessary because it nowhere proved that the Deluge 'might not have been brought upon the earth by the Almighty power of God' (*An Examination of Dr Burnet's Theory of the Earth: with some remarks on Mr Whiston's new Theory of the Earth* (1698), 1734, p. 26).

26 *A New Theory of the Earth*, 1696, *passim*, but especially pp. 357–8, and *A Vindication of the New Theory of the Earth*, 1698, Preface and *passim*.

27 *Novum Organum*, 1620, lxxxiv.

28 *Scepsis Scientifica*, 1665, p. 26.

INDEX